THIRD EDITION

5

D1649151

Skills for Success
READING AND WRITING

Nigel A. Caplan | Scott Roy Douglas

OXFORD
UNIVERSITY PRESS

OXFORD
UNIVERSITY PRESS

198 Madison Avenue
New York, NY 10016 USA

Great Clarendon Street, Oxford, OX2 6DP, United Kingdom

Oxford University Press is a department of the University of Oxford.
It furthers the University's objective of excellence in research, scholarship,
and education by publishing worldwide. Oxford is a registered trade
mark of Oxford University Press in the UK and in certain other countries

ISBN: 978 0 19 490396 7   Student Book 5 with iQ Online pack
ISBN: 978 0 19 490372 1   Student Book 5 as pack component
ISBN: 978 0 19 490432 2   iQ Online student website

Printed in China

This book is printed on paper from certified and well-managed sources

ACKNOWLEDGMENTS

Back cover photograph: Oxford University Press building/David Fisher

Illustrations by: 5W Infographics pp.69, 70, 73, 74; Marc Kolle p.89; Karen
Minot p.164.

*The Publishers would like to thank the following for their kind permission to reproduce
photographs and other copyright material*: Alamy: pp.2 (language signs/Lori
Labrecque), 22 (learning sign language/Oleksandr Rupeta), 63 (busy road
crossing/KHALED KASSEM), 99 (seeds in tubes/Hemis), 105 (astronaut
water training/NG Images), 112 (astronauts from different nations/NASA/S.
Dupuis), 114 (fruit on truck/JJM Stock Photography), 126 (Moscow metro/
Jim Grover), 132 (inside the Stata Center/Pablo Valentini), 135 (Bryant
Park/Goran Bogicevic), 157 (city pedestrianised zone/dov makabaw),
158 (tree sculpture/Hemis), 183 (volunteers litter picking/Hero Images
Inc.), 193 (steam locomotive/Lordprice Collection), 194 (textile factory/
INTERFOTO), 198 (old agricultural scene/Chronicle), (old industrial
landscape/INTERFOTO), 208 (old lightbulbs/gary warnimont), 223 (drone
carrying package/Kiyoshi Takahase Segundo), 255 (white water rafting/
robertharding); Getty: pp.cover (orange cables/Volker Schlichting/
EyeEm), 5 (three girls talking/Drazen_), 15 (students in exam hall/The
Asahi Shimbun), 34 (cycle couriers with cellphones/GERARD JULIEN),
37 (man working at home/visualspace), 44 (man buying online/domoyega),
58 (media interviewing woman/THET AUNG), 82 (antique globe/Felipex),
93 (optical illusion/MICHAEL URBAN), 94 (United Nations Building/
Entienou), 97 (exterior of Global Seed Vault/JUNGE, HEIKO), 98 (interior
of Global Seed Vault/NOEL CELIS), 106 (Chris Hadfield/PETER MUHLY),
113 (cargo ship navigating rough seas/Miguel Navarro), 146 (traffic jam/Levi
Bianco), 160 (landfill site/Nick Vedros), 162 (ecotourists on Pulau Semakau/
ROSLAN RAHMAN), 167 (road on Pulau Semakau/ROSLAN RAHMAN),
176 (filling fuel tank with vegetable oil/fluxfoto), 189 (vertical garden/
Cristian Bortes/EyeEm), 190 (robot restaurant waiter/PRAKASH MATHEMA),
202 (glass windows/Guy Lambrechts), 224 (hikers in the mountains/Ascent
Xmedia), 229 (woman sleeping/andresr), 240 (woman using light therapy
lamp/Philippe TURPIN); NASA: p.116 (earth and satellite/NASA); National
Geographic: p.76 (Bedouin camel riders/GAHAN, GORDON); Oxford
University Press: pp.33 (language dictionaries/Dean Ryan), 178 (recycling
bins/Claire Plumridge/Shutterstock); Shutterstock: pp.8 (college students
in classroom/LStockStudio), 14 (language notes/Eiko Tsuchiya), 21 (student
using language phone app/Daxiao Productions), 42 (woman working in
coffee shop/Monkey Business Images), 45 (tired driver/Nicoleta Ionescu),
51 (congested road/Kevin Hellon), 52 (wildlife photographer/Volodymyr
Burdiak), 64 (optical illusion public art/Joe Pepler), 125 (multi ethnic hands/
BlueDesign), 134 (modern library/Aleksandra Suzi), 135 (Stata Center/
Marco Rubino), 152 (coffee/ViewFinder nilsophon), 212 (eggs/montse sabat),
220 (snowmobiles/irina02), 227 (woman preparing salad/MintImages),
238 (winter day in Edmonton/LisaBourgeault), 243 (carbohydrate rich
foods/beats1); Third party: pp.139 (Drachten, Holland/Jerry Michalski),
170 (repairing lamp/Christina Cooke), 171 (two people repairing at table/
Christina Cooke).

*The authors and publisher are grateful to those who have given permission to
reproduce the following extracts and adaptations of copyright material*: p.5 Adapted
extract from 'How learning a new language improves tolerance' by Amy
Thompson, December 12, 2016, www.theconversation.com. Reproduced
by permission. p.15 From 'Ignore the panic. There's little point learning
languages at school' by Simon Jenkins, August 25, 2017, www.theguardian.
com. © Guardian News & Media Ltd 2018. Reproduced by permission. p.16
From 'Just speaking English won't get us very far in the world', August
28, 2017, www.theguardian.com. © Guardian News & Media Ltd 2018.
Reproduced by permission. p.37 From 'Who Wins in the Gig Economy, and
Who Loses' by Diane Mulcahy, October 27, 2016, Harvard Business Review.
Reproduced by permission of Harvard Business Publishing. p.68 From
'Infographics Lie. Here's How To Spot The B.S.' by Randy Olsen, January
1, 2014, www.fastcompany.com. Used with permission of FastCompany.
com. Copyright © 2018. All rights reserved. p.76 From 'Phototruth or
Photofiction? Ethics and Media Imagery in the Digital Age' by Thomas
H. Wheeler. Copyright © 2002. Reproduced by permission of Taylor and
Francis Group, LLC, conveyed through Copyright Clearance Center, Inc.
p.97 From 'In Norway, Global Seed Vault Guards Genetic Resources'
by Elisabeth Rosenthal from The New York Times, February 28, 2008
© 2008, The New York Times. All rights reserved. Used by permission
and protected by the Copyright Laws of the United States. The printing,
copying, redistribution, or retransmission of this Content without express
written permission is prohibited. p.131 From "The New Oases" as appeared
in The Economist. © The Economist Newspaper Limited, London April
12, 2008. Reproduced by permission. p.139 From 'A Path to Road Safety
with No Signposts' by Sarah Lyall from The New York Times, January 22,
2005 © 2005, The New York Times. All rights reserved. Used by permission
and protected by the Copyright Laws of the United States. The printing,
copying, redistribution, or retransmission of this Content without
express written permission is prohibited. p.162 From 'Island of trash or
the 'Garbage of Eden'?' by Eric Bland, April 11, 2007, www.newscientist.
com. © 2007 New Scientist Ltd. All rights reserve. Distributed by Tribune
Content Agency. p.193 From 'Oxford Encyclopedia of the Modern World'
Edited by Peter N. Stearns. © 2008 Oxford University Press. Reproduced by
permission. p.202 Adapted from 'Humankind's Most Important Material'
by Douglas Main, April 7, 2018. © 2018 The Atlantic Media Co., as first
published in TheAtlantic.com. All rights reserved. Distributed by Tribune
Content Agency. p.227 From 'How can you boost your energy levels?' by
Maria Cohut, May 25, 2018, Medical News Today, www.medicalnewstoday.
com. © Medical News Today. Reproduced with permission. p.238 From 'The
Scientific Reasons You Feel More Tired During Winter (And How To Combat
It)' by Brandon Hall, December 8, 2016, www.stack.com. Reproduced by
permission

*Although every effort has been made to trace and contact copyright holders before
publication, this has not been possible in some cases. We apologize for any apparent
infringement of copyright and if notified, the publisher will be pleased to rectify any
errors or omissions at the earliest opportunity.*

ACKNOWLEDGMENTS

We would like to acknowledge the teachers from all over the world who participated in the development process and review of *Q: Skills for Success* Third Edition.

USA

Kate Austin, Avila University, MO; **Sydney Bassett**, Auburn Global University, AL; **Michael Beamer**, USC, CA; **Renae Betten**, CBU, CA; **Pepper Boyer**, Auburn Global University, AL; **Marina Broeder**, Mission College, CA; **Thomas Brynmore**, Auburn Global University, AL; **Britta Burton**, Mission College, CA; **Kathleen Castello**, Mission College, CA; **Teresa Cheung**, North Shore Community College, MA; **Shantall Colebrooke**, Auburn Global University, AL; **Kyle Cooper**, Troy University, AL; **Elizabeth Cox**, Auburn Global University, AL; **Ashley Ekers**, Auburn Global University, AL; **Rhonda Farley**, Los Rios Community College, CA; **Marcus Frame**, Troy University, AL; **Lora Glaser**, Mission College, CA; **Hala Hamka**, Henry Ford College, MI; **Shelley A. Harrington**, Henry Ford College, MI; **Barrett J. Heusch**, Troy University, AL; **Beth Hill**, St. Charles Community College, MO; **Patty Jones**, Troy University, AL; **Tom Justice**, North Shore Community College, MA; **Robert Klein**, Troy University, AL; **Patrick Maestas**, Auburn Global University, AL; **Elizabeth Merchant**, Auburn Global University, AL; **Rosemary Miketa**, Henry Ford College, MI; **Myo Myint**, Mission College, CA; **Lance Noe**, Troy University, AL; **Irene Pannatier**, Auburn Global University, AL; **Annie Percy**, Troy University, AL; **Erin Robinson**, Troy University, AL; **Juliane Rosner**, Mission College, CA; **Mary Stevens**, North Shore Community College, MA; **Pamela Stewart**, Henry Ford College, MI; **Karen Tucker**, Georgia Tech, GA; **Loreley Wheeler**, North Shore Community College, MA; **Amanda Wilcox**, Auburn Global University, AL; **Heike Williams**, Auburn Global University, AL

Canada

Angelika Brunel, Collège Ahuntsic, QC; **David Butler**, English Language Institute, BC; **Paul Edwards**, Kwantlen Polytechnic University, BC; **Cody Hawver**, University of British Columbia, BC; **Olivera Jovovic**, Kwantlen Polytechnic University, BC; **Tami Moffatt**, University of British Columbia, BC; **Dana Pynn**, Vancouver Island University, BC

Latin America

Georgette Barreda, SENATI, Peru; **Claudia Cecilia Díaz Romero**, Colegio América, Mexico; **Jeferson Ferro**, Uninter, Brazil; **Mayda Hernández**, English Center, Mexico; **Jose Ixtaccihusatl**, Instituto Tecnológico de Tecomatlán, Mexico; **Andreas Paulus Pabst**, CBA Idiomas, Brazil; **Amanda Carla Pas**, Instituição de Ensino Santa Izildinha, Brazil; **Allen Quesada Pacheco**, University of Costa Rica, Costa Rica; **Rolando Sánchez**, Escuela Normal de Tecámac, Mexico; **Luis Vasquez**, CESNO, Mexico

Asia

Asami Atsuko, Women's University, Japan; **Rene Bouchard**, Chinzei Keiai Gakuen, Japan; **Francis Brannen**, Sangmyung University, South Korea; **Haeyun Cho**, Sogang University, South Korea; **Daniel Craig**, Sangmyung University, South Korea; **Thomas Cuming**, Royal Melbourne Institute of Technology, Vietnam; **Jissen Joshi Daigaku**, Women's University, Japan; **Nguyen Duc Dat**, OISP, Vietnam; **Wayne Devitte**, Tokai University, Japan; **James D. Dunn**, Tokai University, Japan; **Fergus Hann**, Tokai University, Japan; **Michael Hood**, Nihon University College of Commerce, Japan; **Hideyuki Kashimoto**, Shijonawate High School, Japan; **David Kennedy**, Nihon University, Japan; **Anna Youngna Kim**, Sogang University, South Korea; **Jae Phil Kim**, Sogang University, South Korea; **Jaganathan Krishnasamy**, GB Academy, Malaysia; **Peter Laver**, Incheon National University, South Korea; **Hung Hoang Le**, Ho Chi Minh City University of Technology, Vietnam; **Hyon Sook Lee**, Sogang University, South Korea; **Ji-seon Lee**, Iruda English Institute, South Korea; **Joo Young Lee**, Sogang University, South Korea; **Phung Tu Luc**, Ho Chi Minh City University of Technology, Vietnam; **Richard Mansbridge**, Hoa Sen University, Vietnam; **Kahoko Matsumoto**, Tokai University, Japan; **Elizabeth May**, Sangmyung University, South Korea; **Naoyuki Naganuma**, Tokai University, Japan; **Hiroko Nishikage**, Taisho University, Japan; **Yongjun Park**, Sangji University, South Korea; **Paul Rogers**, Dongguk University, South Korea; **Scott Schafer**, Inha University, South Korea; **Michael Schvaudner**, Tokai University, Japan; **Brendan Smith**, RMIT University, School of Languages and English, Vietnam; **Peter Snashall**, Huachiew Chalermprakiet University, Thailand; Makoto Takeda, Sendai Third Senior High School, Japan; **Peter Talley**, Mahidol University, Faculty of ICT, Thailand; **Byron Thigpen**, Sogang University, South Korea; **Junko Yamaai**, Tokai University, Japan; **Junji Yamada**, Taisho University, Japan; **Sayoko Yamashita**, Women's University, Japan; **Masami Yukimori**, Taisho University, Japan

Middle East and North Africa

Sajjad Ahmad, Taibah University, Saudi Arabia; **Basma Alansari**, Taibah University, Saudi Arabia; **Marwa Al-ashqar**, Taibah University, Saudi Arabia; **Dr. Rashid Al-Khawaldeh**, Taibah University, Saudi Arabia; **Mohamed Almohamed**, Taibah University, Saudi Arabia; **Dr Musaad Alrahaili**, Taibah University, Saudi Arabia; **Hala Al Sammar**, Kuwait University, Kuwait; **Ahmed Alshammari**, Taibah University, Saudi Arabia; **Ahmed Alshamy**, Taibah University, Saudi Arabia; **Doniazad sultan AlShraideh**, Taibah University, Saudi Arabia; **Sahar Amer**, Taibah University, Saudi Arabia; **Nabeela Azam**, Taibah University, Saudi Arabia; **Hassan Bashir, Edex**, Saudi Arabia; **Rachel Batchilder**, College of the North Atlantic, Qatar; **Nicole Cuddie**, Community College of Qatar, Qatar; **Mahdi Duris**, King Saud University, Saudi Arabia; **Ahmed Ege**, Institute of Public Administration, Saudi Arabia; **Magda Fadle**, Victoria College, Egypt; **Mohammed Hassan**, Taibah University, Saudi Arabia; **Tom Hodgson**, Community College of Qatar, Qatar; **Ayub Agbar Khan**, Taibah University, Saudi Arabia; **Cynthia Le Joncour**, Taibah University, Saudi Arabia; **Ruari Alexander MacLeod**, Community College of Qatar, Qatar; **Nasir Mahmood**, Taibah University, Saudi Arabia; **Duria Salih Mahmoud**, Taibah University, Saudi Arabia; **Ameera McKoy**, Taibah University, Saudi Arabia; **Chaker Mhamdi**, Buraimi University College, Oman; **Baraa Shiekh Mohamed**, Community College of Qatar, Qatar; **Abduleelah Mohammed**, Taibah University, Saudi Arabia; **Shumaila Nasir**, Taibah University, Saudi Arabia; **Kevin Onwordi**, Taibah University, Saudi Arabia; **Dr. Navid Rahmani**, Community College of Qatar, Qatar; **Dr. Sabah Salman Sabbah**, Community College of Qatar, Qatar; **Salih**, Taibah University, Saudi Arabia; **Verna Santos-Nafrada**, King Saud University, Saudi Arabia; **Gamal Abdelfattah Shehata**, Taibah University, Saudi Arabia; **Ron Stefan**, Institute of Public Administration, Saudi Arabia; **Dr. Saad Torki**, Imam Abdulrahman Bin Faisal University, Dammam, Saudi Arabia; **Silvia Yafai**, Applied Technology High School/Secondary Technical School, UAE; **Mahmood Zar**, Taibah University, Saudi Arabia; **Thouraya Zheni**, Taibah University, Saudi Arabia

Turkey

Sema Babacan, Istanbul Medipol University; **Bilge Çöllüoğlu Yakar**, Bilkent University; **Liana Corniel**, Koc University; **Savas Geylanioglu**, Izmir Bahcesehir Science and Technology College; **Öznur Güler**, Giresun University; **Selen Bilginer Halefoğlu**, Maltepe University; **Ahmet Konukoğlu**, Hasan Kalyoncu University; **Mehmet Salih Yoğun**, Gaziantep Hasan Kalyoncu University; **Fatih Yücel**, Beykent University

Europe

Amina Al Hashamia, University of Exeter, UK; **Irina Gerasimova**, Saint-Petersburg Mining University, Russia; **Jodi**, Las Dominicas, Spain; **Marina Khanykova**, School 179, Russia; **Oksana Postnikova**, Lingua Practica, Russia; **Nina Vasilchenko**, Soho-Bridge Language School, Russia

CRITICAL THINKING

The unique critical thinking approach of the *Q: Skills for Success* series has been further enhanced in the Third Edition. New features help you analyze, synthesize, and develop your ideas.

Unit question

The thought-provoking unit questions engage you with the topic and provide a critical thinking framework for the unit.

UNIT QUESTION

What is the value of learning a new language?

A. Discuss these questions with your classmates.

1. Which languages can you speak? How and why did you learn them?
2. Do you think that learning languages has changed any of your ideas or opinions?
3. Look at the photo. Is there another language you would like to learn? What is it, and why?

 B. Listen to *The Q Classroom* **online. Then answer these questions.**

Analysis

You can discuss your opinion of each reading text and analyze how it changes your perspective on the unit question.

WRITE WHAT YOU THINK

A. DISCUSS Discuss the questions in a group. Think about the Unit Question, "How is work changing?"

1. How has the gig economy changed the way we work?
2. Would you prefer to have gig work or a traditional full-time job?
3. Are there other winners and losers in the gig economy apart from those discussed in Reading 1?

B. CREATE Choose one of the questions from Activity A and write one to two paragraphs in response. Look back at your Quick Write on page 36 as you think about what you learned.

NEW! Critical Thinking Strategy with video

Each unit includes a Critical Thinking Strategy with activities to give you step-by-step guidance in critical analysis of texts. An accompanying instructional video (available on iQ Online) provides extra support and examples.

NEW! Bloom's Taxonomy

Blue activity headings integrate verbs from Bloom's Taxonomy to help you see how each activity develops critical thinking skills.

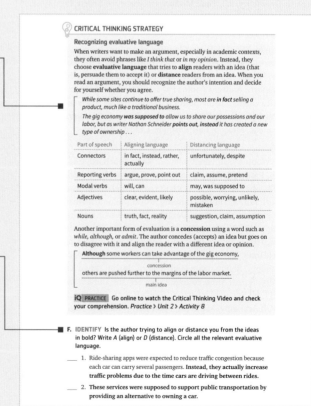

CRITICAL THINKING STRATEGY

Recognizing evaluative language

When writers want to make an argument, especially in academic contexts, they often avoid phrases like *I think that* or *in my opinion*. Instead, they choose **evaluative language** that tries to **align** readers with an idea (that is, persuade them to accept it) or **distance** readers from an idea. When you read an argument, you should recognize the author's intention and decide for yourself whether you agree.

> While some sites continue to offer true sharing, most are **in fact** selling a product, much like a traditional business.
>
> The gig economy **was supposed to** allow us to share our possessions and our labor, but as writer Nathan Schneider **points out**, **instead** it has created a new type of ownership . . .

Part of speech	Aligning language	Distancing language
Connectors	in fact, instead, rather, actually	unfortunately, despite
Reporting verbs	argue, prove, point out	claim, assume, pretend
Modal verbs	will, can	may, was supposed to
Adjectives	clear, evident, likely	possible, worrying, unlikely, mistaken
Nouns	truth, fact, reality	suggestion, claim, assumption

Another important form of evaluation is a **concession** using a word such as *while*, *although*, or *admit*. The author concedes (accepts) an idea but goes on to disagree with it and align the reader with a different idea or opinion.

> **Although** some workers can take advantage of the gig economy,
>
> concession
>
> others are pushed further to the margins of the labor market.
>
> main idea

iQ PRACTICE Go online to watch the Critical Thinking Video and check your comprehension. *Practice > Unit 2 > Activity B*

F. IDENTIFY Is the author trying to align or distance you from the ideas in bold? Write *A* (align) or *D* (distance). Circle all the relevant evaluative language.

___ 1. Ride-sharing apps were expected to reduce traffic congestion because each car can carry several passengers. **Instead, they actually increase traffic problems due to the time cars are driving between rides.**

___ 2. These services were supposed to support public transportation by **providing an alternative to owning a car.**

THREE TYPES OF VIDEO

UNIT VIDEO

The unit videos include high-interest documentaries and reports on a wide variety of subjects, all linked to the unit topic and question. All videos are from authentic sources.

NEW! "Work with the Video" pages guide you in watching, understanding, and discussing the unit videos. The activities help you see the connection to the Unit Question and the other texts in the unit.

CRITICAL THINKING VIDEO

NEW! Narrated by the Q series authors, these short videos give you further instruction into the Critical Thinking Strategy of each unit using engaging images and graphics. You can use them to get a deeper understanding of the Critical Thinking Strategy.

SKILLS VIDEO

NEW! These instructional videos provide illustrated explanations of skills and grammar points in the Student Book. They can be viewed in class or assigned for a flipped classroom, for homework, or for review. One skill video is available for every unit.

Easily access all videos in the Resources section of iQ Online.

WORK WITH THE VIDEO

A. PREVIEW What do you know about sign language? Who uses it, and why?

VIDEO VOCABULARY

deaf (adj.) unable to hear anything or unable to hear very well

hoe (n.) a garden tool with a long handle and a blade, used for breaking up soil and removing weeds

prospect (n.) an idea of what might happen in the future

remote (adj.) far away from places where other people live

iQ RESOURCES Go online to watch the video about a sign-language class in Uganda, a country in East-Central Africa. *Resources > Unit 1 > Unit Video*

B. CATEGORIZE Watch the video two or three times. Take notes in the chart.

Challenges Patrick faces	Benefits of learning sign language

How to compare and contrast

Venn Diagram

Firefighter — fights fires; stays at the station until called

Both — help people; have dangerous jobs

Police Officer — fights crime; works on the street

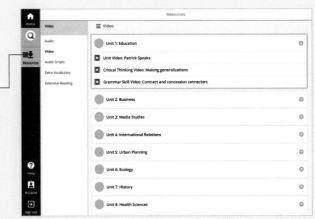

VOCABULARY

A research-based vocabulary program focuses on the words you need to know academically and professionally.

The vocabulary syllabus in *Q: Skills for Success* is correlated to the CEFR (see page 256) and linked to two word lists: the Oxford 5000 and the OPAL (Oxford Phrasal Academic Lexicon).

℞+ OXFORD 5000

The Oxford 5000 is an expanded core word list for advanced learners of English. As well as the Oxford 3000 core list, the Oxford 5000 includes an additional 2,000 words, guiding learners at B2–C1 level on the most useful high-level words to learn.

PREVIEW THE READING

A. PREVIEW Read the title and subheadings of the article. How do you think learning a language can improve tolerance?

B. QUICK WRITE What advantages do bilinguals have? Think about the types of knowledge and ways of communicating that are available to bilinguals but not monolinguals (people who only speak one language). Write for 5–10 minutes. Remember to use this section for your Unit Assignment.

C. VOCABULARY Check (✓) the words and phrases you know. Then work with a partner to locate each word or phrase in the reading. Use clues to help define the words or phrases you don't know. Check your definitions in the dictionary.

acquisition *(n.)* ℞+ OPAL	involve *(v.)* ℞+ OPAL
ambiguity *(n.)*	motivation *(n.)* ℞+ OPAL
bilingual *(adj., n.)*	refer to *(v. phr.)* OPAL
cue *(n.)* ℞+	stereotype *(n.)* ℞+
depending on *(v. phr.)*	the likelihood of *(n. phr.)* OPAL
immersion *(n.)*	tolerance *(n.)* ℞+

℞+ Oxford 5000™ words   OPAL Oxford Phrasal Academic Lexicon

iQ PRACTICE Go online to listen and practice your pronunciation.
Practice › Unit 1 › Activity 2

Vocabulary Key
In vocabulary activities, ℞+ shows you the word is in the Oxford 5000 and **OPAL** shows you the word or phrase is in the OPAL.

OPAL
OXFORD PHRASAL ACADEMIC LEXICON

NEW! The OPAL is a collection of four word lists that provide an essential guide to the most important words and phrases to know for academic English. The word lists are based on the Oxford Corpus of Academic English and the British Academic Spoken English corpus. The OPAL includes both spoken and written academic English and both individual words and longer phrases.

Academic Language tips in the Student Book give information about how words and phrases from the OPAL are used and offer help with features such as collocations and phrasal verbs.

ACADEMIC LANGUAGE
Similar phrases to *the likelihood of* in writing include *the possibility of*, *the probability of*, and *the potential for*. An alternative sentence structure is: *X is more/less likely to (be)*.

――――――――――| OPAL
Oxford Phrasal Academic Lexicon

B. VOCABULARY Here are some words an sentences. Then write each underlined v definition. You may need to change verb

a. Second language <u>acquisition</u> is a long and

b. Students who have strong <u>motivation</u> ten

c. <u>The likelihood of</u> fully learning a new lan

d. You need a high degree of <u>tolerance</u> to de

e. There is a lot of <u>ambiguity</u> in text message communicate emotions well.

f. *Social intelligence* <u>refers to</u> people's ability discussions.

g. In many countries, a <u>stereotype</u> of the Uni learn foreign languages.

EXTENSIVE READING

NEW! Extensive Reading is a program of reading for pleasure at a level that matches your language ability.

There are many benefits to Extensive Reading:

- It helps you to become a better reader in general.
- It helps to increase your reading speed.
- It can improve your reading comprehension.
- It increases your vocabulary range.
- It can improve your grammar and writing skills.
- It's great for motivation—reading something that is interesting for its own sake.

Each unit of *Q: Skills for Success Third Edition* has been aligned to an Oxford Graded Reader based on the appropriate topic and level of language proficiency. The first chapter of each recommended graded reader can be downloaded from iQ Online Resources.

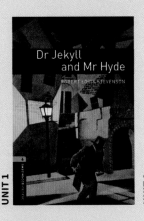

UNIT 1

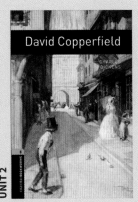

UNIT 2

UNIT 3

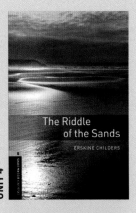

UNIT 4

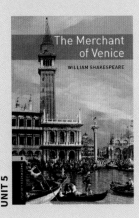

UNIT 5

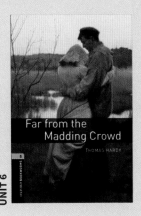

UNIT 6

UNIT 7

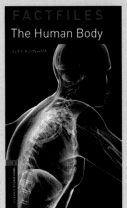

UNIT 8

What is iQ ONLINE?

iQ ONLINE extends your learning beyond the classroom.

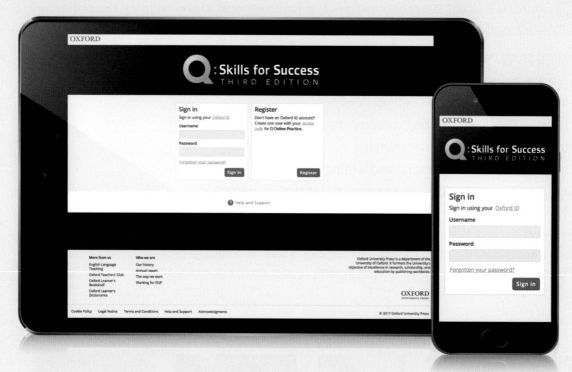

- Practice activities provide essential skills practice and support.
- Automatic grading and progress reports show you what you have mastered and where you need more practice.
- Discussion Board to discuss the Unit Questions helps you develop your critical thinking.
- Writing Tutor helps you practice your academic writing skills.
- Essential resources such as audio and video are easy to access anytime.

NEW TO THE THIRD EDITION

- Site is optimized for mobile use so you can use it on your phone.
- An updated interface allows easy navigation around the activities, tests, resources, and scores.
- New Critical Thinking Videos expand on the Critical Thinking Strategies in the Student Book.
- Extensive Reading program helps you improve your vocabulary and reading skills.

How to use iQ ONLINE

Go to **Practice** to find additional practice and support to complement your learning in the classroom.

Go to **Resources** to find
- All Student Book video
- All Student Book audio
- Critical Thinking videos
- Skills videos
- Extensive Reading

Go to **Messages** and **Discussion Board** to communicate with your teacher and classmates.

Online tests assigned by your teacher help you assess your progress and see where you still need more practice.

Progress bar shows you how many activities you have completed.

View your scores for all activities.

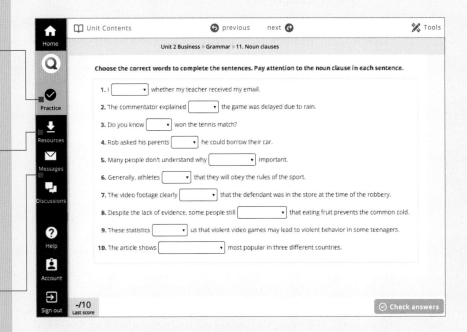

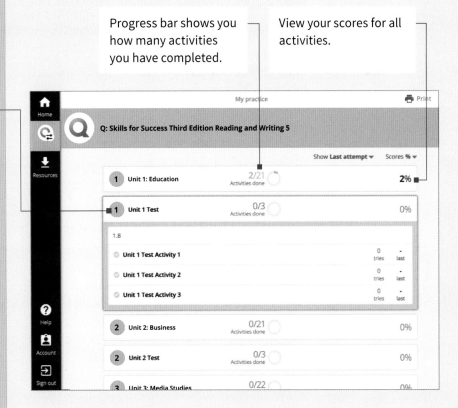

CONTENTS

Education

READING	distinguishing main ideas from details
CRITICAL THINKING	making generalizations
VOCABULARY	using a thesaurus
WRITING	writing an effective email
GRAMMAR	contrast and concession connectors

What is the value of learning a new language?

A. Discuss these questions with your classmates.

1. Which languages can you speak? How and why did you learn them?

2. Do you think that learning languages has changed any of your ideas or opinions?

3. Look at the photo. Is there another language you would like to learn? What is it, and why?

B. Listen to *The Q Classroom* online. Then answer these questions.

1. Why do Sophy and Felix think it's useful to learn a new language?

2. Why does Marcus disagree?

iQ PRACTICE   Go to the online discussion board to discuss the Unit Question with your classmates. *Practice > Unit 1 > Activity 1*

UNIT OBJECTIVE

Read two articles with contrasting opinions on the value of learning a new language. Gather information and ideas to write a persuasive email about a new foreign language program in your school, university, or community.

READING 1

How Learning a New Language Improves Tolerance

OBJECTIVE ▶

You are going to read an article from the website *The Conversation* about the benefits of learning a new language. It was written by an applied linguist, a professional who studies how languages are taught and learned. Use the article to gather information and ideas for your Unit Assignment.

PREVIEW THE READING

A. PREVIEW Read the title and subheadings of the article. How do you think learning a language can improve tolerance?

B. QUICK WRITE What advantages do bilinguals have? Think about the types of knowledge and ways of communicating that are available to bilinguals but not monolinguals (people who only speak one language). Write for 5–10 minutes. Remember to use this section for your Unit Assignment.

C. VOCABULARY Check (✓) the words and phrases you know. Then work with a partner to locate each word or phrase in the reading. Use clues to help define the words or phrases you don't know. Check your definitions in the dictionary.

acquisition *(n.)* &+ OPAL	**involve** *(v.)* &+ OPAL
ambiguity *(n.)*	**motivation** *(n.)* &+ OPAL
bilingual *(adj., n.)*	**refer to** *(v. phr.)* OPAL
cue *(n.)* &+	**stereotype** *(n.)* &+
depending on *(v. phr.)*	**the likelihood of** *(n. phr.)* OPAL
immersion *(n.)*	**tolerance** *(n.)* &+

&+ Oxford 5000™ words   OPAL Oxford Phrasal Academic Lexicon

iQ PRACTICE Go online to listen and practice your pronunciation.
Practice > Unit 1 > Activity 2

WORK WITH THE READING

How Learning a New Language Improves Tolerance

By Amy S. Thompson

1   There are many benefits to knowing more than one language. For example, it has been shown that aging adults who speak more than one language have less **likelihood of** developing dementia[1]. Additionally, the **bilingual** brain becomes better at filtering out distractions, and learning multiple languages improves creativity. Evidence also shows that learning subsequent languages is easier than learning the first foreign language (Thompson, 2013). Unfortunately, not all U.S. universities consider learning foreign languages a worthwhile investment.

Why is foreign language study important at the university level?

2   As an applied linguist, I study how learning multiple languages can have cognitive and emotional benefits. One of these benefits that's not obvious is that language learning improves **tolerance**.

3   This happens in two important ways. The first is that it opens people's eyes to a way of doing things that is different from their own, which is called *cultural competence*. The second is related to the comfort level of a person when dealing with unfamiliar situations, or *tolerance of* **ambiguity**.

Gaining cross-cultural understanding

4   Cultural competence is key to thriving in our increasingly globalized world. How specifically does language learning improve cultural competence? The answer can be illuminated by examining different types of intelligence.

5   Psychologist Robert Sternberg's research on intelligence describes different types of intelligence and how they are related to adult language learning. What he **refers to** as "practical intelligence" is similar to social intelligence in that it helps individuals learn nonexplicit information from their environments,

[1] **dementia:** a serious mental disorder usually caused by old age that affects the ability to think, remember, and behave normally

including meaningful gestures or other social **cues**. Language learning inevitably **involves** learning about different cultures. Students pick up clues about the culture both in language classes and through meaningful **immersion** experiences, such as visiting countries where the language is spoken and interacting with users of the language. Therefore, language learners develop new types of practical intelligence that will help them communicate across cultures.

6   Researchers have also shown that when students learn another language, they develop new ways of understanding culture through analyzing cultural **stereotypes**. This is because "learning a second language involves the **acquisition** not only of linguistic forms but also ways of thinking and behaving" (Nguyen & Kellogg, 2010). With the help of an instructor, students can think critically about stereotypes of different cultures related to food, appearance, and conversation styles.

Dealing with the unknown

7   The second way that adult language learning increases tolerance is related to the comfort level of a person when dealing with tolerance of ambiguity. Someone with a high tolerance of ambiguity finds unfamiliar situations exciting, rather than frightening. My research on **motivation**, anxiety, and beliefs indicates that language learning improves people's tolerance of ambiguity, especially when more than one foreign language is involved (Thompson & Aslan, 2015; Thompson & Erdil-Moody, 2016; Thompson & Lee, 2012).

8   It's not difficult to see why this may be so. Conversations in a foreign language will inevitably involve unknown words. It wouldn't be a successful conversation if one of the speakers constantly stopped to say, "Hang on—I don't know that word. Let me look it up in the dictionary." Those with a high tolerance of ambiguity would feel comfortable maintaining the conversation despite the unfamiliar words involved. Indeed, research shows that those

with experience learning more than one foreign language in an instructed setting have more tolerance of ambiguity (Dewaele & Wei, 2012).

What changes with this understanding

9   A high tolerance of ambiguity brings many advantages. It helps students become less anxious in social interactions and in subsequent language-learning experiences. Not surprisingly, the more experience a person has with language learning, the more comfortable the person gets with this ambiguity.

10   And that's not all.

11   Individuals with higher levels of tolerance of ambiguity have also been found to be more entrepreneurial (i.e., are more optimistic, innovative, and open to taking risks).

12   In the current climate, universities are frequently being judged by the salaries of their graduates. Taking it one step further, based on the relationship of tolerance of ambiguity and entrepreneurial intention, increased tolerance of ambiguity could lead to higher salaries for graduates, which in turn, I believe, could help increase funding for those universities that require foreign language study. Those who have devoted their lives to theorizing about and teaching languages might say, "It's not about the money." But perhaps it is.

Language learning in higher education

13   Most U.S. universities have a minimal language requirement that often varies **depending on** the student's major. However, students can typically opt out of the requirement by taking a placement test or providing some other proof of competency.

14   In contrast to this trend, Princeton University recently announced that all students, regardless of their competency when entering the university, would be required to study an additional language. I'd argue that more universities should follow Princeton's lead, as language study at the university level could lead to an increased tolerance of the different cultural norms

represented in U.S. society. There have been many examples recently of conflicts on university campuses between students of different backgrounds and opinions. A little more tolerance would help everyone.

15 Knowledge of different languages is crucial to becoming global citizens. As former Secretary of Education[2] Arne Duncan noted, "Our country needs to create a future in which all Americans understand that by speaking more than one language, they are enabling our country to compete successfully and work collaboratively with partners across the globe."

16 Considering the evidence that studying languages as adults increases tolerance in two important ways, the question shouldn't be, "Why should universities require foreign language study?" but rather, "Why in the world wouldn't they?"

[2]**Secretary of Education:** the person in the U.S. government responsible for the country's educational system

References

Dewaele, J.-M., & Wei, L. (2012). Is multilingualism linked to a higher tolerance of ambiguity? *Bilingualism: Language and Cognition, 16,* 231–240.

Nguyen, H.T., & Kellogg, G. (2010). "I had a stereotype that Americans were fat": Becoming a speaker of culture in a second language. *The Modern Language Journal, 94,* 56-73.

Thompson, A.S. (2013). The interface of language aptitude and multilingualism: Reconsidering the bilingual/multilingual dichotomy. *Modern Language Journal, 97,* 685–70. doi: 10.1111/j.1540-4781.2013.12034.x

Thompson, A.S. & Aslan, E. (2015). Multilingualism, perceived positive language interaction (PPLI), and learner beliefs: What do Turkish students believe? *International Journal of Multilingualism, 12,* 259–275. doi: 10.1080/14790718.2014.973413

Thompson, A.S. & Erdil-Moody, Z. (2016). Operationalizing multilingualism: Language learning motivation in Turkey. *International Journal of Bilingual Education and Bilingualism, 19,* 314–331. doi: 10.1080/13670050.2014.985631

Thompson, A.S. & Lee, J. (2012). Anxiety and EFL: Does multilingualism matter? *International Journal of Bilingual Education and Bilingualism, 16,* 730–749.

B. VOCABULARY Here are some words and phrases from Reading 1. Read the sentences. Then write each underlined word or phrase next to the correct definition. You may need to change verbs to their base form.

a. Second language <u>acquisition</u> is a long and complex process.

b. Students who have strong <u>motivation</u> tend to learn languages faster.

c. <u>The likelihood of</u> fully learning a new language decreases with age.

d. You need a high degree of <u>tolerance</u> to deal with unfamiliar situations.

e. There is a lot of <u>ambiguity</u> in text messages because they are short and can't communicate emotions well.

f. *Social intelligence* <u>refers to</u> people's ability to participate in conversations and discussions.

g. In many countries, a <u>stereotype</u> of the United States is that people there do not learn foreign languages.

ACADEMIC LANGUAGE

Similar phrases to **the likelihood of** in writing include *the possibility of, the probability of,* and *the potential for.* An alternative sentence structure is: *X is more/less likely to (be).*

⌐ OPAL

Oxford Phrasal Academic Lexicon

h. Learning basic communication skills in a new language can take 6–12 months, <u>depending on</u> the situation.

i. Many Canadians are <u>bilingual</u> in English and French.

j. She did not recognize the <u>cue</u> that the interview was finished.

k. In an <u>immersion</u> language program, students use only the new language in their classes and conversations.

l. Academic classes <u>involve</u> reading, writing, listening, and speaking.

1. _____ *(verb phrase)* to describe or be connected to somebody or something

2. _____ *(noun)* willingness to accept ideas and beliefs that are different from your own

3. _____ *(noun phrase)* the chance of something happening

4. _____ *(noun)* the state of being difficult to understand or explain because it has many different aspects or possible meanings

5. _____ *(adjective)* able to speak two languages

6. _____ *(noun)* the act of obtaining something, such as knowledge or a skill

7. _____ *(noun)* the feeling of wanting to do something

8. _____ *(noun)* a fixed idea or image that many people have of a particular type of person or thing, but which is often not true in reality

9. _____ *(verb)* having something as a necessary part of an event or activity

10. _____ *(noun)* an action or event that is a signal for somebody to do something

11. _____ *(verb phrase)* according to

12. _____ *(noun)* the state of being completely involved in something

iQ PRACTICE Go online for more practice with the vocabulary.
Practice > Unit 1 > Activity 3

C. IDENTIFY Check (✓) the main benefits of learning a new language, according to the article.

☐ 1. Bilinguals are less easily distracted.

☐ 2. Bilinguals are better at handling new situations.

☐ 3. Bilinguals are better at math.

☐ 4. Learning a new language helps you think more carefully about stereotypes.

☐ 5. Learning a new language helps you read better in your first language.

D. RESTATE Find two pieces of evidence from the article that support each main idea. Write them below the statement. Include the paragraph number where you found the evidence.

1. There are many benefits to the brain of becoming bilingual.

   a. _____

   b. _____

2. Learning a new language improves cross-cultural understanding.

   a. _____

   b. _____

3. Learning a new language helps you tolerate ambiguity.

   a. _____

   b. _____

4. Tolerance for ambiguity is beneficial for the future.

   a. _____

   b. _____

5. Universities should require students to study a foreign language.

   a. _____

   b. _____

E. CATEGORIZE Read the statements. Write *T* (true) or *F* (false). Then correct each false statement to make it true. Write the number of the paragraph where you found the answer.

____ 1. It is easier to learn a third language than a second one. (Paragraph: ____)

____ 2. Learning gestures and other body language is part of social intelligence. (Paragraph: ____)

____ 3. Learning a language only involves learning grammar and vocabulary. (Paragraph: ____)

____ 4. People with high tolerance of ambiguity become very anxious when they speak a second language. (Paragraph: ____)

____ 5. In a successful conversation, speakers often stop to check the meaning of new words in a dictionary. (Paragraph: ____)

____ 6. Language learners become more comfortable taking risks. (Paragraph: ____)

____ 7. All U.S. university students have to study a foreign language. (Paragraph: ____)

____ 8. Princeton University has stopped requiring its students to study a foreign language. (Paragraph: ____)

____ 9. Arne Duncan believes that students should learn languages so they can work with people from different countries. (Paragraph: ____)

____ 10. The author concludes that there is not enough evidence to recommend language study for all university students. (Paragraph: ____)

F. EXTEND Look back at your Quick Write on page 4. What advantages do bilinguals have? Add any new information you learned from the reading.

iQ PRACTICE Go online for additional reading and comprehension.
Practice > Unit 1 > Activity 4

WRITE WHAT YOU THINK

A. EVALUATE Discuss the questions in a group. Think about the Unit Question, "What is the value of learning a new language?"

1. Is learning a new language an advantage when you are looking for a job? What types of jobs require knowledge of additional languages?

2. Should all non-English-speaking countries require students to learn English? Why or why not?

B. CREATE Choose one of the questions from Activity A and write one to two paragraphs in response. Look back at your Quick Write on page 4 as you think about what you learned.

READING SKILL Distinguishing main ideas from details

Main ideas are the major points that support the focus of a piece of writing. If you can find the main ideas and distinguish them from the supporting details, you will understand the purpose and focus of the writing. In most texts, you can find main ideas by doing the following:

- paying attention to repeated vocabulary, which may be key words
- looking for words in the headline or title of the text
- reading subheadings and the captions of any graphs or illustrations
- watching for words that introduce conclusions and main ideas, such as *therefore, as a result, so, (more/most) importantly, finally*, and *to conclude*
- focusing on words in bold, italics, or different colors

The position of the main ideas may depend on the **genre**, or **type of text**, because there are different ways of organizing information.

Academic writing is divided into paragraphs that usually contain one main idea. The main idea is often stated near the beginning of the paragraph and summarized at the end, so read the first and last sentences of each paragraph carefully. Remember that all the main ideas in the text are usually connected to the central focus, argument, or thesis of the paper. This is often stated near the end of the introduction.

News articles, whether in print or online, have to catch readers' attention and then keep them reading. They frequently use headlines and subheadings to give main ideas.

Business communication has to be brief, efficient, and persuasive, so main ideas are often stated early and repeated at the end of the text. Bullet points, bold text, and repetition are often used to draw the readers' attention.

Narratives, including anecdotes (short, amusing stories about a real incident or person), fairy tales, folk tales, and stories told on blogs and in magazines, typically start with an orientation (the place and time of the event), followed by the series of events that occurred. If there is a moral, message, main idea, or lesson, it will usually come at the end of the narrative.

A. IDENTIFY Read the excerpts. Identify the genre of the writing. Then write the main idea in a sentence.

1.

> When people move to a new culture, they usually experience a series of different feelings as they adjust to their new surroundings. A new culture is not necessarily another country or a place where another language is spoken. Therefore, this adjustment can occur in any situation where a person's normal rules of behavior no longer work. The process of adapting to these differences has four stages and is called *culture shock*.

Genre: _____

Main idea: _____

_____

2.

> **Solution: *Say It Again* Language Learning Program**
>
> The company is interested in investing in a language-learning program. There are two suitable programs available: *Say It Again* and *Language Now*. We recommend *Say It Again* for these reasons:
>
> • cost: 19 percent less
>
> • technical support: included in price
>
> *Say It Again* will meet our needs at a lower cost and with better service.

Genre: _____

Main idea: _____

_____

3.

> A few years ago, I had the opportunity to travel to Japan. I was excited because I had never visited Asia before, but I was also nervous because I didn't speak a word of Japanese. I couldn't even guess the meanings of words on menus as I couldn't read any of the characters. I had to rely on the patience of English-speaking waiters and hotel staff, which was a humbling experience. The moral of the story for me was that it is essential to learn even a few basic words of a language before you travel to a new country.

Genre: _____

Main idea: _____

_____

4.

> Languages change through two processes: internal change and language contact. Internal change occurs slowly over time as words or phrases shift in meaning or grammatical structure. For instance, the Old English *a nadder*, meaning "a snake," gradually became *an adder*, the modern word, when the *n* became attached to the article. The second source of change is external, and it occurs when another, usually more powerful, language comes into contact with it.

Genre: _____

Main idea: _____

_____

5.

> This study examined the cultural stereotypes of students who learn a second language. By observing adult students and collecting their discussion board posts and writing assignments, we looked at how students' understanding of the word *stereotype* changed during a semester. Our analysis demonstrates that learning a second language involves the acquisition not only of linguistic forms but also ways of thinking and behaving in new cultural contexts.

Genre: _____

Main idea: _____

_____

B. DISCUSS How would you find the main ideas in the following types of writing? Discuss your answers with a partner.

1. an email

_____

2. a business letter

_____

3. an advertisement

_____

4. a newspaper editorial

_____

iQ PRACTICE Go online for more practice with distinguishing between main ideas and details. *Practice > Unit 1 > Activity 5*

Is Learning Languages a Waste of Time?

You are going to read an opinion column about teaching languages from the British newspaper *The Guardian*, followed by three letters sent to the editor in response. Use the article and letters to gather information and ideas for your Unit Assignment.

PREVIEW THE READING

TIP FOR SUCCESS

Reading opinion columns and letters to the editor in newspapers is a good way to learn how to make good arguments in writing.

A. PREVIEW Look at the article and responses. Does each writer believe that language learning is beneficial or a waste of time?

B. QUICK WRITE Do you think that it is a waste of time for students in English-speaking countries to learn another language? Write for 5–10 minutes. Remember to use this section for your Unit Assignment.

C. VOCABULARY Check (✓) the words and phrases you know. Then work with a partner to locate each word or phrase in the reading. Use clues to help define the words or phrases you don't know. Check your definitions in the dictionary.

is based on *(adj. phr.)* OPAL	**fallacy** *(n.)*
cognitive *(adj.)* 🔑+	**lingua franca** *(n.)*
contemporary *(adj.)* 🔑+ OPAL	**measure** *(v.)* 🔑+ OPAL
enhanced *(adj.)* 🔑+ OPAL	**plummet** *(v.)*
equip *(v.)* 🔑+	**specialist** *(adj.)* 🔑+ OPAL
exploration *(n.)* 🔑+ OPAL	**spread the myth** *(v. phr.)*

🔑+ Oxford 5000™ words   OPAL Oxford Phrasal Academic Lexicon

iQ PRACTICE Go online to listen and practice your pronunciation.
Practice > Unit 1 > Activity 6

WORK WITH THE READING

A. INVESTIGATE Read the article and letters and gather opinions about the value of learning languages in English-speaking countries.

Is Learning Languages a Waste of Time?

BY SIMON JENKINS

1   Education policy is like defense policy. It is always fighting the last war but one. Predictable woe¹ has greeted the **plummeting** number of pupils studying modern languages, which has fallen by roughly 10% in a year and German by one-third since 2010. Only Chinese and Arabic look reasonably healthy.

2   Students are not stupid. They take subjects they find relevant to their future lives. European languages are not that. Europe is universally adopting English as a **lingua franca**. European universities are increasingly English environments. In addition, translation, spoken as well as written, has (like math) proved susceptible to computerization².

3   Those who need to learn German to live or work there can do so in an immersion class faster, more efficiently, and far more cheaply than by sitting in a schoolroom for an hour a week for years—the perfect way not to learn a language but to forget one. German should be a **specialist** skill for those who love or need it, and can be taught as such.

4   Languages are beloved of reactionary educators for one reason: they are easy to test, quantify, and regiment³. Challenge the usefulness of such subjects, and teachers fall back on the medieval saying that "they train the mind." They used to say that of Latin. They then switch and claim language students "earn more." It never occurs to them that, as with Latin, successful students are those who know how to please their teachers.

5   Computerization is clearly transforming education. It is also showing what computers cannot do, and good teachers can. A computer cannot inspire students with the wonders of the scientific world. It cannot guide them through the glories and horrors of Europe's history. It cannot unfold the human drama of literature or the full mystery of the global environment. A computer cannot teach the life skills of speaking, listening, debating, personal presentation, and confidence.

6   The mad month of August (when national exam results are released) gets ever madder, as the education system plunges deeper each year into the one thing that obsesses it: how many students and institutions did exactly how well in an exam. It is the greatest of political **fallacies**, to make what is measurable important, not what is important measurable.

7   Germany is Europe's most important country of our day. Teach its history, revel in⁴ its culture, analyze the strength of its economy. Visit its cities and countryside—and see how much better they are planned and protected than ours. In comparison, learning Germany's language is not that important.

¹ **woe:** great sadness
² **computerization:** the process of converting a system, device, etc. to be operated by computers
³ **regiment:** to organize strictly
⁴ **revel in:** to enjoy something very much

Now read these letters to the editor written in response to Jenkins's article and published in the following issue of *The Guardian*.

8   Simon Jenkins is accurate in reporting the falling numbers studying languages in the UK. Almost everything else in his article flies in the face of[5] the evidence. All the evidence shows clearly that speaking English is not enough in the **contemporary** world. The concept of "global English" **is based on** the very high numbers of people internationally who have learned English as a second language and who are, therefore, by definition, bilingual or multilingual, benefiting from all the well-attested advantages—cognitive and other—of speaking more than one language.

9   Contrary to the idea that languages are "easy to test, quantify, and regiment," many of the less quantifiable but crucial skills to be gained hinge on **enhanced** relationships and deep cultural understanding, both of which impact profoundly on business, politics, and peace. Language is inextricably bound up with history, culture, and economics, whose importance Jenkins fully acknowledges.

10   It is time to stop **spreading the myth** that we are not good at learning languages and will, in any case, only ever need English. Comments such as these, alongside arguments about languages as "specialist" skills, serve only to perpetuate the perceived elitism of language learning at post-primary level.

Prof. Wendy Ayres-Bennett, *University of Cambridge;* **Prof. Janice Carruthers**, *Queen's University Belfast;* **Prof. Charles Forsdick**, *University of Liverpool;* **Prof. Stephen Hutchings**, *University of Manchester;* **Prof. Katrin Kohl**, *University of Oxford*

11   There are different ways to get up a hill: walking up, practicing navigation, exploring the landscape, getting exercise—or choosing a cable car and taking a selfie on the top. Likewise, education can be a path of **exploration**, in which not only the final result counts but everything learned on the way. Or it can be an exam selfie, "been there, done it."

12   Simon Jenkins criticizes the current trend to reduce education to league tables[6], replacing the path of learning experience through a screenshot of exam results. But his argument against learning foreign languages attacks precisely what he is defending. He praises "speaking, listening, debating," guiding students through "the human drama of literature," and "reveling in culture." Well, that's exactly what language learning is about: a path of exploration (to use a popular German term: *Wanderung*) through the landscapes of history and culture, science and technology, politics and economics. It makes you understand people, their way of thinking and doing things. It is also a mental exercise which, as recent research shows, improves attention and understanding of other points of view, delays **cognitive** ageing and dementia, and leads to a better recovery from stroke[7]. It is an example of learning for

[5] **fly in the face of:** to go against; to be the opposite of
[6] **league table:** a table that shows how well institutions such as schools are performing in comparison with each other
[7] **stroke:** a sudden serious illness when a blood vessel (= tube) in the brain bursts or is blocked

life rather than just for exams. And it is not easy to **measure**; testing vocabulary tells us as much about knowledge of languages as listing dates does about understanding history. I agree that we should focus on "what is important." That's why we need languages.

13 If all you want from Germany is a selfie in front of the Brandenburg Gate[8], you won't need any German. But to understand German history, culture and people, do business with them, and learn from them, you'll be better off learning at least a bit of their language.

Dr. Thomas H. Bak, *University of Edinburgh*

14 Simon Jenkins thinks learning languages at school is a waste of time. We disagree.

15 It's not true, as he claims, that "Europe is universally adopting English as a lingua franca." Get away from the big tourist resorts, and you're probably lost without some knowledge of the local language. Only 38% of Europeans claim to be able to operate in English. And what arrogance to make others do the hard work. European languages are relevant to young people.

16 It is true, as he admits, that a language such as German may be needed by some; and it is true that such a language can be learned later in life—but how much harder if you've never learned any foreign language at all at school! According to the national curriculum (of England and Wales), that's what school language lessons are for: "Language teaching should provide the foundation for learning further languages, **equipping** pupils to study and work in other countries."

17 It's not true that languages are only taught because "they are easy to test, quantify, and regiment." In fact, they're very hard to test fairly. There's a much better reason for teaching them: that they're really interesting and mind-opening, and appeal to the same mental faculties as math.

Richard Hudson, *Emeritus Professor of Linguistics, University College London;* **Dr. Louise Courtney**, *University of Reading;* **Dr. Marcello Giovanelli**, *Aston University;* **Dr. René Koglbauer**, *Newcastle University;* **Prof. Terry Lamb**, *University of Westminster;* **Dr. Gee Macrory**, *Manchester Metropolitan University;* **Dr. Emma Marsden**, *University of York*

[8] **Brandenburg Gate:** a famous monument and tourist attraction in Berlin, Germany

B. VOCABULARY Here are some words and phrases from Reading 2. Read their definitions. Then complete each sentence.

is based on *(adj. phr.)* using or developing an idea
cognitive *(adj.)* connected with mental processes of understanding
contemporary *(adj.)* belonging to the present time
enhanced *(adj.)* increased or improved
equip *(v.)* to prepare somebody for an activity or task
exploration *(n.)* an examination of something in order to find out about it
fallacy *(n.)* a false idea that many people believe is true
lingua franca *(n.)* a common language used between people whose native languages are different
measure *(v.)* to judge the importance, value, or effect of something
plummet *(v.)* to fall suddenly and quickly
specialist *(adj.)* having or involving expert knowledge of a particular, specific area of work or study
spread the myth *(v. phr.)* to tell a story that many people believe but that is not true

1. A good education will _____ students for their future career.

2. English is the _____ for air-traffic controllers.

3. Bilinguals have a(n) _____ advantage because they are less easily distracted.

4. Some people continue to believe the _____ that children get confused by learning two languages.

5. The number of students taking foreign language classes will _____ if universities stop requiring them.

6. The report _____ a survey of 100 schools.

7. Newspapers should not _____ that the whole world speaks English.

8. Reading and writing tests are often used to _____ students' progress in language learning.

9. In _____ society, speaking more than one language is a huge benefit.

10. Researchers usually focus on _____ topics.

11. This course includes a(n) _____ of the history of the English language.

12. Students who learn another language have a(n) _____ ability to understand other cultures.

iQ PRACTICE Go online for more practice with the vocabulary.
Practice > Unit 1 > Activity 7

C. CATEGORIZE Read the points that Jenkins makes in his argument against language learning in English-speaking countries. Then use the letters to complete the table with the reasons for learning a foreign language.

Against	For
People who speak English don't need to learn another language.	Only 38% of people in Europe speak English.
Computers can translate languages, so schools should focus on important skills such as speaking, listening, debating, and culture.	
Schools should only focus on what's important.	
Schools only teach languages because they are easy to test.	
Languages are a specialist knowledge that only a few people will need.	
If you want to learn about Germany, you should learn about and visit the country, not learn German.	

TIP FOR SUCCESS

In academic references, *et al.* means "and others" and is used to abbreviate a list of three or more authors.

D. IDENTIFY Which writers made these arguments? Write *Jenkins, Ayres-Bennett et al., Bak,* or *Hudson et al.* on the lines and write the paragraph number where you found the answer.

_____ 1. Education is about exploration. (Paragraph: ____)

_____ 2. It is untrue that the British are not good at learning languages. (Paragraph: ____)

_____ 3. Learning a language in school is not efficient or effective. (Paragraph: ____)

_____ 4. Politicians are only interested in test scores. (Paragraph: ____)

_____ 5. It is harder to learn a language as an adult if you didn't learn a language when you were in school. (Paragraph: ____)

_____ 6. It is wrong to expect people in other countries to learn English. (Paragraph: ____)

_____ 7. Around the world, large numbers of people have learned English, which shows that they value the benefits of language learning. (Paragraph: ____)

_____ 8. Learning a second language can improve cognitive function and help you recover faster from some brain diseases. (Paragraph: ____)

_____ 9. Students don't choose to learn languages because they know they won't need them in the future. (Paragraph: ____)

_____ 10. Some students don't choose to learn languages because they believe the myth that only a small group of people have the time to learn them. (Paragraph: ____)

E. EVALUATE Do you agree or disagree with these statements about learning a new language? Discuss your answers in a group, giving examples or reasons from Reading 2.

1. If you speak English, you don't need any other language to live in Europe.

2. You shouldn't learn another language if you don't need it immediately.

3. Because foreign languages can be translated by computers, we don't need to learn how to speak and understand them.

 CRITICAL THINKING STRATEGY

Making generalizations

When you make a **generalization**, you use specific information to make general rules or draw broad conclusions. Generalizations are an important way to show that you understand the information you have read or heard thoroughly. A good generalization finds relevant similarities from different situations and makes a claim that you can defend with evidence. To form a valid generalization, you need to have enough different examples: for instance, you might make a generalization about the students in your class after speaking to at least half of them.

Specific information	Generalization
I looked at all the articles on the front page of three different newspapers and asked where the main idea is stated.	In newspaper articles, the main idea is usually stated in the headline and again near the beginning of the article.
Learning a new language helps you concentrate and multitask better, and it can protect against the loss of memory.	Learning a language has cognitive benefits.

However, an **overgeneralization** is a type of logical fallacy. This means that your conclusion is not supported by the information you have. At worst, overgeneralizations can become stereotypes. For example, if you know some British people who have tried to learn French unsuccessfully, it would be an overgeneralization to say that the British are bad at learning languages. When you make a generalization, ask yourself whether it is a reasonable conclusion from the information that is available.

iQ PRACTICE Go online to watch the Critical Thinking Video and check your comprehension. *Practice › Unit 1 › Activity 8*

F. EVALUATE Read some specific information followed by an overgeneralization. Discuss the information in a group and then write a valid generalization.

1. There are more non-native speakers of English than native speakers. English is used for communication among pilots, business people, and scientists even when it is nobody's first language. Eighty percent of the world's electronic information is stored in English.

   Overgeneralization: Everyone in the world must be learning English.

   _____

2. My university has dropped its foreign language requirement, but one of my friends has to take at least two semesters of language classes at her university. Meanwhile, my other friend goes to a university where there has never been a language requirement.

   Overgeneralization: Universities in my country are not interested in teaching foreign languages.

   _____

3. Bilinguals score a little higher on math and reading tests than monolinguals. Also, bilinguals usually have a larger vocabulary than monolinguals if you include all the words they know in both languages. Bilinguals perform better than monolinguals on most cognitive tasks.

   Overgeneralization: Monolinguals are not as smart as bilinguals.

   _____

WORK WITH THE VIDEO

A. PREVIEW What do you know about sign language? Who uses it, and why?

VIDEO VOCABULARY

deaf (adj.) unable to hear anything or unable to hear very well

hoe (n.) a garden tool with a long handle and a blade, used for breaking up soil and removing weeds

prospect (n.) an idea of what might happen in the future

remote (adj.) far away from places where other people live

iQ RESOURCES Go online to watch the video about a sign-language class in Uganda, a country in East-Central Africa. *Resources > Unit 1 > Unit Video*

B. CATEGORIZE Watch the video two or three times. Take notes in the chart.

Challenges Patrick faces	Benefits of learning sign language

C. DISCUSS In the video, you saw one person traveling around Uganda to teach sign language. Do you think this is a good solution for the deaf community in countries such as Uganda? What else could be done to make sure that children like Patrick can learn sign language? Discuss your ideas with a group.

WRITE WHAT YOU THINK

SYNTHESIZE Think about Reading 1, Reading 2, and the video as you discuss these questions. Then choose one question and write a paragraph in response.

1. Do you believe that learning a second or foreign language should be required in schools or universities?

2. Do you think that sign languages should be offered as second or foreign language classes in schools and universities?

3. Do you think we will ever have or want a global lingua franca?

WRITING TIP

Use *could, might,* or *would* to write about hypothetical situations or predictions about the future when you cannot be certain they will happen. For example, *languages might disappear* or *important local knowledge would be lost.*

VOCABULARY SKILL Using a thesaurus

A thesaurus is a reference book that gives you **synonyms**, words with similar meanings, and **antonyms**, words with opposite meanings. Learning synonyms and antonyms is a good way to build your vocabulary, and it allows you to use more variety in your writing and speaking. You should always be sure to check the meaning and use of new words carefully. The *Oxford Learner's Thesaurus* lists collocations and appropriate contexts for using each synonym correctly.

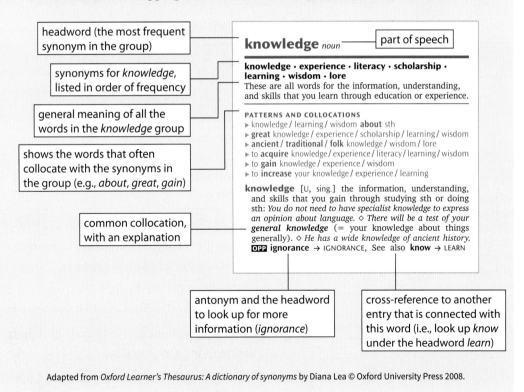

headword (the most frequent synonym in the group)

knowledge *noun* — part of speech

synonyms for *knowledge*, listed in order of frequency

general meaning of all the words in the *knowledge* group

shows the words that often collocate with the synonyms in the group (e.g., *about, great, gain*)

common collocation, with an explanation

knowledge · experience · literacy · scholarship · learning · wisdom · lore
These are all words for the information, understanding, and skills that you learn through education or experience.

PATTERNS AND COLLOCATIONS
▸ knowledge / learning / wisdom **about** sth
▸ **great** knowledge / experience / scholarship / learning / wisdom
▸ **ancient / traditional / folk** knowledge / wisdom / lore
▸ to **acquire** knowledge / experience / literacy / learning / wisdom
▸ to **gain** knowledge / experience / wisdom
▸ to **increase** your knowledge / experience / learning

knowledge [U, sing.] the information, understanding, and skills that you gain through studying sth or doing sth: *You do not need to have specialist knowledge to express an opinion about language.* ◇ *There will be a test of your* **general knowledge** (= your knowledge about things generally). ◇ *He has a wide knowledge of ancient history.* **OPP** ignorance → IGNORANCE, See also **know** → LEARN

antonym and the headword to look up for more information (*ignorance*)

cross-reference to another entry that is connected with this word (i.e., look up *know* under the headword *learn*)

Adapted from *Oxford Learner's Thesaurus: A dictionary of synonyms* by Diana Lea © Oxford University Press 2008.

A. IDENTIFY Complete each sentence with a different word from the thesaurus entry for *knowledge*. Discuss your choices with a partner.

---

knowledge *noun*

knowledge · experience · literacy · scholarship · learning · wisdom · lore
These are all words for the information, understanding, and skills that you learn through education or experience.

PATTERNS AND COLLOCATIONS
▸ knowledge / learning / wisdom **about** sth
▸ **great** knowledge / experience / scholarship / learning / wisdom
▸ **ancient / traditional / folk** knowledge / wisdom / lore
▸ to **acquire** knowledge / experience / literacy / learning / wisdom
▸ to **gain** knowledge / experience / wisdom
▸ to **increase** your knowledge / experience / learning

knowledge [U, sing.] the information, understanding, and skills that you gain through studying sth or doing sth: *You do not need to have specialist knowledge to express an opinion about language.* ◇ *There will be a test of your **general knowledge** (= your knowledge about things generally).* ◇ *He has a wide knowledge of ancient history.* **OPP ignorance** → IGNORANCE, See also **know** → LEARN

experience [U] the knowledge and ability that you have gained through doing sth for a period of time; the process of gaining this: *I have over ten years' teaching experience.* ◇ *Do you have any **previous experience** of this type of work?* ◇ *She didn't get paid much, but it was all **good experience**.* ◇ *We all **learn by experience**.* **OPP inexperience** → IGNORANCE
literacy [U] the ability to read and write: *The government is running a campaign to promote **adult literacy** (= the ability of adults to read and write).* **OPP illiteracy**
scholarship [U] the serious study of an academic subject and the knowledge and methods involved: *Oxford became one of the great centers of medieval scholarship.*
learning [U] knowledge that you get from reading and studying: *He is a teacher of great intellect and learning.* See also **learned** → INTELLECTUAL 2
wisdom [U] the knowledge that a society or culture has gained over a long period of time: *We need to combine ancient wisdom and modern knowledge.* See also **wise** → WISE
lore [U] knowledge and information related to a particular subject, especially when this is not written down; the stories and traditions of a particular group of people: *an expert in ancient Celtic lore*

Adapted from *Oxford Learner's Thesaurus: A dictionary of synonyms* by Diana Lea © Oxford University Press 2008.

1. Jenkins's _____knowledge_____ of the field of applied linguistics is limited.

2. Modern medicine is turning to traditional cultures for their _____.

3. Thompson's _____ focuses on motivation and multilingualism.

4. Learners need _____ in using the new language in real contexts.

5. Cultures without written languages pass on traditional _____ through storytelling and ritual.

6. Students do not always learn to write well in the foreign language, meaning there is a problem with their _____ in the language.

7. In traditional cultures, the oldest people are responsible for sharing their _____ with the next generation.

TIP FOR SUCCESS
No two words have exactly the same meaning and use. Check the exact meaning of new words in a dictionary or thesaurus before you use them.

B. IDENTIFY Write an appropriate synonym for each underlined word. Use your thesaurus or dictionary.

1. _____: New immigrants face many <u>problems</u> with language.

2. _____: The <u>shift</u> from native languages to Spanish can be seen across Central and South America.

3. _____: Multiculturalism is the <u>idea</u> that people of different cultures and ethnicities can live and learn together.

4. _____: One <u>opinion</u> about multiculturalism is that it puts national unity in jeopardy.

5. _____: There are some concepts in other languages that are difficult to <u>say</u> in English.

iQ PRACTICE Go online for more practice with using a thesaurus.
Practice › Unit 1 › Activity 9

WRITING

OBJECTIVE ▶

At the end of this unit, you will write a persuasive email about a new foreign language program in your school, university, or community. Your email will include specific information from the readings and your own ideas.

WRITING SKILL Writing an effective email

Although emails are often informal, sometimes you need to write emails to important people: teachers, administrators, employers, or community leaders. In these situations, you need to use appropriate format and persuasive appeals.

In a formal email, be sure to include these elements:

Email section	Example
A clear subject line	Application for exchange program
Polite greeting	Dear Dr. Stevens,
Self-introduction and purpose of the email	I am a first-year student, and I am writing to apply for next year's exchange program to Germany.
Thanks	Thank you for considering my application.
Closing	Sincerely, Jack Brody

You should also consider what kind of arguments and evidence the reader will find persuasive. You can appeal to emotions, logic, or authority.

Appeal	Explanation	Example
Emotion	An appeal to the reader's emotions, beliefs, or values	I would like to study in Europe because my great-grandparents emigrated from there, and I have always wanted to trace my family history.
Logic	Arguments that use explanations, causes, consequences, or conditions	If I study abroad, I will develop intercultural skills that will make me a better leader.
Authority	Using experts' opinions to support your claims	Research has demonstrated that language learners perform better in other academic subjects.

Your choice of appeals depends on the reader, the situation, and the type of email you are writing.

A. WRITING MODEL Read the email. How could the writer improve it? Complete the chart below.

To: lang@univ.edu

From: mps22@univ.edu

Subject: class

Hi teacher!

I really want to enroll in your beginner's Greek class, but I missed the deadline. Last night, I was so sad because I had to take my cat to the vet, and I completely forgot to go online and complete my class registration.

Can you help me?

Meg

Element	What did the writer do wrong?	How could it be improved?
Subject	unclear subject line	Permission to enroll
Greeting		
Self-introduction and purpose		
Appeal (authority, emotion, or logic?)		
Thanks		
Closing		

B. EVALUATE Imagine you are writing an email to persuade your manager to pay for you to take a language course. Which appeals do you think would be effective? Explain your answers to a partner.

	Type of appeal	Effective?
1. Our company is expanding in Asia, so my Korean language skills will help us win more business.	Logic	Yes
2. Researchers have found that bilingual employees are better able to understand social cues and prevent miscommunication.		
3. If I can read and write Korean better, we won't need to pay for a translator.		
4. This company is proud to be multicultural, so employees should have the chance to learn a new language.		
5. According to a recent study, learning a language helps prevent memory loss.		
6. I am so excited about learning Korean because I find the culture fascinating.		

C. APPLY Read the email and answer the questions below.

To: lrw@protravel.com

From: workshops@icbtraining.com

Subject: ICB Training intercultural communication workshops

Hi Lin,

1 This is Bella Warner from ICB Training. We met at the travel industry conference last week, and I promised I would send you some more information about our intercultural communication workshops.

2 ICC Training's workshops are ideal for small businesses like yours because they help you and your employees understand their cultural competencies and how to develop a more global perspective. Participants will follow a sequence of three activities. First, they will complete an intercultural communication inventory, which is a series of questions that help people at all levels of your business recognize their strengths and weaknesses when working with clients and colleagues from different cultural backgrounds. Next, our expert trainers engage participants in role plays that simulate situations in which cultural miscommunications can occur. Finally, we discuss participants' behavior and responses in the simulations, and your team will set goals for improved intercultural communication.

3 Our workshops were developed by leading voices in the field of intercultural communication based on the latest research. We have been in business for over 20 years, helping companies become more welcoming work environments and more successful global competitors. One recent client wrote, "ICB Training is the gold standard! Thanks to their workshops, we have doubled our international business and improved worker satisfaction."

4 Please let me know when we can talk by phone to discuss the pricing and timing of workshops for your company. We are running a special discount this month for new clients that I would really like to offer you!

5 I look forward to continuing our conversation soon.

Bella

Bella Warner
Sales Manager
ICB Training, Inc.

1. Why do you think the writer uses first names for the greeting and closing?

2. What is the purpose of the second paragraph? What type of appeal is used?

3. What is the purpose of the third paragraph? What type of appeal is used?

4. How does the writer use an emotional appeal?

5. Do you think this is an effective persuasive email? Why or why not?

iQ PRACTICE Go online for more practice writing effective emails.
Practice > Unit 1 > Activity 10

Contrast and concession connectors join ideas with different meanings. In a *contrast*, you show that two ideas disagree. In a *concession*, you acknowledge an opposing idea and then show that it is less important than your main idea. In persuasive writing, introducing a counter-argument with one of these connectors allows you to make your own opinion stronger.

The coordinating conjunctions *but* and *yet* are used to join two contrasting independent clauses of equal importance. *Yet* is stronger than *but* and introduces an unexpected contrast or concession with the first clause. Use a comma between the clauses.

> English is spoken in many countries, **but** tourists should still know basic phrases in the local language.
>
> Online translators can give you the basic meaning, **yet** they struggle with complex sentences.

The subordinators *although, though,* or *even though* are used to introduce a contrast or concession in a dependent clause. *Even though* is a little stronger than *although* and *though*. *While* introduces a direct contrast or opposition to the idea in the main clause. Use a comma to separate the clauses when there is a contrast or concession.

> **Although** studying abroad is expensive, it is one of the best ways to understand a culture.
>
> It is important to offer classes in less commonly taught languages, **even though** fewer students may take them.

Transitions are adverbs and phrases that show the relationship between the ideas in one sentence and the ideas in the next. A period or semicolon is necessary to punctuate the independent clauses.

However, the most common transition in writing, can be used to show differences of various kinds. It is followed by a comma when used as a transition word.

> I learned Japanese for ten years. **However**, there were still words I could not understand.

On the other hand introduces opposite ideas, often with a positive versus a negative contrast. It is usually followed by a comma at the beginning of a sentence and set between commas if in the middle of a sentence.

> Some universities have dropped their foreign-language requirement. Eastern State University, **on the other hand**, asks all students to take a language for four semesters.

iQ RESOURCE Go online to watch the Grammar Skill Video.
Resources > Video > Unit 1 > Grammar Skill Video

A. APPLY Circle the best connector to complete each sentence.

1. *But / Although* computers can translate written language quite well, they are less successful with live speech.

2. Sign language consists of hand signals instead of words. *On the other hand / However*, it is still learned like any other language.

3. Learning Latin is useful for understanding other languages, *even though / but* Latin has not been spoken for centuries.

4. The word *algebra* looks like a Latin or Greek word, *yet / however* it comes from Arabic.

5. Children of immigrants usually speak both their parents' language and the local language. *However / Although*, their children—the third generation— rarely speak the heritage language.

6. In many countries, school children learn the country's official language in school, *while / even though* they speak a native language at home.

7. Speaking two languages has many benefits, *but / yet* few schools in English-speaking countries have bilingual immersion programs.

8. *Even though / Yet* adults learners find pronunciation difficult, they can learn grammar and vocabulary more quickly than children.

B. APPLY Connect each pair of sentences using the connector in parentheses. Punctuate your sentences correctly.

1. The children did not all speak the same language. They learned to communicate. (although)

   Although the children did not all speak the same language, they learned
   to communicate.

2. There are more than 6,000 languages in the world. The United Nations operates with only six official languages. (while)

   _____

   _____

3. The translation was accurate. The book was extremely difficult to understand. (yet)

   _____

   _____

4. Researchers have studied most of the world's languages. New languages are still being discovered. (however)

_____

_____

5. Some research indicates that immersion environments are best for very young language learners. Learning languages in a classroom seems more effective for teenagers. (on the other hand)

_____

_____

iQ PRACTICE Go online for more practice with contrast and concession connectors. *Practice > Unit 1 > Activity 11*

iQ PRACTICE Go online for the Grammar Expansion: Reduced adverbial clauses of time and reason. *Practice > Unit 1 > Activity 12*

UNIT ASSIGNMENT **Write a persuasive email**

OBJECTIVE ▶

In this assignment, you are going to write a persuasive email about a new foreign language program in your school, university, or community. As you prepare to write, think about the Unit Question, "What is the value of learning a new language?" Use information from Reading 1, Reading 2, the unit video, and your work in this unit to support your ideas. Refer to the Self-Assessment checklist on page 32.

iQ PRACTICE Go online to the Writing Tutor to read a persuasive email writing model. *Practice > Unit 1 > Activity 13*

PLAN AND WRITE

A. BRAINSTORM Answer the questions to choose an audience, context, and purpose for your email. Discuss your ideas with a partner.

1. What type of language program are you going to write about (e.g., a new class, a new language lab, a foreign exchange, a conversation group, a book club, an online program, etc.)?

_____

2. Which language or languages will the program teach?

_____

3. Who are you going to write to?

_____

4. What arguments can you use to persuade the reader to support your program? You might not want to use all three types of appeal.

Emotion:

_____

_____

Logic:

_____

_____

Authority:

_____

_____

B. PLAN Complete the outline for your email. Use ideas from your brainstorming.

Subject line: _____

Greeting: _____

Introduction and purpose: _____

_____

_____

Arguments (make an organized list): _____

_____

_____

Thanks: _____

Closing: _____

iQ RESOURCES Go online to download and complete the outline for your email.
Resources > Writing Tools > Unit 1 > Outline

C. WRITE Use your planning notes to write your persuasive email.

1. Write your email. Format it correctly and use effective appeals to persuade the reader. Use contrast and concession connectors to express counterarguments where appropriate.

2. Look at the Self-Assessment checklist to guide your writing.

iQ PRACTICE Go online to the Writing Tutor to write your assignment.
Practice > Unit 1 > Activity 14

REVISE AND EDIT

iQ RESOURCES Go online to download the peer review worksheet.
Resources > Writing Tools > Unit 1 > Peer Review Worksheet

A. PEER REVIEW Read your partner's email. Then use the peer review worksheet. Discuss the review with your partner.

B. REWRITE Based on your partner's review, revise and rewrite your email.

C. EDIT Complete the Self-Assessment checklist as you prepare to write the final draft of your email. Be prepared to hand in your work or discuss it in class.

SELF-ASSESSMENT	Yes	No
Did you format your email correctly?	☐	☐
Did you choose persuasive appeals?	☐	☐
Did you make valid generalizations?	☐	☐
Did you use appropriate contrast and concession connectors?	☐	☐
Did you check new words and collocations in a dictionary or thesaurus?	☐	☐
Does the email include vocabulary from the unit?	☐	☐
Did you check the email for punctuation, spelling, and grammar?	☐	☐

D. REFLECT Discuss these questions with a partner or group.

1. What is something new you learned in this unit?

2. Look back at the Unit Question—What is the value of learning a new language? Is your answer different now than when you started the unit? If yes, how is it different? Why?

iQ PRACTICE Go to the online discussion board to discuss the questions.
Practice > Unit 1 > Activity 15

TRACK YOUR SUCCESS

iQ PRACTICE   Go online to check the words and phrases you have learned in this unit. *Practice > Unit 1 > Activity 16*

Check (✓) the skills you learned. If you need more work on a skill, refer to the page(s) in parentheses.

READING	☐ I can distinguish main ideas from details. (p. 11)
CRITICAL THINKING	☐ I can make generalizations and avoid overgeneralizations. (p. 20)
VOCABULARY	☐ I can use a thesaurus. (p. 23)
WRITING	☐ I can write an effective email. (p. 25)
GRAMMAR	☐ I can use contrast and concession connectors. (p. 28)
OBJECTIVE ▶	☐ I can gather information and ideas to write a persuasive email about a new foreign language program in my school, university, or community.

Business

READING	identifying contrasting ideas
CRITICAL THINKING	recognizing evaluative language
VOCABULARY	reporting verbs
WRITING	using evidence to support an argument
GRAMMAR	noun clauses

How is work changing?

A. Discuss these questions with your classmates.

1. What kinds of jobs do you think will not be needed in the future?

2. How has the workplace changed since your parents or grandparents were your age?

3. Look at the photo. Have you ever used services provided by people doing "gigs" (temporary jobs), such as delivering food? What type of service was it? How was your experience?

B. Listen to *The Q Classroom* online. Then answer these questions.

1. How do Marcus, Sophy, Yuna, and Felix think that work is changing?

2. What do you think about their ideas?

iQ PRACTICE Go to the online discussion board to discuss the Unit Question with your classmates. *Practice > Unit 2 > Activity 1*

UNIT OBJECTIVE ▶ Read two articles that support and criticize the "gig economy." Gather information and ideas to write an article for your school or university career services newsletter arguing why a particular job is a good choice in the changing workplace.

READING

READING 1

Who Wins in the Gig Economy, and Who Loses?

OBJECTIVE ▶

You are going to read an article by Diane Mulachy from *Harvard Business Review* about the winners and losers in the sharing, or "gig," economy. Use the article to gather information and ideas for your Unit Assignment.

PREVIEW THE READING

A. PREVIEW Who do you think benefits from sharing services that pay you to drive your car, rent a room, or do small jobs for other people?

B. QUICK WRITE Do you prefer to use taxis or ride-sharing services? Do you prefer hotels or rooms rented directly from the owner? What services could you offer that people would pay for? Write for 5–10 minutes. Remember to use this section for your Unit Assignment.

C. VOCABULARY Check (✓) the words and phrases you know. Use a dictionary to define any new or unknown words or phrases. Then discuss with a partner how the words and phrases will relate to the unit.

automate *(v.)*	labor *(n.)* ϗ+
benefits *(pl. n.)* ϗ+ OPAL	on the margins *(prep. phr.)*
discrimination *(n.)* ϗ+ OPAL	substitute *(v.)* ϗ+ OPAL
expertise *(n.)* ϗ+ OPAL	take advantage of *(v. phr.)*
gig *(n.)* ϗ+	the other end of the spectrum *(n. phr.)* OPAL
job security *(n. phr.)*	wage *(n.)* ϗ+

ϗ+ Oxford 5000™ words   OPAL Oxford Phrasal Academic Lexicon

iQ PRACTICE Go online to listen and practice your pronunciation.
Practice › Unit 2 › Activity 2

WORK WITH THE READING

🔊 **A. INVESTIGATE** Read the article and gather information about winners and losers in the gig economy.

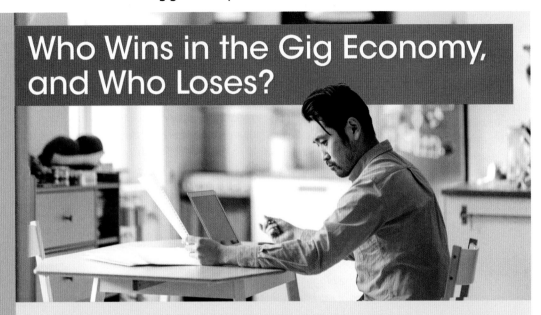

Who Wins in the Gig Economy, and Who Loses?

1   The winners and losers in the U.S. economy have traditionally been easy to identify. If you had a full-time job, you won. A full-time job provided the steady income needed to support our traditional version of the American Dream: the house, the cars, the latest consumer goods. A full-time job was also the only way to access important employer-provided **benefits**, such as health insurance and a pension[1], as well as protections against workplace injuries, **discrimination**, and harassment. Without a full-time job, a true sense of security was elusive, benefits were inaccessible, and you were more likely to be stranded **on the margins** of the **labor** market, observing rather than living the American Dream.

2   All of that is changing. Work is being disaggregated[2] from jobs and reorganized into a variety of alternative arrangements, such as consulting projects, freelance assignments, and contract opportunities. Independent workers can obtain health insurance and save for retirement without an employer. The American Dream is transforming to prioritize experiences over material goods and quality of life over quantity of stuff. Most important, the absence of **job security** opens up new possibilities for a portfolio of **gigs** to provide a more meaningful and robust sense of income security than any full-time job can.

3   As the jobs-based economy gives way to the gig economy, winners and losers are determined by the type of worker you are—or can become.

4   Workers with specialized skills, deep **expertise**, or in-demand experience win in the gig economy. They can command attractive **wages**, garner[3] challenging and interesting work, and structure their own working lives. Workers who possess strong technical, management, leadership, or creative abilities can best **take advantage of** the opportunity to create a working life that incorporates flexibility, independence, and meaning.

[1] **pension:** an amount of money paid regularly to somebody who is considered to be too old to work
[2] **disaggregate:** to separate
[3] **garner:** to obtain or collect

5   Entrepreneurial[4] workers also win. Independent workers who are comfortable with and excited about developing their own income, marketing themselves, and connecting with others are best positioned to take advantage of the many opportunities the gig economy offers. These skilled and entrepreneurial workers win in the gig economy by moving from good jobs to great work.

6   On **the other end of the spectrum**, retail and service workers currently in low-skill, low-wage jobs can also win in the gig economy. In the jobs economy, these individuals work in what Zeynep Ton at MIT's Sloan School of Management refers to as "bad jobs"—poorly paid, insecure, part-time roles with limited or no benefits and no control over schedules. Their wages are staying flat or declining, and their jobs are at risk of being **automated**.

7   In the gig economy, these workers have the chance to gain more control and have more flexibility and autonomy in their working lives. Uber drivers work under similar economic circumstances as most taxi drivers: they are contractors with low pay and no benefits, no overtime or minimum wage, and no access to unemployment insurance. But there are many more people willing to be Uber drivers than taxi drivers, in part because they can control when and how much they work.

8   Bad jobs won't disappear in the gig economy, but the gig economy gives low-skill workers a way to move from bad jobs to better work. It's not a sufficient change, but it's moving in the right direction.

9   Among the biggest winners in the gig economy are workers who have been stuck on the margins of our traditional economy. Stay-at-home parents, retired people, the elderly, students, and people with disabilities now have more options to work as much as they want, and when, where, and how they want, in order to generate income, develop skills, or pursue a passion. Because it is now so much easier to work and earn income from home, part-time, and on a flexible schedule, the gig economy can provide choice, dignity[5], and a measure of financial control and opportunity to workers who previously had little of those things. Formerly marginalized workers win because, in the gig economy, they can move from no job to some work.

10   The people who struggle most in the gig economy are corporate workers whose skills are common or less in demand. Their jobs are most likely to be automated, eliminated, or outsourced to cheaper labor. Their incomes are not growing, their benefits are shrinking, and they are too slowly coming to terms with the reality that there is no longer any job security. If these workers lose their good jobs, they are the most likely to have difficulty finding good work.

11   It's clear that our current way of working isn't working well for many Americans. The employee-in-a-single-job model isn't the best option for everyone. Many studies also reveal high levels of stress and dissatisfaction among employees. The gig economy offers a much-needed alternative model of work that can supplement or **substitute** for being a full-time employee in a full-time job.

12   There's no way to avoid the truth that fundamental changes in the ways we work are here to stay and are creating a new set of winners and losers. But the growth of new opportunities in the gig economy to choose how, how much, where, and when to work is one big win for all.

---

[4] **entrepreneurial:** connected with making money by starting businesses, especially when this involves taking financial risks

[5] **dignity:** the fact of being given honor or respect by other people

B. VOCABULARY Complete the sentences with the vocabulary from Reading 1.

ACADEMIC LANGUAGE
The corpus shows that
*the other end of the
spectrum* is a useful
phrase in academic
writing for showing
contrast. It is often used
at the start of a sentence
with the prepositions
at or *on*. The phrase
is not as common in
spoken English.

⌐_____⌐ OPAL
Oxford Phrasal Academic Lexicon

automated	gig	substitute
benefits	job security	take advantage of
discrimination	labor	the other end of the spectrum
expertise	on the margins	wage

1. The job requires _____ in coding and website design.

2. People without a high school education often live _____ of society.

3. You can _____ this new opportunity by visiting our website today!

4. I don't have _____, so I can be fired at any time.

5. The job includes _____ such as health insurance and vacation time.

6. If your work can be _____, you might be replaced by a robot.

7. Many countries have a minimum _____, which is the lowest amount you can be paid for an hour of work.

8. On one sharing website, you can rent a small room in someone's house or, on _____, you can rent an entire luxury house.

9. Older people may suffer _____ when they apply for a new job because some companies prefer to hire young workers.

10. The _____ market refers to the number of people who are available for work in relation to the number of jobs available.

11. Fast-food restaurants are starting to _____ touch screens for employees to take your order.

12. In the _____ economy, workers may have many small jobs instead of one full-time job.

iQ PRACTICE Go online for more practice with the vocabulary.
Practice ⟩ Unit 2 ⟩ Activity 3

C. **CATEGORIZE** Will the following workers benefit or lose in the gig economy, according to the article? Check (✓) the correct column and write the paragraph number where you found the answer.

Workers	Win	Lose	Paragraph
1. People with special skills	✓		4
2. People with creative ideas who can start new businesses			
3. Retail workers in part-time jobs with low wages			
4. Older workers and retired people			
5. People who work for traditional companies			

D. **APPLY** Which of the following people are likely to benefit from the gig economy, according to the article? Which people may lose their jobs? Write the jobs from the box in the correct column and add at least one of your own examples to each category.

website designers	accountants	supermarket cashiers
people with disabilities	doctors	small-business owners
part-time salespeople	taxi drivers	customer-service representatives

Benefit from the gig economy	Lose in the gig economy

E. **RESTATE** Read the statements. Write one reason from the reading that supports each idea.

1. In the past, the only path to a secure lifestyle was a full-time job.

   You could only get good wages and benefits with a full-time job.

2. Today, independent workers don't need a single job to have a good quality of life.

3. Retail and service workers today have "bad jobs."

4. Retail and service workers have more control over their work in the gig economy than in traditional jobs.

_____

5. People who live on the margins of society benefit from the gig economy.

_____

6. Corporate workers have less job security today.

_____

F. INTERPRET Answer the questions. Use examples from the reading.

1. The author uses the words *work* and *job* with different meanings. What is the difference between a *good job* and *good work*?

   _____

   _____

   _____

2. "Winners and losers are determined by the type of worker you are—or can become." What is the author implying in the words "or can become"?

   _____

   _____

   _____

3. Does the author suggest that the gig economy will provide workers who now have "bad jobs" with "good jobs"? Explain your answer.

   _____

   _____

   _____

G. EXTEND Look back at your Quick Write on page 36. Who wins and who loses in the gig economy? Add any new ideas or information you learned from the reading.

iQ PRACTICE Go online for additional reading and comprehension.
Practice > Unit 2 > Activity 4

? WRITE WHAT YOU THINK

A. DISCUSS Discuss the questions in a group. Think about the Unit Question, "How is work changing?"

1. How has the gig economy changed the way we work?

2. Would you prefer to have gig work or a traditional full-time job?

3. Are there other winners and losers in the gig economy apart from those discussed in Reading 1?

B. CREATE Choose one of the questions from Activity A and write one to two paragraphs in response. Look back at your Quick Write on page 36 as you think about what you learned.

READING SKILL Identifying contrasting ideas

Authors often present several different opinions in order to provide a balanced argument. They may also add their own opinion, which might differ from those of other experts.

To follow the authors' arguments and main ideas, it is important to recognize whose opinion you are reading and to be aware of different opinions in a text. Here are some words and phrases you can look for to identify a new opinion or a different opinion.

Phrases that introduce an opinion	Phrases that show a different opinion
according to . . .	however / on the other hand . . .
in a recent study, . . .	in contrast (to), as opposed to . . .
a recent report found that . . .	X points out that . . .
advocates claim that . . .	. . . but rather/instead . . .
a critic might say . . .	his/her concern is that . . .
some people regard/see this as . . .	other experts argue that . . .

A. IDENTIFY Read the paragraph. Circle phrases that introduce an opinion, and underline phrases that show a different opinion. Compare your answers with a partner.

Economists agree that the sharing economy represents a major change in the world of work. However, they disagree about whether the changes will be positive or negative for people who want to earn money through these platforms. Advocates[1] such as Sundararajan (2016) claim that these new working conditions will give workers more control over their earnings. Some economists regard this as positive because it will increase the efficiency of the sector. On the other hand, Hill's (2015) concern is that gig work is unstable, and workers can be easily exploited. In a recent study, Shor and Attwood-Charles (2017) found wide variation in workers' experiences. Some spoke very positively about labor conditions, while others were highly critical. According to Shor and Attwood-Charles, each company is different, and their policies change over time, so it is impossible to say whether the sector as a whole offers good or bad employment.

[1] **advocate:** a person who supports an idea

Adapted from J. B. Schor & W. Attwood-Charles (2017). The "sharing" economy: Labor, inequality, and social connection on for-profit platforms. *Sociology Compass 11*(8).

B. CATEGORIZE Complete the chart with the different opinions about the effects of the sharing economy on workers. Use your annotations from Activity A to help you.

Is the sharing economy good or bad for workers?	
Sundararajan's opinion	
Hill's opinion	
Shor and Attwood-Charles's opinion	

iQ PRACTICE Go online for more practice with identifying contrasting opinions. *Practice > Unit 2 > Activity 5*

READING 2 The Dark Side of the Gig Economy

OBJECTIVE ▶

You are going to read a magazine article about the problems of the gig economy. Use the article to gather information and ideas for your Unit Assignment.

PREVIEW THE READING

A. PREVIEW Read the first and last sentences of each paragraph. What problems with the gig economy do you expect the article to discuss?

B. QUICK WRITE What might be the negative consequences of working in the sharing economy? Who makes money from ride-sharing services and other sharing platforms? Is flexibility more important than job security? Write for 5–10 minutes. Remember to use this section for your Unit Assignment.

C. VOCABULARY Check (✓) the words and phrases you know. Use a dictionary to define any unknown words or phrases. Then discuss with a partner how the words and phrases will relate to the unit.

accumulate *(v.)* 🔑+ OPAL	hypothetical *(adj.)* OPAL
algorithm *(n.)*	scraps *(pl. n.)*
at stake *(prep. phr.)*	supply *(n.)* 🔑+ OPAL
demand *(n.)* 🔑+ OPAL	take a cut *(v. phr.)*
entry-level *(adj.)*	the degree of *(n. phr.)* OPAL
freelancer *(n.)*	transaction *(n.)* 🔑+

🔑+ Oxford 5000™ words　　　　　　　　　　OPAL Oxford Phrasal Academic Lexicon

iQ PRACTICE Go online to listen and practice your pronunciation.
Practice ⟩ Unit 2 ⟩ Activity 6

WORK WITH THE READING

 A. INVESTIGATE Read the article and gather information about problems with the sharing economy.

The Dark Side of the Gig Economy

For Jackie, the gig economy means unsociable hours and low pay.

1   We are taught from an early age that "sharing is caring." We tell our children to share their toys. "A trouble shared is a trouble halved," the saying goes. The sharing economy certainly sounds like a good thing. Advocates claim that the sharing economy is driven by the desire to benefit society. Thanks to popular websites and apps, users can share their cars, their spare bedrooms, their power tools, and even their own time and talents. And because both parties—the borrower (or seller) and the lender (or buyer)—review each other, these digital platforms create a trusting environment even among complete strangers. According to one of its earliest supporters, author Rachel Botsman, the gig economy takes advantage of "idle capacity" to better utilize assets. This should be good for the owner, the community, and the environment.

2   More than a decade after the first sharing sites emerged, the reality is starkly different. Most of the major players in the new sharing economy are for-profit companies, which **take a cut** of every **transaction**. While some sites continue to offer true sharing, most are in fact selling a product, much like a traditional business. With so much money **at stake**, the new world of work can be a dark, unfriendly place.

3   Consider the case of Jackie, a **hypothetical** worker in a coffee shop, profiled by writer Matthew Biggins in a recent newspaper article. Compared with her **entry-level** job, driving for a ride-sharing service sounds like a dream come true. Jackie can choose her own hours, she is her own boss, and she doesn't need to worry about long shifts[1] and small tips. Unfortunately, the dream is too good to be true. Because there are so many people like Jackie who turn to the gig economy, the **supply** of drivers quickly outpaces the **demand** for rides, so naturally prices fall. Jackie also realizes that she has expenses: she has to pay for gas, insurance, and maintenance of her car, which is costly because she is driving so much more. The only way to earn more money is to work unsociable hours or less desirable routes, where there are fewer other drivers. As a result, she isn't entirely her own boss: the ride-sharing service's **algorithm** determines when she should work, who she picks up, and how much money she makes. As Biggins explains, "gig workers do have a boss, and that boss is an algorithm."

4   Former U.S. Secretary of Labor Robert Reich calls this the "share-the-**scraps**" economy. He argues that only the software companies earn

[1] **shift:** a period of time worked by a group of people who start work as another group finishes

real money; gig workers have to make do with the scraps. The gig economy promised extra income, an opportunity for people to "monetize their own downtime," as economist Arun Sundararajan claimed. On the other hand, Reich points out that this "downtime" might be your family time or time you need to relax for your own health. In return, gig workers earn low wages without any guarantee of a predictable income, retirement savings, or other benefits.

5   Sundararajan looks forward to a brave new world of "micro-entrepreneurs"[2] as flexible freelance work replaces the traditional full-time job. However, as sociologists Juliet Schor and William Attwood-Charles found in their research, people who depend on the gig economy as their primary source of income are less likely to be satisfied than those who still have a regular job. In other words, the shift toward freelance work will probably cause greater dissatisfaction as well as less stable, less safe, and more competitive labor conditions.

6   In Canada, for example, a recent report by a human resources agency found that as much as 30% of the workforce comprises "non-traditional workers." These are people without a full-time job who work as independent contractors or "on-demand workers" in the gig economy. Worryingly, for over half of these gig-based workers, it is "the only way to make a living right now," according to research from the Canadian Centre for Policy Alternatives. Furthermore, 71% of those working on-demand jobs are young people under 40.

7   Why should we be concerned about this large number of young people with gigs rather than full-time jobs? Andrew Cash, a former member of the Canadian parliament, told *Global News* that "there are two kinds of **freelancers**. Freelancers by choice, and freelancers by force." His concern is that the lack of stability and security in the gig economy may have unintended social consequences, such as delaying the age at which people get married, buy a

house, or have children. Supporters of the sharing economy argue that the flexibility of on-demand work gives individuals more freedom than the traditional full-time job. However, that freedom may come at a heavy price and leave workers just as dependent on the technology companies as on a corporate employer.

8   That **degree of** dependence should alarm people who drive cars for a ride-share service, or rent their rooms online, or provide freelance services through an app. Their ability to earn money is based on their reputation, which is calculated separately on each platform. This data gives the owners of the technology a great deal of control to decide who gets the best paid work. The gig economy was supposed to allow us to share our possessions and our labor, but as writer Nathan Schneider points out, instead it has created a new type of ownership: the owners of the sharing platforms make profit, not the users, and they can decide which workers will benefit most from their gig work. If a worker wants to leave, they lose all the social credit they have **accumulated** on that site, which can feel like a trap.

9   Some social entrepreneurs like Antonin Léonard, co-founder of the French online network OuiShare, remain optimistic. Léonard has built a network that supports projects and events around the world in which members have true shared ownership. The OuiShare model is similar to an old idea, the cooperative. A cooperative is a farm or small business that is owned by its members, who share the work and the profits. Léonard admits, though, that cooperatives are rarely successful, and it is not clear how a truly cooperative sharing platform could compete against the major players that already dominate the gig economy and make money from it. Ironically, these companies might not be willing to share their success, and the real losers could turn out to be the users who provide the labor that makes the platforms work at all.

---

[2] **micro-entrepreneurs:** people who start small businesses

B. VOCABULARY Read these sentences with some words and phrases from Reading 2. Then write each bold word or phrase next to the correct definition.

a. The website uses a complex **algorithm** to decide how many people will want a ride at each hour during the week.

b. It is important to check your résumé carefully for errors as there is a lot **at stake** when you submit a job application.

c. When you rent a room on an online website, the software company **takes a cut** of the money, usually about 1 to 5 percent.

d. Many teenagers work **entry-level** jobs in supermarkets or fast-food restaurants.

e. Ahmed quit his job for a newspaper and became a **freelancer**, so now he writes for many different publications.

f. After working a number of different gigs, Jing only **accumulated** a small amount of money in her savings account.

g. The **demand** for hotel rooms has dropped because so many travelers are renting rooms and apartments online.

h. House prices go down when there is an increase in the **supply** of new homes.

i. **The degree of** risk with a new business depends on the number of competitors in the market.

j. Let me ask a **hypothetical** question: what would you do if you could have any job in the world?

k. At the end of the meal, we gave the **scraps** of food to the dog.

l. Websites need strong safety measures to keep credit-card **transactions** secure.

1. _____ *(pl. n.)* small pieces or amount of something

2. _____ *(n.)* a person who works for many different organizations rather than being employed by them

3. _____ *(n.)* an act of buying or selling

4. _____ *(adj.)* based on situations which are possible and imagined rather than real and true

5. _____ *(n.)* a set of rules that are followed to solve a problem, especially by a computer

6. _____ (adj.) at the lowest rank in a company

7. _____ (n.) the amount of something that is provided or available for use

8. _____ (prep. phr.) that can be won or lost, depending on the success of a particular action

9. _____ (n. phr.) the amount or level of something

10. _____ (v.) to gradually increase over time

11. _____ (v. phr.) to keep a share of the money

12. _____ (n.) the desire or need of customers for goods or services

iQ PRACTICE Go online for more practice with the vocabulary.
Practice ⟩ Unit 2 ⟩ Activity 7

C. **IDENTIFY** Which of these statements describe a problem with the gig economy that is discussed in the article? Check (✓) the correct statements and write the number of the paragraph that contains each idea.

☐ 1. Freelance workers are dependent on computer algorithms to earn a living. (Paragraph: ____)

☐ 2. Customers' personal data can be stolen from sharing websites. (Paragraph: ____)

☐ 3. Many sharing sites are motivated by profit, not the goal of improving society. (Paragraph: ____)

☐ 4. When people work for sharing sites in their spare time, they may be harming their family life or mental health. (Paragraph: ____)

☐ 5. Freelance work is more flexible than a full-time job. (Paragraph: ____)

☐ 6. Freelancers might change major life choices, such as marriage, because they do not have a stable job. (Paragraph: ____)

☐ 7. There are unexpected costs to working for ride-sharing sites. (Paragraph: ____)

☐ 8. Gig work can be less satisfying than a full-time job. (Paragraph: ____)

☐ 9. Not all freelancers choose to work in the gig economy. Some are forced into it by the lack of traditional jobs. (Paragraph: ____)

☐ 10. Canadian laws make it difficult for some sharing sites to operate. (Paragraph: ____)

It is important to keep track of the source for different ideas in a text like Reading 2. Sometimes, the author introduces other authors' voices in order to disagree or agree with them.

D. IDENTIFY Who made these arguments? Match the sources to the statements from Reading 2. One of the names won't be used.

a. Andrew Cash

b. Antonin Léonard

c. Canadian Centre for Policy Alternatives

d. Juliet Schor and William Attwood-Charles

e. Matthew Biggins

f. Rachel Botsman

g. Arun Sundararajan

h. Robert Reich

_____ 1. The sharing economy takes advantage of "idle capacity."

_____ 2. Only the software companies earn real money; gig workers have to make do with the scraps.

_____ 3. The lack of stability and security in the gig economy may have unintended social consequences.

_____ 4. For over half of all gig-based workers, freelancing is the only way to make a living right now.

_____ 5. Thanks to "micro-entrepreneurs," flexible freelance work will replace traditional full-time jobs.

_____ 6. People who depend on the gig economy as their primary source of income are less likely to be satisfied than those who still have a regular job.

_____ 7. Online networks could be like cooperatives, although these are rarely successful.

E. EXPLAIN Write answers to these questions about Reading 2.

1. How can the sharing economy benefit "the owner, the community, and the environment"?

_____

2. How do sharing websites and apps make money?

_____

3. Why might freelance or on-demand workers such as Jackie be less satisfied with gigs than traditional full-time jobs?

_____

4. How are on-demand workers dependent on technology companies?

_____

5. Why does the author find the statistics about freelance workers in Canada worrying?

_____

CRITICAL THINKING STRATEGY

Recognizing evaluative language

When writers want to make an argument, especially in academic contexts, they often avoid phrases like *I think that* or *in my opinion*. Instead, they choose **evaluative language** that tries to **align** readers with an idea (that is, persuade them to accept it) or **distance** readers from an idea. When you read an argument, you should recognize the author's intention and decide for yourself whether you agree.

> *While some sites continue to offer true sharing, most are **in fact** selling a product, much like a traditional business.*
>
> *The gig economy **was supposed to** allow us to share our possessions and our labor, but as writer Nathan Schneider **points out, instead** it has created a new type of ownership . . .*

Part of speech	Aligning language	Distancing language
Connectors	in fact, instead, rather, actually	unfortunately, despite
Reporting verbs	argue, prove, point out	claim, assume, pretend
Modal verbs	will, can	may, was supposed to
Adjectives	clear, evident, likely	possible, worrying, unlikely, mistaken
Nouns	truth, fact, reality	suggestion, claim, assumption

Another important form of evaluation is a **concession** using a word such as *while, although,* or *admit*. The author concedes (accepts) an idea but goes on to disagree with it and align the reader with a different idea or opinion.

> **Although** some workers can take advantage of the gig economy,
>
> concession
>
> others are pushed further to the margins of the labor market.
>
> main idea

iQ PRACTICE Go online to watch the Critical Thinking Video and check your comprehension. *Practice > Unit 2 > Activity 8*

F. IDENTIFY Is the author trying to align or distance you from the ideas in bold? Write *A* (align) or *D* (distance). Circle all the relevant evaluative language.

___ 1. Ride-sharing apps were expected to reduce traffic congestion because each car can carry several passengers. **Instead, they actually increase traffic problems due to the time cars are driving between rides.**

___ 2. **These services were supposed to support public transportation by providing an alternative to owning a car.**

_____ 3. **The reality is that ride-sharing service are attracting customers away from buses and subways.**

_____ 4. A spokesperson for one app claimed that **cities should cooperate with ride-sharing services because they increase access to transportation.**

_____ 5. **Although one study shows that traffic congestion may have dropped slightly in San Francisco because of ride-sharing apps**, cities like Chicago, which add a tax to shared rides, are much more likely to improve their roads.

_____ 6. Although one study shows that traffic congestion may have dropped slightly in San Francisco because of ride-sharing apps, **cities like Chicago, which add a tax to shared rides, are much more likely to improve their roads.**

_____ 7. Supporters of ride-sharing apps were mistaken in their assumption that **this new technology would benefit the environment.**

_____ 8. Taxi drivers also point out that **many drivers for these ride-sharing services are clearly inexperienced and potentially dangerous.**

WORK WITH THE VIDEO

A. PREVIEW Do you think you can travel full-time and still earn a living? How?

iQ RESOURCES Go online to watch the video about earning a living while traveling full-time. *Resources > Video > Unit 2 > Unit Video*

B. CATEGORIZE Watch the video two or three times. Write down all the gigs the couple does. How do they make money? Infer the answer if it is not explained in the video.

Gig	How do they make money?

C. EXTEND What other gigs could you do to earn money while traveling? Add them to the table above.

WRITE WHAT YOU THINK

SYNTHESIZE Think about Reading 1, Reading 2, and the unit video as you discuss these questions. Then choose one question and write one to two paragraphs in response.

1. Which arguments do you find more persuasive: the ones about the benefits or the ones about the problems of the gig economy? Why?

2. Which should be the main goal of sharing apps and businesses in general: improving the society or making a profit?

3. The video shows two people who lead an "alternative lifestyle" with the support of gigs such as photography and podcasting. What other alternative lifestyles could the sharing economy support?

VOCABULARY SKILL Reporting verbs

When writing academic papers, you often need to report information, ideas, or research by other authors. The choice of verb in the main clause can show your attitude toward the source. The verb can imply a supporting, distancing, or neutral attitude. Use a dictionary to help you understand the exact meaning and use of different verbs so that you can accurately express your opinion and recognize other authors' attitudes.

Example	Type of verb	Explanation
The authors **prove** that freelance work has negative social consequences.	Supporting	*Prove* means "to use facts or evidence to show that something is true." The authors have provided enough support to convince you that freelance work has negative consequences.
The authors **say** that freelance work has negative social consequences.	Neutral	*Say* means "to give information." You are reporting the authors' information without expressing your own opinion.
The authors **claim** that freelance work has negative social consequences.	Distancing	*Claim* means "to say that something is true, although it has not been proved and other people may not believe it." You do not completely accept the authors' conclusion about freelance work.

Adverbs can also have a supporting or distancing effect on a sentence. For example, "The authors argue **convincingly** . . . " means you are persuaded by the argument, whereas "The authors **supposedly** prove that . . . " shows doubt about their conclusions.

iQ RESOURCES Go online to watch the Vocabulary Skill Video.
Resources > Video > Unit 2 > Vocabulary Skill Video

A. IDENTIFY Read the sentences. Do the words in bold have a supporting, neutral, or distancing effect? Circle the correct answer.

1. Some companies **contend** that employees prefer flexibility to regular pay and benefits.

    a. supporting   b. neutral   c. distancing

2. Research **clearly demonstrates** that job satisfaction affects people's overall happiness.

    a. supporting   b. neutral   c. distancing

3. Economists **state** that a certain degree of unemployment is unavoidable.

    a. supporting   b. neutral   c. distancing

4. The evidence **validates** the argument that entrepreneurs create new jobs.

    a. supporting   b. neutral   c. distancing

5. The authors **incorrectly suggest** that most unemployed people have chosen not to work.

    a. supporting   b. neutral   c. distancing

6. The graph **shows** the relationship between supply and demand of taxi rides on weekends.

    a. supporting   b. neutral   c. distancing

B. CREATE Choose five ideas, opinions, facts, or statistics about the changing workplace from Reading 1, Reading 2, or the video. Use a reporting verb and evaluative language (see Critical Thinking Strategy) to show your attitude.

1. _____

2. _____

3. _____

4. _____

5. _____

C. IDENTIFY Exchange your sentences from Activity B with a partner. Read each sentence. Identify your partner's attitude.

iQ PRACTICE   Go online for more practice with reporting verbs.
Practice > Unit 2 > Activity 9

WRITING

OBJECTIVE ▶

At the end of this unit, you will write an article for the opinion section of your school or university career services newsletter arguing why a particular job is a good choice in the changing world of work. Your article will include specific information from the readings and your own ideas.

WRITING SKILL Using evidence to support an argument

Most academic writing requires you to make an argument and try to persuade the reader that your opinion is correct. Writers use evidence (examples, quotations, statistics, explanations, etc.) to make their arguments more convincing. All evidence must be relevant (meaningful and connected to the topic), or it will confuse and not convince the reader.

The author of Reading 2, for example, used several types of evidence to support the argument about the dark side of the gig economy, including:

- **statistics** (71% of freelance workers are under 40)

- **expert sources** (a member of parliament, sociologists, economists)

- **a hypothetical example** (Jackie)

- **analysis and predictions** (freelance work is likely to lead to greater dissatisfaction)

- **cause and effect** (because workers' ability to earn money is based on their reputation, the sharing sites exert a lot of control)

TIP FOR SUCCESS

Different academic subjects have different rules for good evidence, so always find out what kind of evidence your reader will accept. Ask your teacher or look closely at your readings for examples.

A. WRITING MODEL Read each section of this draft of an article on why journalism is a good career for the changing workplace. Answer the questions after each section.

News Matters

The news media landscape has changed dramatically in a short time. For my parents, news meant the radio, a nightly TV broadcast, and the newspaper delivered to our house every morning. Today, we have a 24-hour news cycle with stories—true and false—pushed at us through websites and social media at all hours of the day and night. At the other end of the spectrum, newspapers are going out of business, and the traditional media channels seem less relevant in an age when everyone thinks they are a citizen-journalist. However, I still believe that journalism is an important career, even though the job of the journalist will look very different in the future.

1. Which types of evidence does the writer provide to support the claim that the news media landscape has changed? Check (✓) all the correct answers.

☐ a. personal examples

☐ b. statistics

☐ c. the writer's observations

☐ d. expert opinions

2. Which of these additional pieces of evidence would support the claim? Choose one answer and discuss with a partner how you would add it to the paragraph.

a. According to the Pew Research Center, the number of journalists working for U.S. newspapers has decreased by almost 50% in the last decade.

b. Newspaper editors earn about 30% more on average than reporters, according to U.S. government data.

c. Sunday newspapers have slightly higher sales than weekday newspapers.

> There is no doubt that technology has made it possible for anyone to write and share news stories by writing a blog, taking a picture with their smartphone, or posting a link on social media. However, there will always be a need for professional journalists who report on stories that are important, not just those that are convenient and attractive. According to the American Press Institute, unlike amateur reporters, journalists are focused on improving the public's knowledge and checking the accuracy of the news they produce. Furthermore, a recent poll in Australia found that an astonishing 93% of respondents say they want good quality investigative journalism. Because there is a demand for in-depth, ethical reporting, journalism remains an exciting career.

3. Highlight the words and phrases in the paragraph that introduce an opinion or a contrasting opinion.

4. Which types of evidence does the writer provide to support the claim that there will always be a need for professional journalists?

☐ a. personal examples

☐ b. statistics

☐ c. contrasting examples

☐ d. expert opinions

☐ e. cause/effect arguments

However, journalism is a different career now than it was in the past. Although the sales of printed newspapers are declining, more and more people are visiting newspaper websites. Data from the Pew Research Center show that over 11 million people a day access the top 50 U.S. newspapers online. Meanwhile, almost half of all cell phone owners in the U.S. have tuned in to the radio online using an app, and podcasts continue to grow in popularity. Many of these are serious news sources. For example, I listen to current events and politics podcasts from different countries two or three times a week. The people behind these websites, online radio broadcasts, and podcasts are still journalists, but they are working under very different conditions now.

5. Which types of evidence does the writer use to explain the changes in journalism?

☐ a. personal examples

☐ b. statistics

☐ c. cause/effect arguments

☐ d. expert opinions

Consequently, the type of work available to journalists is certainly changing. In the past, reporters were employed full-time by newspapers or TV channels. Those jobs still exist, but reporters need to be more flexible and willing to work across different media without needing additional photographs and camera operators. For example, Australian journalist Ashlynne McGhee used her smartphone and other simple, portable equipment to report from a refugee camp. In one day, she produced a four-minute piece for national TV news and an online article, complete with photos and video.

In reality, though, there will be fewer traditional full-time jobs, but that's not the end of the profession. Media companies need flexible and reliable freelancers who can investigate stories and produce content that will appeal to readers across digital platforms. These journalists need expertise in using social media to find contacts and research stories.

6. Which of these examples would be the most effective to complete the last paragraph?

a. For example, digital advertising accounts for a growing proportion of revenue for media companies, mostly on mobile devices rather than desktop computers.

b. For example, investigative journalists use specialized search tools to look through the enormous amount of data on blogs, social media, and photo-sharing websites in order to find details for their stories.

c. For example, citizens can send tips about news stories as well as photos and videos to TV stations, which use them instead of paying for local reporters.

7. Which would be a good conclusion for this article? Remember that it will appear in a career services newsletter as part of a discussion of good jobs for the changing world of work. Discuss your answer with a partner.

a. Repeat the main ideas and conclude that journalism is a good career in the changing workplace.

b. Summarize the main ideas to show that journalists can be successful in the gig economy if they are flexible freelancers with technology expertise.

c. Suggest universities and majors that could lead to a career in journalism.

iQ PRACTICE Go online for more practice with using evidence to support an argument. *Practice › Unit 2 › Activity 10*

When writers include other people's speech, thoughts, questions, or results in their writing, they often use **noun clauses**. A noun clause is a dependent clause that can replace a noun or pronoun as a subject or object.

> main clause   noun clause
>
> Some economists say that the sharing economy is bad for workers.

There are three types of noun clauses:

- Noun clauses formed from statements

> noun clause
>
> Many smartphone users report (**that**) they use ride-sharing apps.

- Noun clauses formed from *wh-* questions

> noun clause
>
> Jackie explained **why** she quit her part-time job.

- Noun clauses formed from *yes/no* questions

> noun clause
>
> Researchers asked **if/whether** freelancers were satisfied with their work.

Noun clauses formed from questions always have sentence word order (subject-verb). They do not have the inverted word order typically used in questions, and they omit the form of *do* that is needed to form questions.

> ✗   Jackie explained why **did she quit** her part-time job.

Remember that you can use different verbs in the main clause to show your attitude toward the information in the noun clause. (See page 53.)

TIP FOR SUCCESS

The word *that* may be deleted in a noun clause, but it is usually kept in academic writing.

A. APPLY Complete the paragraph by forming correct noun clauses with *that, if, whether, how, where, why,* or *who.*

It can be hard to come up with a great idea for a new sharing business. For example, a Chinese start-up lends umbrellas to people in big cities for a small deposit and hourly fee. However, they soon discovered _____ they had lost
1
300,000 umbrellas. They wondered _____ the umbrellas had gone. The
2
company knew _____ had borrowed the umbrellas, so the problem seemed
3
to be reliability not theft. People simply forgot _____ they had to return the
4
umbrellas. The deposit was so low that users did not care _____ they lost
5
their money. However, the company could not afford to lose all their umbrellas.
Successful sharing sites have to consider _____ their product or service
6
will be used, and ask themselves _____ their customers can be trusted.
7

B. APPLY Complete each sentence using a noun clause with an appropriate reporting verb from the box in the correct form. Use each verb once.

| argue | ask | claim | discuss | ~~feel~~ | wonder |

1. A job is part of a person's identity.

   Many Americans _feel that a job is part of their identity._

2. What will the jobs of the future look like?

   Young people _____

3. Will we still need teachers and doctors?

   Experts _____

4. Freelance work is more flexible than full-time jobs.

   Supporters of the gig economy _____

5. How do sharing websites work in developing countries?

   The article _____

6. The potential benefits of the gig economy are greater than its current problems.

   Some economists _____

iQ PRACTICE Go online for more practice with noun clauses.
Practice > Unit 2 > Activities 11–12

UNIT ASSIGNMENT Write a persuasive newsletter article

OBJECTIVE ▶

In this assignment, you are going to write an article for a newsletter arguing why a particular career is a good choice. As you prepare to write, think about the Unit Question, "How is work changing?" Use information from Reading 1, Reading 2, the unit video, and your work in this unit to support your article. Refer to the Self-Assessment checklist on page 62.

---

iQ PRACTICE Go online to the Writing Tutor to read a model persuasive article. *Practice > Unit 2 > Activity 13*

PLAN AND WRITE

A. BRAINSTORM Think of two or three jobs. Brainstorm reasons why they are good choices in the changing world of work.

_____

_____

_____

_____

B. PLAN Follow these steps to plan your article.

1. Choose one of the jobs. Discuss the reasons to choose this job with a partner. Write down any new ideas. Underline at least three of the best ideas that support your argument.

_____

_____

_____

_____

_____

_____

_____

2. For each reason, find specific evidence from statistics, examples, hypothetical situations, experts, cause/effect logic, or other sources. Write the evidence next to each reason.

iQ RESOURCES Go online to download and complete the outline for your article. _Resources > Writing Tools > Unit 2 > Outline_

C. WRITE Use your planning notes from B to write your article.

1. Write your newsletter article, arguing why a particular job is a good choice. Support each main idea with evidence from your knowledge, experience, or reading.

2. Look at the Self-Assessment checklist on page 62 to guide your writing.

iQ PRACTICE Go online to the Writing Tutor to write your assignment. _Practice > Unit 2 > Activity 14_

REVISE AND EDIT

iQ RESOURCES Go online to download the peer review worksheet. *Resources > Writing Tools > Unit 2 > Peer Review Worksheet*

A. PEER REVIEW Read your partner's article. Then use the peer review worksheet. Discuss the review with your partner.

B. REWRITE Based on your partner's review, revise and rewrite your article.

C. EDIT Complete the Self-Assessment checklist as you prepare to write the final draft of your article. Be prepared to hand in your work or discuss it in class.

SELF-ASSESSMENT	Yes	No
Does the article build a convincing argument using main ideas supported with good evidence?	☐	☐
Are contrasting ideas introduced clearly?	☐	☐
Did you use noun clauses effectively?	☐	☐
Are there a variety of reporting verbs?	☐	☐
Does the article include vocabulary from the unit?	☐	☐
Did you check the article for punctuation, spelling, and grammar?	☐	☐

D. REFLECT Discuss these questions with a partner or group.

1. What is something new you learned in this unit?

2. Look back at the Unit Question—How is work changing? Is your answer different now than when you started the unit? If yes, how is it different? Why?

iQ PRACTICE Go to the online discussion board to discuss the questions. *Practice > Unit 2 > Activity 15*

TRACK YOUR SUCCESS

iQ PRACTICE Go online to check the words and phrases you have learned in this unit. *Practice > Unit 2 > Activity 16*

Check (✓) the skills you learned. If you need more work on a skill, refer to the page(s) in parentheses.

READING ☐ I can identify contrasting ideas. (p. 42)

CRITICAL THINKING ☐ I can recognize evaluative language. (p. 50)

VOCABULARY ☐ I can recognize and use reporting verbs. (p. 53)

WRITING ☐ I can use evidence to support an argument. (p. 55)

GRAMMAR ☐ I can recognize and use noun clauses. (p. 59)

OBJECTIVE ▶ ☐ I can gather information and ideas to write a persuasive argumentative newsletter article about a job.

3 Media Studies

UNIT QUESTION

How well does a picture illustrate the truth?

A. Discuss these questions with your classmates.

1. How can a photograph change what we see?

2. How can advertisements alter your view of a product or service?

3. Look at the photo. Which parts of it are real?
   What visual tricks are being used? Why?

B. Listen to *The Q Classroom* online. Then answer these questions.

1. How did the students answer the question?

2. Do you agree or disagree with their ideas? Why?

iQ PRACTICE   Go to the online discussion board to discuss the
Unit Question with your classmates. *Practice > Unit 3 > Activity 1*

**UNIT
OBJECTIVE**

Read an article from *Fast Company* and an excerpt from a textbook about the
manipulation of images. Gather information and ideas to create a proposal for a print
or online advertisement.

READING 1

OBJECTIVE ▶

Infographics Lie: Here's How

You are going to read an article about infographics (graphs, figures, maps, and other ways of displaying data) by Randy Olson from the business magazine *Fast Company*. Use the article to gather information and ideas for your Unit Assignment.

READING SKILL Previewing a text

Before you read a text, it is helpful to make guesses about its content. **Preview a text** by following these steps:

- Look at the text without reading it: What type of text is it? Who wrote it? Who is it written for?

- Read the title and subtitles or headings: What is the topic of each section?

- Look at the pictures, illustrations, and graphs, and read the captions: What do you expect to read about in the text?

Previewing a text helps you:

- predict the content of the reading using your existing knowledge about the topic.

- read faster because you have already thought about the ideas.

- make connections between the text and the graphics.

- recognize main ideas and details or examples.

A. IDENTIFY Preview Reading 1 on pages 68–70. Circle the answer that best completes each statement.

1. This reading is probably from ____.

   a. an online magazine

   b. an academic book

   c. a student essay

2. According to the title and first sentence, the article is probably about ____.

   a. the benefits of using infographics

   b. ways that infographics can trick readers

   c. techniques for creating infographics on computers

3. The three headings within the text are probably recommendations for ___.

   a. readers of infographics

   b. designers of infographics

   c. critics of infographics

4. Color and structural cues are ___.

   a. features of data presentation

   b. parts of the data source

   c. types of data alterations

5. Excluding data, transforming data, and the use of statistics are ___.

   a. features of data presentation

   b. aspects of the data source

   c. types of data alterations

B. DISCUSS Look at the infographics (the graphs and maps) in Reading 1. Discuss your predictions with a partner.

1. Which states in the map in Figure 1 stand out to you the most? Why?

   _____

2. Could the two graphs in Figure 2 represent the same data? Why or why not?

   _____

3. What do you think Figure 3 means?

   _____

iQ PRACTICE Go online for more practice previewing a text.
Practice > Unit 3 > Activity 2

PREVIEW THE READING

A. PREVIEW Based on the preview you have just done, predict three main ideas you will read in the article.

1. _____

2. _____

3. _____

B. QUICK WRITE How do you think graphs and other graphical representations of data might be unreliable? Write for 5–10 minutes in response. Remember to use this section for your Unit Assignment.

C. VOCABULARY Check (✓) the words you know. Use a dictionary to define any unknown words or phrases. Then discuss with a partner how the words and phrases will relate to the unit.

campaign *(n.)* 🔑+	scale *(n.)* 🔑+ OPAL
distort *(v.)* 🔑+	skyrocket *(v.)*
error-prone *(adj.)*	take . . . with a grain of salt *(v. phr.)*
manipulate *(v.)* 🔑+	transformation *(n.)* 🔑+ OPAL
misleading *(adj.)* 🔑+	unprecedented *(adj.)* 🔑+
prominent *(adj.)* 🔑+	visualize *(v.)*

🔑 Oxford 5000™ words   OPAL Oxford Phrasal Academic Lexicon

iQ PRACTICE Go online to listen and practice your pronunciation.
Practice > Unit 3 > Activity 3

WORK WITH THE READING

 A. INVESTIGATE Read the article and gather information on how well a picture illustrates the truth.

INFOGRAPHICS LIE: HERE'S HOW
by Randy Olson

1   We live in an age of Big: Big Computers, Big Data, and Big Lies.

2   Faced with an **unprecedented** torrent[1] of information, data scientists have turned to the visual arts to make sense of big data. The results of this unlikely marriage—often called *data visualizations* or *infographics*—have repeatedly provided us with new and insightful perspectives on the world around us.

3   However, time and time again, we have seen that data visualizations can easily be **manipulated** to lie. By misrepresenting, **distorting**, or faking the data they **visualize**, data scientists can twist public opinion to their benefit and even profit at our expense. We have a natural tendency to trust images more than text. As a result, we're easily fooled by data visualizations. Fortunately, there are three easy steps we can follow to save ourselves from getting duped[2] in the data deluge.

CHECK THE DATA PRESENTATION

4   The subtlest way a data visualization can fool you is by using visual cues to make data stand out that normally wouldn't. Be on the lookout for these visual tricks.

5   1. Color cues: Color is one popular tool for making certain data more **prominent** than the rest. When considering the map in Figure 1, Kentucky and Utah (the darkest and the lightest) will most likely stand out to us first.

[1] **torrent:** a large amount of something that comes suddenly and violently
[2] **dupe:** to trick or cheat someone

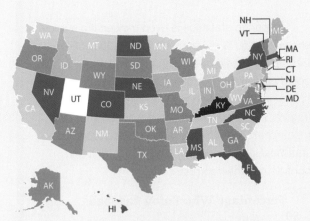

Figure 1: Percentage of smokers by U.S. state

6   If the map in Figure 1 were showing percentage of the population that smokes (where dark colors indicate more smokers and light colors fewer smokers), we might quickly conclude that Kentucky has a serious smoking problem. But what if we looked at the raw numbers and saw that 27% of Kentuckians and 23% of Utahans smoke? Now, there's not so big of a difference after all. Make sure to look at what the colors actually represent before drawing a conclusion from the visualization.

7   2. Structural cues: Structure is another popular tool for making data immediately stand out. In the bar charts in Figure 2, we're looking at the same data but with different **scales** on the y-axes[3]. Notice how such a simple structural change can make differences in the data look much more significant. Is an increase of 15 fraudulent visualizations from last year really "**skyrocketing**"? Don't let the structure of the visualization decide that for you. Always check the numbers that the visualization is representing.

CHECK THE DATA SOURCE

8   Make sure the data source is reliable. Data collected by an amateur is more **error-prone** than data collected by a professional scientist. Do a quick Web search to see if the people who collected and organized the data have a good track record of collecting and distributing data.

9   You should also make sure the data source isn't biased. A drug company may be inclined to present fake data showing that their latest drug is more effective than it really is, or a political **campaign** may manipulate data to discredit their political opponents. Think twice when considering data provided by biased groups.

10   Generally, we can trust data provided by government organizations, university research centers, and non-partisan[4] organizations.

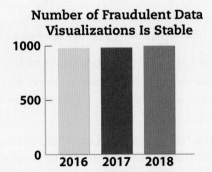

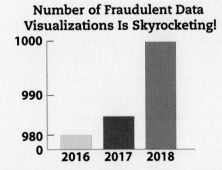

Figure 2: Changes in fraudulent visualizations, 2016–2018

---

[3] **y-axis:** the vertical axis (a fixed line against which the positions of points on a graph are measured)

[4] **non-partisan:** not supporting the ideas of one particular political party or group of people strongly

However, we should look more closely at data provided by for-profit companies, political organizations, and advocacy groups. If the data source isn't listed, **take the data visualization with many grains of salt.**

CHECK THE DATA ALTERATIONS

11   Many data sets require a little bit of housecleaning before they can be visualized, but excessive editing can be a sign of misrepresented data. Every good data visualization will come with explanations describing how the data was manipulated from its raw form into the visualization you see. Read the explanations, and watch out for the following data alterations.

12   1. Excluded data: Ensure that the explanations for excluding that data are reasonable. Sometimes the "explanation" may be that the data inconveniently contrasted with the story the author wanted to tell.

13   2. Transformed data: Data **transformation**, the process of converting data from one format to another format, can complicate the relationships between data. It's difficult to interpret a finding such as "The log transform[5] of a city's productivity is related to the log transform of the city's population." See how that doesn't make any sense to us in practical terms? While a transformation can make complicated mathematics accessible, it can also potentially be **misleading**. Be wary if several transformations have been applied to the data.

14   3. Statistics: Statistics are an often-abused tool in data science. "Fatal shark attacks have risen 100% this year" sounds like an alarming statistic until you realize that only one person was fatally attacked by a shark last year. Check the raw numbers when data visualizations present only the statistics.

15   Comparing statistics is even trickier. If a survey shows that 50% of Latinos and only 30% of Caucasians[6] enjoy watching baseball, those results could easily have been purely due to chance if the survey interviewed only 20 people of each ethnicity (Figure 3). If the visualization doesn't indicate the researchers' confidence in the comparison (called *statistical significance*), then we shouldn't be confident in their comparisons.

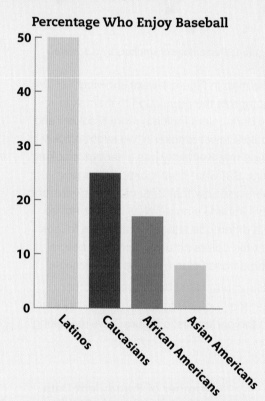

Figure 3: Baseball supporters by ethnicity

16   If the details on the data alterations aren't provided with the visualization, always keep in mind how easy it is to make data lie when it's visualized.

17   Remember: to save yourself from getting tricked by deceitful data, check the presentation, data source, and alterations.

---

[5] **log transform:** a statistical procedure that can be applied to raw data to show more regular patterns
[6] **Caucasian:** a member of any of the races of people who have pale skin

**VOCABULARY
SKILL REVIEW**

In Unit 1, you learned how to use a thesaurus to check the meaning of synonyms. Look up *distort*, *manipulate*, and *misleading* in your dictionary or thesaurus to find other similar words.

B. VOCABULARY Here are some words and phrases from Reading 1. Choose one to complete each sentence. You may need to change the form of the word or phrase to make the sentence grammatically correct.

campaign *(n.)*	misleading *(adj.)*	take . . . with a grain of salt *(v. phr.)*
distort *(v.)*	prominent *(adj.)*	transformation *(n.)*
error-prone *(adj.)*	scale *(n.)*	unprecedented *(adj.)*
manipulate *(v.)*	skyrocket *(v.)*	visualize *(v.)*

1. A graph must not _____ important data by making differences look greater than they actually are.

2. The photograph was in a(n) _____ position on the home page of the website.

3. The _____ of the map made the distance look short, but it took all day to drive between the two cities.

4. Our last advertising _____ was successful; a week's worth of ads increased sales by 20 percent.

5. A good graph helps readers to _____ the data described in the text.

6. The number of complaints _____ last year as readers became more aware of data misrepresentation.

7. _____ any email promising large cash rewards _____.

8. The picture has been _____ to hide imperfections.

9. Analyzing data can often be a complex and _____ process.

10. The chart is _____ because it does not state the number of people interviewed.

11. After so many _____, it was impossible to extract the raw data.

12. The newspaper took the _____ decision to publish an article explaining its policy for creating infographics.

C. IDENTIFY Put the main ideas of the article in the correct order. Write the number(s) of the paragraph(s) where you found them. Two of the sentences are NOT main ideas. Write *X* next to them.

_____ a. Graphical choices in data representations can be deliberately deceptive.
(Paragraph(s): _____)

_____ b. More Latinos than Caucasians enjoy watching baseball.
(Paragraph(s): _____)

_____ c. Infographics help us visualize large amounts of information.
(Paragraph(s): _____)

_____ d. Some sources of data should not be trusted to present data accurately.
(Paragraph(s): _____)

_____ e. It is important to know how the information in an infographic has been changed from the raw numbers.
(Paragraph(s): _____)

_____ f. Pharmaceutical companies may produce infographics that exaggerate the benefits of drugs they make.
(Paragraph(s): _____)

_____ g. It is easy to be manipulated by infographics because most people believe what they see more than what they read.
(Paragraph(s): _____)

D. CATEGORIZE Look again at the infographics in the article. Complete the table using information from the text.

Figure	What does it appear to show?	What does it actually mean?
1		
2		
3		

E. IDENTIFY Which pieces of advice are recommended in the article? Check (✓) the correct answers and write the number of the paragraph containing the advice.

☐ 1. Make sure the scientists who collected the data are experienced professionals. (Paragraph: ____)

☐ 2. Be cautious about infographics that use color to show differences. (Paragraph: ____)

☐ 3. Read the scale on the vertical axis (or y-axis) carefully. (Paragraph: ____)

☐ 4. You should be highly suspicious of infographics that do not indicate the source of the data. (Paragraph: ____)

☐ 5. It is important to check the actual numbers when reading a graph that displays percentages. (Paragraph: ____)

☐ 6. You should look carefully for the date when the information was collected, as infographics sometimes present old information. (Paragraph: ____)

F. APPLY Why should readers be careful if they see the following infographics? Support your answer with ideas from the article.

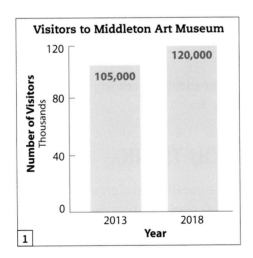

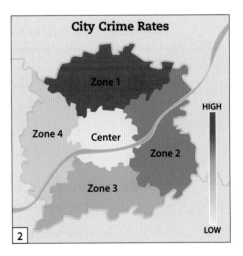

1. _____

_____

2. _____

_____

Customers Prefer Shop Smart Orange Juice

3 Our Brand   Other Brands

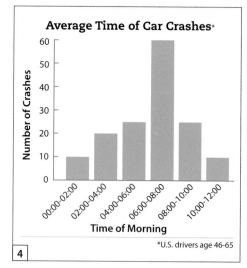

Average Time of Car Crashes*

Number of Crashes

60
50
40
30
20
10
0

00:00–02:00 02:00–04:00 04:00–06:00 06:00–08:00 08:00–10:00 10:00–12:00

Time of Morning

*U.S. drivers age 46-65

4

3. _____

_____

4. _____

_____

G. EXTEND Look back at your Quick Write on page 67. How well do graphs and figures show the truth? Add any new ideas or information you learned from the reading.

iQ PRACTICE Go online for additional reading and comprehension.
Practice > Unit 3 > Activity 5

WRITE WHAT YOU THINK

A. EVALUATE Discuss the questions in a group. Think about the Unit Question, "How well does a picture illustrate the truth?"

1. Have you seen graphs, tables, or infographics that have been distorted using the tricks described in Reading 1? Why do you think this was done?

2. Do you agree with the author that people are more easily persuaded by images than by text? Why or why not?

3. In what other ways can graphs, infographics, maps, or diagrams be misleading?

B. COMPOSE Choose one question and write a paragraph in response. Look back at your Quick Write on page 67 as you think about what you learned.

Phototruth or Photofiction?

OBJECTIVE ▶

You are going to read an excerpt from the college textbook *Phototruth or Photofiction? Ethics and Media Imagery in the Digital Age* by Thomas Wheeler. It asks how far journalists can go when manipulating photographs. Use the excerpt to gather information and ideas for your Unit Assignment.

PREVIEW THE READING

A. PREVIEW Think about the title and look at the picture on page 76. What do you predict the writer will say about manipulating photographs in journalism?

☐ It is always acceptable.

☐ It is sometimes acceptable.

☐ It is never acceptable.

B. QUICK WRITE Why might someone want to change a photo? Write for 5–10 minutes in response. Remember to use this section for your Unit Assignment.

C. VOCABULARY Check (✓) the words and phrases you know. Use a dictionary to define any unknown words or phrases. Then discuss with a partner how the words and phrases will relate to the unit.

alteration *(n.)* OPAL	**document** *(v.)* OPAL	**legitimate** *(adj.)* ᴷ+
bias *(n.)* ᴷ+ OPAL	**ethical** *(adj.)* ᴷ+ OPAL	**provoke** *(v.)* ᴷ+
concoct *(v.)*	**inherent** *(adj.)* ᴷ+ OPAL	**scrutinize** *(v.)*
credible *(adj.)* ᴷ+	**leave in the dark** *(v. phr.)*	**tempting** *(adj.)* ᴷ+

ᴷ+ Oxford 5000™ words   OPAL Oxford Phrasal Academic Lexicon

iQ PRACTICE Go online to listen and practice your pronunciation.
Practice > Unit 3 > Activity 6

WORK WITH THE READING

 A. INVESTIGATE Read the textbook extract and gather information on how well a picture illustrates the truth.

PHOTOTRUTH OR PHOTOFICTION?

1   Any discussion of "manipulated" photography must begin with the recognition that photography itself is an **inherent** manipulation—a manipulation of light, a process with many steps and stages, all subject to the **biases** and interpretations of the photographer, printer, editor, or viewer. Photography is not absolute "reality." It is not unqualified "truth." It is not purely "objective." It was never any of those things, and it has always been subject to distortion. Indeed, many of its earliest practitioners were more concerned with **concocting** fantasy than **documenting** reality. They were artists, not journalists.

2   Still, one branch of photography—called *photojournalism*—has acquired a special standing in the public mind. Newspaper and magazine readers generally believe that a photo can *reflect* reality in a **credible** way.

3   But why? Why has photography seemed so inherently realistic for so long? Much of the trust in photojournalism comes from average citizens' everyday experiences with personal photography. We point our cameras and cell phones at ourselves, our families, friends, and vacation sights and view the files and prints as **legitimate** documents that "capture" the events and scenes in meaningful ways. Countless millions of us take "selfies" and snapshots or collect our photos in albums, on social media, and on hard drives for future generations, not only for entertainment or curiosity value but as evidence of the way we once looked and the way the world once worked. As Dartmouth College professor Marianne Hirsch has said, "People say if there was a fire, the first thing they would save is their photo albums. We almost fear we'll lose our memories if we lose our albums." The same is probably true now of digital photo collections.

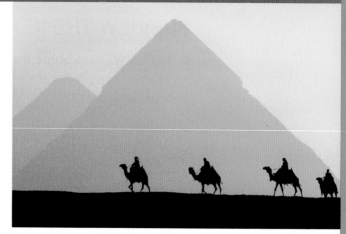

National Geographic's February 1982 photo of the Great Pyramids of Giza

4   This credibility has survived despite photography's history of occasional duplicity[1]. However, digital manipulation may challenge this trust more than a century and a half of other methods of fakery. Commentators have observed, "There's nothing new about faking photos," but that is not quite right. There is something new. Computer technology has made photo doctoring much easier to do and accessible to many more people with nothing more sophisticated than the phone in their pockets.

5   It seems that with each new graphics software program or photo app, the opportunities for fictionalizing images become ever more numerous and **tempting**. One result is that "the objective 'truth' of photographs has become something of a quaint[2] concept" (*American Photo*). Michael Morse of the National Press Photographers Association agrees: "People have no idea how much **alteration** is going on." This raises thorny **ethical** challenges for professionals, educators, and students alike.

[1] **duplicity:** dishonest behavior that is intended to make people believe something that is not true
[2] **quaint:** attractive in an unusual or old-fashioned way

6   For decades, photojournalists and editors have opposed misleading alterations, particularly in "hard news" photos (images of war, crime scenes, political events, natural disasters, etc.). As computer manipulations have become more common, however, adherence to photojournalistic norms has given way to the temptations of commerce, even in respected newspapers and news magazines.

7   For example, during the processing of *National Geographic*'s February 1982 photo of the Great Pyramids of Giza, a pyramid was digitally shifted to make the image fit the cover. The alteration **provoked** much controversy, not so much because it was drastic (it was relatively insignificant) but because it appeared in a magazine long respected for its authenticity.

8   In 1998, *National Geographic* editor Bill Allen said, "Nearly two decades ago we moved one pyramid to get the same effect as if the photographer had walked perhaps fifty yards to the left before taking the photograph. And yet after all that time, one of the most common questions I'm asked is, 'Do you guys still move pyramids?' This reminds all of us of just how fragile our credibility is. If you lose it, it's almost impossible to ever get it back. It's why we're such fanatics about disclosure[3] now at *National Geographic*."

9   Kenneth Brower's article in the May 1998 *Atlantic Monthly* listed a number of faked nature photos and sequences, including a polar bear in Antarctica that appeared in a full-page ad for *National Geographic Online*. (There are no polar bears in Antarctica; there are polar bears in the Arctic—and also in the Ohio zoo where this particular animal was photographed!)

10   The following are just some of the many other examples of "photomanipulation" that have appeared in print:

- The winner of a spelling bee[4] sponsored by the *New York Daily News* was photographed for a story in the *New York Post*, which removed the name of its rival newspaper from the image of the winner's identification card.

- In all of their outdoor photos of the 1984 Summer Olympic Games, editors at the *Orange County Register* changed the color of the Los Angeles sky (notorious for its smog) to clear blue.

11   There are many more recent examples of digital deception, such as these:

- In March 2012, after a number of tornadoes in the American Midwest, a graphic design student in Michigan posted a photo of a tornado on a popular social media site. The photo quickly spread until it was posted on the web page of a local TV station and was even broadcast on the evening news. The student then admitted it was a fake. WNEM news director Ian Rubin said, "We've used this experience as a reminder to the whole news team to review viewer-submitted photos with the meteorologists before they go on the air."

- In Sydney, Australia, in 2013, a man called Dimitri di Angelis tricked investors into giving him $8 million, in part by showing them photographs of himself with world leaders and movie stars. The photos were, of course, created using computer software, and di Angelis was sent to prison for 12 years.

12   Some professionals might consider a few of this chapter's examples to be relatively innocuous[5], but in most cases, readers and viewers were **left in the dark** until the truth was revealed. In these images, photography's presumed relationship to reality was disrupted. Readers might have a simpler description: they might call the photos lies.

13   The inherent trustworthiness once attributed to photography is withering[6], even as amateur photos flood the Internet. From now on, assumptions about the ability of photos to tell the truth will increasingly be **scrutinized**—for good reason. Visual journalists will have to accommodate these shifts and re-examine their own practices and ethics if they are to successfully separate their work from cartoons, fantasy, and fiction.

---

[3] **disclosure:** the act of making information public

[4] **spelling bee:** a competition in which participants have to spell difficult words correctly

[5] **innocuous:** not harmful or dangerous

[6] **withering:** growing weaker before disappearing completely

B. VOCABULARY Here are some words and a phrase from Reading 2. Read the paragraphs. Then write each bold word or phrase next to the correct definition. Write verbs in their base form and nouns in the singular.

> Newspaper articles can never tell the entire truth: some element of lying is **inherent** in all journalism because it is impossible for one article to include all the details of the story. Journalists may also manipulate the order in which they present information to achieve more drama or other effects in their writing. Choosing details and the order to describe them is considered proper and **ethical** behavior for journalists. Editors can even reflect their paper's political **bias** when writing opinion pieces about elections and politics.
>
> In book publishing, many companies do not always **scrutinize** the information authors write. A best-selling book can make a lot of money, so some authors find it **tempting** to make up lies. In one famous case, a writer **concocted** a completely fictitious history about himself. The writing seemed **credible**, so most readers believed his story. However, the writer later was unable to **document** the facts in the book, and he was revealed as a fake, which **provoked** controversy for him and his publisher. Although the writer's tale was not **legitimate**, many people still found it meaningful. Even these readers agree that they would rather not be **left in the dark**, wondering whether or not a story is true. They would rather be aware of any major **alteration** of facts that could turn a good true story into just a good story.

1. _____ (v.) to cause a particular reaction or have a particular effect

2. _____ (v. phr.) to prevent from learning something

3. _____ (v.) to invent a story, an excuse, etc.

4. _____ (n.) a strong feeling in favor of or against one group of people or one side in an argument, often not based on fair judgment

5. _____ (n.) a change to something

6. _____ (v.) to look at or examine somebody or something carefully

7. _____ (adj.) that can be believed or trusted

8. _____ (adj.) morally correct or acceptable

9. _____ (adj.) valid; fair

10. _____ (adj.) existing as a basic or permanent part of somebody or something

11. _____ (v.) to prove or support something with evidence

12. _____ (adj.) attractive; making people want to have it or do it

iQ PRACTICE Go online for more practice with the vocabulary.
Practice > Unit 3 > Activity 7

C. IDENTIFY Answer these questions. Write the number of the paragraph where you found each answer. Then compare your answers with a partner.

1. Why are photographs always manipulated in some way? (Paragraph: ____)

_____

2. Why do most people trust the photographs they see in the news media? (Paragraph: ____)

_____

3. How is digital fakery different from earlier forms of photographic manipulation? (Paragraph: ____)

_____

4. What does the example of the pyramid in *National Geographic* say about the credibility of photojournalism? (Paragraph: ____)

_____

5. Why are the examples in this reading important even though many of them are relatively minor changes? (Paragraph: ____)

_____

D. IDENTIFY Match each sentence with the correct person or publication.

____ 1. Photographs have such great value for many people that we are almost afraid of losing our memories if our photo albums are lost.

____ 2. It is old-fashioned to believe that photographs are inherently objective.

____ 3. Most magazine readers do not realize how much photographs have been manipulated.

____ 4. When people stop believing in your honesty, it is very hard to convince them otherwise.

____ 5. Many nature photographs in magazines have been faked (for example, showing a polar bear in Antarctica).

a. Bill Allen of *National Geographic*

b. *Atlantic Monthly* article by Kenneth Brower

c. *American Photo* magazine

d. Professor Marianne Hirsch

e. Michael Morse

E. EVALUATE What is your opinion? Rank the examples of manipulated photographs in the article from 1 (least serious) to 6 (most serious). Then justify your rankings to a partner with evidence from the reading.

____ a. *National Geographic*'s pyramids

____ b. *National Geographic Online*'s polar bears

____ c. The *New York Daily News*'s report on a spelling bee

____ d. The *Orange County Register*'s photograph of Los Angeles

____ e. The social media photo of a tornado

____ f. Dimitri di Angelis's fake photographs

F. IDENTIFY Write the phrases from the text the pronouns in bold refer to.

1. **It** is not purely "objective." (Paragraph 1) _____*photography*_____

2. **They** were artists, not journalists. (Paragraph 1) _____

3. However, digital manipulation may challenge **this** trust more than a century and a half of other methods of fakery. (Paragraph 4) _____

4. **This** raises thorny ethical challenges for professionals, educators, and students alike. (Paragraph 5) _____

5. **It** was relatively insignificant. (Paragraph 7) _____

CRITICAL THINKING STRATEGY

Interpreting graphs and charts

As you saw in Reading 1, it is important to read graphs and charts critically. In academic and newspaper articles, you will sometimes find the most important information in the graphs and charts (or *figures*). Here are some questions you can answer to interpret different types of graphs and charts carefully:

Figure	Interpretations
Table	What categories and variables are presented? What are the most important statistics?
Line graph	What are the trends and patterns in the numerical data?
Bar chart	What are the similarities and differences between the categories?
Pie chart	What are the proportions and percentages of the categories?
Map	Where are the geographical trends and patterns?
Diagram	What is the process or what are the important components of the figure?

iQ PRACTICE Go online to watch the Critical Thinking Video and check your comprehension. *Practice ▸ Unit 3 ▸ Activity 8*

G. INTEPRET Use the graphs below to answer the questions.

1. What does Figure 1 tell you about young people's preferred news sources?

2. According to Figure 2, what are the differences between generations in newspaper readership?

3. Do Figures 1 and 2 suggest that companies should stop buying advertisements in newspapers? Why?

4. What trend in newspaper sales is shown in Figure 3?

5. Some daily newspapers have reported that the number of people reading their articles is increasing. According to Figures 1 and 3, how is this possible?

ACADEMIC LANGUAGE

As well as *according to*, the phrases *as shown in*, *can be seen in* and *indicate(s) that* are commonly used in academic writing to refer to information in graphs and charts.

⎤ **OPAL**

Oxford Phrasal Academic Lexicon

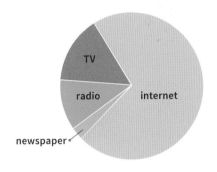

Figure 1: Where do young people get their news?

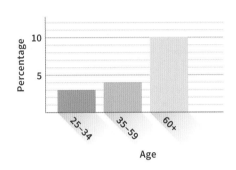

Figure 2: Who reads newspapers?

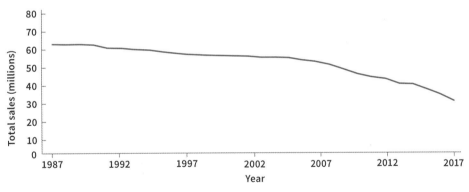

Figure 3: Sales of daily newspapers

H. DISCUSS Discuss these questions in a group. Look back at your Quick Write on page 75 as you think about what you have learned.

1. Are photographs important to you? Why or why not?

2. Do you think of photography more as an art form or a type of journalism? Please explain.

3. Do you care if a photograph in a magazine or newspaper has been manipulated? Why or why not?

WORK WITH THE VIDEO

VIDEO VOCABULARY

survey (v.) to measure and record the features of an area of land

cartography (n.) the art or process of drawing or making maps

navigate (v.) to find your position or the position of your ship, plane, car, etc. and the direction you need to go in

two-dimensional (adj.) flat

aerial (adj.) from the air, often from a plane

topography (n.) the physical features of an area of land

A. PREVIEW Do you ever use maps? What do you use them for?

iQ RESOURCES Go online to watch the video about maps.
Resources > Video > Unit 3 > Unit Video

B. CATEGORIZE Watch the video two or three times. What type of information do you find in different kinds of maps? Take notes in the table.

Map	Information
Two-dimensional drawings	
Thematic maps	
Satellite imagery	
Sonar maps	

C. EXTEND Many people today do not use printed maps because they have navigation technology in their cars and smartphones. Do you think it is still important for everyone to learn how to read a map, or is this a skill that only experts in specific fields need? Discuss your ideas in a small group.

WRITE WHAT YOU THINK

SYNTHESIZE Think about Reading 1, Reading 2, and the video as you discuss these questions. Then choose one question and write a paragraph in response.

1. Both readings suggest that images are persuasive but often untruthful. How confident should we be that maps tell the objective truth? How could they be manipulated or distorted?

2. How could marketers use the manipulation techniques described in the readings to advertise products and services?

VOCABULARY SKILL Latin and Greek roots

Identifying **Greek and Latin roots** (or **stems**) will help you recognize and understand new words. Words with these roots are especially common in formal written English, so using these words will aid in reading comprehension and add sophistication to your writing.

Common roots

Root	Meaning	Examples
mot- / mov- / mob-	move	promote, immobile
just- / jur-	right, legal	justify, jury
her- / hes-	stick	coherent, cohesive
vid- / vis-	see, notice	evidence, visible

You should also watch for other roots when you recognize groups of words with similar meanings.

iQ RESOURCES Go online to watch the Vocabulary Skill Video.
Resources > Video > Unit 3 > Vocabulary Skill Video

A. APPLY Read each sentence. Using your knowledge of roots, circle the word or phrase that best matches the meaning of each bold word.

1. The patient reported reduced **mobility**.

   a. ability to speak   b. ability to read   c. ability to move

2. You need to choose an **adhesive** that works on wood.

   a. paint   b. pencil   c. glue

3. I don't **envisage** any problem with this plan.

   a. remember   b. create   c. expect

4. She was angry at the **injustice** of the professor's decision.

    a. humor   b. unfairness   c. danger

5. The student was **motivated** to study hard by her teacher.

    a. moved   b. told   c. warned

6. There is an **inherent** problem with this type of car.

    a. unusual   b. unavoidable   c. annoying

7. She was unable to provide a **justification** for her behavior.

    a. plan   b. wish   c. good explanation

8. Successful companies are often led by great **visionaries**.

    a. people with a lot of money

    b. people with a lot of power

    c. people with a lot of imagination

TIP FOR SUCCESS

Learning Latin and Greek roots can improve your English spelling. For example, if you know *millimeter* comes from *milli-*, you will remember to write it with a double *l*.

B. INTERPRET Look at the sets of words below the box. The common root is bold. Choose the answer in the box that best defines each bold root. Then explain your choices to a partner.

break	follow	life	thousand
circle/round	law	other/different	write

1. hemi**sphere**, **spher**ical, atmo**sphere**   sphere   = _____

2. **alter**native, **alter**ation, **alter**   alter-   = _____

3. **sequ**ence, **sec**ond, **sequ**el   sequ-/sec- = _____

4. sur**viv**e, **viv**id, re**viv**e   viv-   = _____

5. de**scrip**tion, post**script**, **scrib**ble   scrip-/scrib- = _____

6. **leg**itimate, **leg**al, **leg**islation   leg-   = _____

7. **mill**ennium, **milli**meter, **milli**pede   milli-   = _____

8. **frag**ile, **frag**ment, **fract**ion   frag-/fract- = _____

iQ PRACTICE Go online for more practice with Latin and Greek roots. *Practice > Unit 3 > Activity 9*

WRITING

OBJECTIVE ▶

At the end of this unit, you will write an advertisement proposal. Your proposal will include information from the readings, the unit video, and your own ideas.

WRITING SKILL Writing with unity

In good writing, each paragraph has **unity**: it explores one idea. This helps readers understand all the main ideas in a text. If you mix different ideas in a paragraph, your readers may become confused, and your writing will not be effective. Sometimes, one idea needs several paragraphs, in which case each paragraph should describe one part of the idea. This keeps the reader focused on one point at a time.

The complete piece of writing (essay, article, report, etc.) also needs unity. All the points and ideas in the paragraphs should support one topic, argument, thesis, or purpose. This will keep your writing clear, interesting, and persuasive.

WRITING TIP

In Unit 2, you learned to give evidence to support an argument. A proposal is another kind of persuasive writing, so you should give details and reasons to support your recommendations.

A. EVALUATE Read these paragraphs from an advertisement proposal for a cafe. Cross out one sentence to improve the unity of each paragraph. Explain your reason to a partner.

1. At the top of the web page advertising Roy's Silver Spoon Cafe, three images will rotate. The first image is a digitally enhanced photograph of a cup of coffee that appears to show steam rising perfectly from the smooth surface of the drink. In the second picture, two friends are shown sitting at a table in the cafe. The web page also shows the menu and weekly special coffees. The final photograph is of Roy himself, but we will manipulate the photo to make it look as if he is standing on top of the building to welcome customers.

2. The most important part of our proposed website design is your new logo. A shiny silver spoon stands proudly in the center of the cafe's name. A new, more modern font has been chosen to bring your business up to date. Roy's name appears in silver to make it more prominent and to match the color of the spoon. The next change we recommend is to include customer comments on the web page.

3. The first page of your current website is dominated by a map of the town, showing the location of the cafe. We recommend moving this to another page, with directions and hours of operation. The home page is the first impression a new customer gets of your business, and while it is important to be able to find your cafe, thanks to navigation software and smartphones, an address is probably enough. There will also be a page to promote upcoming events at the cafe. In place of the map, we would like to write a paragraph explaining the history of the cafe and the atmosphere you create there.

B. CATEGORIZE A graphic designer working for an advertising agency is writing a proposal for a magazine advertisement for a local business, Rudy's Plumbing Supply. Look at the designer's notes in the cluster diagram. Then follow the instructions below.

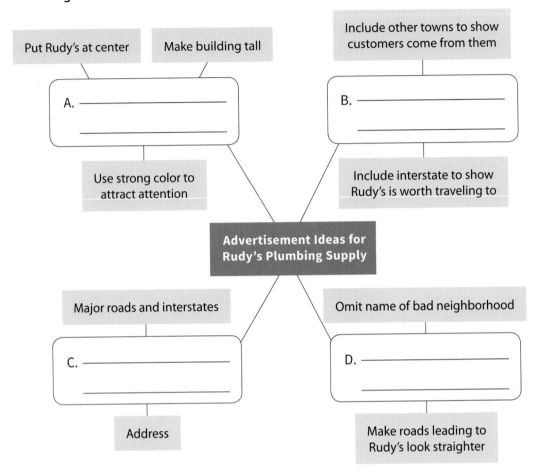

Put Rudy's at center   Make building tall

Include other towns to show customers come from them

A. _____

B. _____

Use strong color to attract attention

Include interstate to show Rudy's is worth traveling to

Advertisement Ideas for Rudy's Plumbing Supply

Major roads and interstates

Omit name of bad neighborhood

C. _____

D. _____

Address

Make roads leading to Rudy's look straighter

1. Label each cluster with an idea from the box. You will not use one idea.

Basic features of the map   Make Rudy's look more accessible

Information about other businesses   Stimulate demand

Make Rudy's look impressive

2. Check (✓) each idea that the designer could include without affecting the unity of the proposal. Write X if an idea does not fit anywhere.

____ a. Add this line of copy (text): "Just around the corner!"

____ b. Include Rudy's website.

____ c. Print a customer's review of Rudy's service.

____ d. Suggest that people don't mind traveling a long way to go to Rudy's.

____ e. Put a photograph of Rudy at the top to add personal appeal.

TIP FOR SUCCESS

Notice the format of this proposal, which is a common form of business writing. Proposals always include the company's name and address as well as the date.

Tildon Advertising
290 West Main, Tildon, PA

From: Liz Madison, Account Executive
To: Mr. Rudy Swenson, Manager, Rudy's Plumbing Supply
Date: March 14
Re: Ad Proposal

Dear Mr. Swenson,

1   Thank you for asking us to design a magazine advertisement for your store. Please find below a description of the ad we are proposing.

2   The centerpiece of the ad is a map. Maps are excellent attention-getters. The map will contain all the practical information customers need to find your business: the address, the major roads, and the nearby interstates. Obviously, most of your customers are local, and few of them need the interstate to get to your store. However, we want to show them that your store is so good that a number of customers might also come from far away. In this way, we can stimulate a great deal of demand for your business.

3   In addition to including the interstate, we will mention the names of several neighboring towns. You might attract a few customers from other towns, but mainly we will show that your business is popular and known throughout the region.

4   In our meeting, you asked us to stress the accessibility of your business, and our ad will make customers feel comfortable about visiting you. You told us you were concerned that your business is not located in the best part of town. Therefore, we recommend omitting the name of your neighborhood and some road names. The ad will encourage new customers to visit you and judge the quality of your service, not the neighborhood.

5   A good impression is also achieved by using strong colors in the ad and drawing your building from an angle that increases its scale. The building will be at the center of the ad, and its prominent position and size will bring in plenty of new business.

6   We hope you approve of this proposal. We feel that it tells a truthful and persuasive story about Rudy's Plumbing Supply. Please do not hesitate to contact me if you have any questions.

1. Write the purpose or main idea of each paragraph. Use the cluster diagram in Activity B to help you.

Paragraph 1: _____

Paragraph 2: _____

Paragraph 3: _____

Paragraph 4: _____

Paragraph 5: _____

Paragraph 6: _____

2. What idea does the writer use to give unity through the entire proposal?

_____

D. APPLY Work with a partner. Add a new paragraph between paragraphs 5 and 6 of the writing model. Your paragraph should be about a slogan for Rudy's Plumbing Supply.

1. Choose a slogan from the suggestions below or write your own.

☐ "For service you can trust, call Rudy today!"

☐ "Your local plumbing expert"

☐ "Rudy's goes the extra mile!"

☐ Your idea: _____

2. Brainstorm ideas for your paragraph by answering these questions.

a. Why does Rudy's need a good slogan?

_____

b. Why have you chosen this slogan?

_____

c. How will you use the slogan in the ad?

_____

3. Organize your ideas and add a clear first and final sentence, plus any other ideas you have to write a paragraph that has unity.

4. Swap your paragraph with another pair. Discuss these questions.

a. Does the paragraph have unity? Is every sentence related to the slogan?

b. Are the ideas in the paragraph in a clear and logical order?

c. What advice would you give the writers to improve their paragraph?

iQ PRACTICE Go online for more practice with writing with unity.
Practice > Unit 3 > Activity 10

Quantifiers are words that modify nouns and noun phrases and indicate amounts. They give information about *how much* (for a noncount noun) and *how many* (for a plural count noun). Quantifiers generally come before the noun.

Noncount nouns

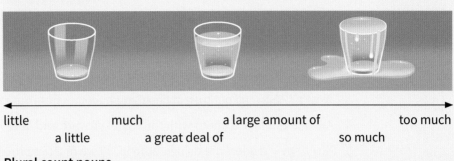

little   much   a large amount of   too much
    a little   a great deal of   so much

Plural count nouns

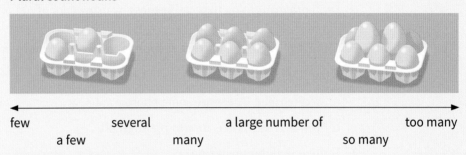

few   several   a large number of   too many
    a few   many   so many

Both count and noncount nouns

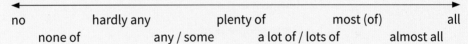

no   hardly any   plenty of   most (of)   all
    none of   any / some   a lot of / lots of   almost all

Be especially careful with these quantifiers:

A few / A little have positive meanings: the quantity is small but still important.

☐ There is **a little** demand for the product, so we will keep selling it.

Few / Little have negative meanings: the quantity is almost zero.

☐ There is **little** demand for the product, so we will stop selling it.

Use *a lot of* instead of *much* in affirmative sentences.

☐ ✓ We did **a lot of** advertising this year.
    ✗ We did much advertising this year.

Any is used in negative sentences and questions to mean *some*.

☐ Do you have **any** questions? Yes, I have **some** questions.

However, *any* can also mean "it doesn't matter which" in affirmative sentences with a singular count or noncount noun.

☐ Look in **any** book for an example at **any** time.

Almost all means nearly 100 percent.

Note: Do not use *almost* by itself before a noun; it is an adverb, not a quantifier.

- ✓ **Almost all** people take photographs.
- ✗ Almost people take photographs.

A. IDENTIFY Circle the correct quantifier to complete each sentence.

1. *Some / Any* magazine photographs are manipulated.

2. Your ad should not contain *too much / too many* details.

3. *Almost / Almost all* our trust in photography comes from our experience with it.

4. Anyone can fake a photo with the right software and *little / a little* experience.

5. *Few / A few* readers are using our map, so we must improve it.

6. I will draw attention to your business by using *a lot of / much* color.

B. EXTEND Circle the correct response to each comment or question.

1. I don't like this book. There's too much text, and there aren't enough pictures.

   a. You're right. There are some photographs.

   b. You're right. There are few photographs.

2. Is this a popular magazine?

   a. No, few people read it.

   b. No, a few people read it.

3. Why do you think this ad uses a map?

   a. It has so much good information.

   b. It has hardly any good information.

4. Can you finish the proposal by tomorrow?

   a. I don't think so. I need little more time.

   b. I don't think so. I need a little more time.

5. The survey found that 45 percent of people expect magazines to manipulate photographs.

   a. OK, but plenty of people still trust photojournalists!

   b. OK, but almost all people still trust photojournalists!

C. IDENTIFY Look back at the model proposal in Activity C of the Writing Skill on page 87. Circle the quantifiers in the proposal.

iQ PRACTICE Go online for more practice with quantifiers.
Practice ⟩ Unit 3 ⟩ Activity 11

iQ PRACTICE Go online for the Grammar Expansion: Articles.
Practice > Unit 3 > Activity 12

UNIT ASSIGNMENT Write a proposal

OBJECTIVE ▶

In this assignment, you will pretend that you work for an advertising agency that designs print or online advertisements. You will write a proposal for a client, describing your ideas for an ad. As you prepare your proposal, think about the Unit Question, "How well does a picture illustrate the truth?" Use information from Reading 1, Reading 2, the unit video, and your work in this unit to support your ideas. Refer to the Self-Assessment checklist on page 92.

iQ PRACTICE Go online to the Writing Tutor to read a model proposal.
Practice > Unit 3 > Activity 13

PLAN AND WRITE

A. BRAINSTORM Complete the following tasks.

1. Work with a partner. Choose a product or service for another pair of students to advertise: for example, your school, a business you know, a product you use, or something that does not exist yet. Imagine you represent that product or service. Write a paragraph describing it and the type of advertisement you want to create, such as a poster, a website, or a newspaper ad.

2. Exchange paragraphs with another pair. Read and discuss the paragraphs. Ask for clarification as necessary. You are going to write a proposal to convince the other pair to hire you to design an ad for their product or service.

3. With your partner, answer these questions.

    a. What type of graphic will you use in the ad? Draw or describe in words the photograph, drawing, infographic, map, or other graphic you will use.

    _____

    b. How will the graphic make the ad persuasive?

    _____

    c. How will the graphic help promote the product or service?

    _____

B. PLAN Draw a cluster diagram and write your main ideas for the ad in the circles. Then connect supporting details, explanations, and examples outside each circle. Refer to the cluster diagram on page 86 if you need.

iQ RESOURCES Go online to download and complete the outline for your proposal. *Resources > Writing Tools > Unit 3 > Outline*

C. WRITE Use your planning notes from B to write your proposal.

1. Write your proposal using your cluster diagram and any other ideas from your discussions in Activity A. Think about the unity of each paragraph and of the entire proposal.

2. Look at the Self-Assessment checklist below to guide your writing.

iQ PRACTICE Go online to the Writing Tutor to write your assignment.
Practice > Unit 3 > Activity 14

REVISE AND EDIT

iQ RESOURCES Go online to download the peer review worksheet.
Resources > Writing Tools > Unit 3 > Peer Review Worksheet

A. PEER REVIEW Read your partner's proposal. Then use the peer review worksheet. Discuss the review with your partner.

B. REWRITE Based on your partner's review, revise and rewrite your proposal.

C. EDIT Complete the Self-Assessment checklist as you prepare to write the final draft of your proposal. Be prepared to hand in your work or discuss it in class.

SELF-ASSESSMENT	Yes	No
Is each paragraph written with unity?	☐	☐
Does the entire proposal have unity?	☐	☐
Are quantifiers varied and used correctly?	☐	☐
Does the proposal include vocabulary from the unit?	☐	☐
Does the proposal use a chart, map, or graphic effectively?	☐	☐
Did you check the proposal for punctuation, spelling, and grammar?	☐	☐

D. REFLECT Discuss the questions with a partner or group.

1. What is something new you learned in this unit?

2. Look back at the Unit Question—How well does a picture illustrate the truth? Is your answer different now than when you started the unit? If yes, how is it different? Why?

iQ PRACTICE Go to the online discussion board to discuss the questions.
Practice > Unit 3 > Activity 15

TRACK YOUR SUCCESS

iQ PRACTICE Go online to check the words and phrases you have learned in this unit. *Practice > Unit 3 > Activity 16*

Check (✓) the skills you learned. If you need more work on a skill, refer to the page(s) in parentheses.

READING	☐ I can preview a text. (p. 66)
CRITICAL THINKING	☐ I can interpret graphs and charts. (p. 80)
VOCABULARY	☐ I can use Latin and Greeks roots to understand words. (p. 83)
WRITING	☐ I can write with unity. (p. 85)
GRAMMAR	☐ I can use quantifiers correctly. (pp. 89–90)

OBJECTIVE ▶   ☐ I can gather information and ideas to create a proposal for a print or online advertisement.

International Relations

Why is global cooperation important?

A. Discuss these questions with your classmates.

1. Have you ever worked with someone from another country? What were the benefits of cooperating with this person?

2. What issues or problems in your country do other countries also have? How do they affect you personally? Would cooperating with other countries help solve these problems?

3. Look at the photo of the United Nations headquarters in Geneva, Switzerland. What are some of the ways this organization promotes global cooperation? What other organizations do you know that promote global cooperation?

B. Listen to *The Q Classroom* online. Then answer these questions.

1. What ideas do Marcus, Felix, Yuna, and Sophy have about why global cooperation is important?

2. What ideas do you have to add to their discussion?

iQ PRACTICE Go to the online discussion board to discuss the Unit Question with your classmates. *Practice > Unit 4 > Activity 1*

UNIT OBJECTIVE ▶ Read an article from *The New York Times* and an article from *Maclean's* news magazine about global cooperation initiatives. Gather information and ideas to write an essay about the importance of global cooperation.

READING

READING 1

In Norway, Global Seed Vault Guards Genetic Resources

OBJECTIVE ▶

You are going to read an article from *The New York Times* that reports on the international response to the dangers threatening the genetic diversity of the world's food supply. Use the article to gather information and ideas for your Unit Assignment.

PREVIEW THE READING

A. PREVIEW What do you think might cause plants to become extinct? Write three possible reasons.

1. _____

2. _____

3. _____

WRITING TIP
Brainstorming ideas before you write can help you write more fluently.

B. QUICK WRITE How could countries work together to protect the world's plant life? Take a couple of minutes to brainstorm ideas. Then write for 5–10 minutes in response. Remember to use this section for your Unit Assignment.

C. VOCABULARY Work with a partner to find these words in the reading. Circle clues in the text that help you understand the meaning of each word. Then use a dictionary to define any unknown words.

confront (v.) 🕮+	devastating (adj.) 🕮+	inevitable (adj.) 🕮+
conserve (v.) 🕮+ OPAL	erosion (n.)	plan B (n.)
consolidate (v.) 🕮+	extinct (adj.)	urgency (n.)
crucial (adj.) 🕮+ OPAL	genetic (adj.) 🕮+	vulnerability (n.) 🕮+

🕮+ Oxford 5000™ words   OPAL Oxford Phrasal Academic Lexicon

iQ PRACTICE Go online to listen and practice your pronunciation.
Practice > Unit 4 > Activity 2

WORK WITH THE READING

 A. INVESTIGATE Read the article and gather information about why global cooperation is important.

In Norway, Global Seed Vault Guards Genetic Resources

By Elisabeth Rosenthal

1   LONGYEARBYEN, Norway – With plant species disappearing at an alarming rate, scientists and governments are creating a global network of plant banks to store seeds and sprouts[1]—precious **genetic** resources that may be needed for man to adapt the world's food supply to climate change.

2   This week, the flagship of that effort, the Global Seed Vault, received its first seeds here—millions of them. Bored[2] into the middle of a snow-topped Arctic mountain, the seed vault has as its goal the storing of every kind of seed from every collection on the planet. While the original seeds will remain in ordinary seed banks, the seed vault's stacked gray boxes will form a backup in case natural disaster or human error erases the seeds from the outside world.

3   The seed vault is part of a far broader effort to gather and classify information about plants and their genes. In Leuven, Belgium, scientists are scouring[3] the world for banana samples and cryo-preserving their shoots[4] in liquid nitrogen before they become **extinct**. A similar effort is under way in France on coffee plants. A number of plants, most from the tropics, do not produce seeds that can be stored.

4   For years, a hodgepodge network of seed banks has been amassing[5] seed and shoot collections. Labs in Mexico banked corn species. Those in Nigeria banked cassava. These scattershot efforts are being **consolidated** and systematized, in part because of better technology to preserve plant genes and in part because of rising alarm about the trajectory[6] of climate change and its impact on world food production.

---

[1] **sprout:** a new part growing on a plant
[2] **bore:** to make a long, deep hole with a tool or by digging
[3] **scour:** to search a place thoroughly in order to find something
[4] **shoot:** the part that grows up from the ground when a plant starts to grow
[5] **amass:** to collect something, especially in large quantities
[6] **trajectory:** the direction that something is taking; progression

5   "We started thinking about this post-9/11 and on the heels of Hurricane Katrina," said Cary Fowler, president of the Global Crop Diversity Trust, the nonprofit group that runs the vault. "Everyone was saying, 'Why didn't anyone prepare for a hurricane before?'

6   "Well, we are losing biodiversity every day—it's a kind of drip, drip, drip. It's also **inevitable**. We need to do something about it."

7   This week, the **urgency** of the problem was underscored as wheat prices reached record highs and wheat stores dropped to the lowest level in 35 years. Droughts[7] and new diseases cut wheat production in many parts of the world.

8   "The **erosion** of plants' genetic resources is really going fast," said Rony Swennen, head of crop biotechnics at the Catholic University of Leuven, who has cryo-preserved half of the world's 1,200 banana varieties. "We're at a critical moment, and if we don't act fast, we're going to lose a lot of plants that we may need."

Interior of the Global Seed Vault

9   The United Nations International Treaty on Plant Genetic Resources, ratified[8] in 2004, created a formal global network for banking and sharing seeds, as well as studying their genetic traits. Last year, its database received thousands of new seed varieties.

10   A well-organized system of plant banks could be **crucial** in responding to climate crises because it could identify genetic material and plant strains that are better able to cope with a changed environment. At the Global Seed Vault, hundreds of gray boxes containing seeds from Syria to Mexico were being moved this week into a freezing vault to be placed in suspended animation. Collectively they harbor[9] a vast range of characteristics, including the ability to withstand a drier, warmer climate.

11   Climate change is expected to bring new weather stresses as well as new plant pests into agricultural regions. Heat-trapping carbon dioxide emissions will produce not only global warming but also an increase in extreme weather events, like floods and droughts, the Intergovernmental Panel on Climate Change concluded.

12   Already, three-quarters of biodiversity in crops has been lost in the last century, according to the UN Food and Agriculture Organization. Eighty percent of corn varieties that existed in the 1930s no longer exist today, for example. In the United States, 94 percent of peas are no longer grown.

13   Seed banks have operated for decades, but many are based in agricultural areas, and few are as technologically advanced or secure as the Global Seed Vault. Earlier efforts had been regarded as resources for gardeners, scientists, farmers, and food aficionados rather than a tool for human survival.

14   The importance and **vulnerability** of seed banks have become apparent in recent years. Centers in Afghanistan and Iraq were destroyed during conflicts by looters who were after the plastic containers that held the seeds. In the Philippines, a typhoon demolished the wall of a seed bank, destroying many samples.

15   In reviewing seed bank policies a few years ago, experts looked at the banks in a new light, said Fowler of the Global Crop Diversity Trust. "We said, 'We may have some of the best seed banks in the world, but look at where they are: Peru, Colombia, Syria, India, Ethiopia, and the Philippines.' So a lot of us were asking, 'What's **plan B**?'"

[7] **drought:** a long period of time when there is little or no rain
[8] **ratify:** to make an agreement officially valid by voting for or signing it
[9] **harbor:** to contain something and allow it to develop

16   The goal of the new global plant bank system is to protect the precious stored plant genes from the vagaries[10] of climate, politics, and human error. Many banks are now "in countries where the political situation is not stable and it is difficult to rely on refrigeration," said Swennen, the biotechnics expert. Seeds must be stored at minus 20 degrees Celsius (minus 4 Fahrenheit), and plant sprouts that rely on cryo-preservation must be far colder.

17   "We are inside a mountain in the Arctic because we wanted a really, really safe place that operates by itself," Fowler said.

18   Underground in Longyearbyen, just 1,000 kilometers, or 600 miles, from the North Pole, the seeds will stay frozen regardless of power failures. The Global Crop Diversity Trust is also funding research into methods for storing genetic material from plants like bananas and coconuts that cannot be stored as seed.

19   The vault was built by Norway, and its operations are financed by government and private donations, including $20 million from the United Kingdom, $12 million from Australia, $11 million from Germany, and $6.5 million from the United States.

20   The effort to preserve a wide variety of plant genes in banks is particularly urgent because many farms now grow just one or two crops. They are particularly vulnerable to pests, disease, and climate change.

21   Just as efforts to preserve biodiversity increase, economics encourages farmers to focus on fewer crops. But those seeds may contain traits that will prove advantageous in another place or another time. Scientists at Cornell University recently borrowed a gene from a South American potato to make potatoes that resist late blight, a **devastating** disease that caused the Irish potato famine[11] in the nineteenth century.

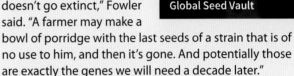

Seeds preserved in the Global Seed Vault

22   "You need a system to **conserve** the variety so it doesn't go extinct," Fowler said. "A farmer may make a bowl of porridge with the last seeds of a strain that is of no use to him, and then it's gone. And potentially those are exactly the genes we will need a decade later."

23   Scientists are also working to learn more about the genetic characteristics of each banked seed—crucial knowledge that is often not recorded. Ultimately, plant breeders will be able to consult a global database to find seeds with genes suitable for the particular challenge **confronting** a region, like corn with a stalk that is strong enough to resist high winds or wheat that needs less water.

24   "The seed vault is adding a new dimension to an evolving global system," Swennen said. "We should have done it sooner. But the technology and the global interest weren't available."

[10] **vagaries:** changes that are difficult to predict or control
[11] **famine:** a lack of food during a long period of time in a region

---

VOCABULARY SKILL REVIEW

In Unit 3, you learned to identify Latin and Greek roots (or stems) in new words. As you work through this unit, look for Latin and Greek roots and use them to help you understand new vocabulary.

B. VOCABULARY Here are some words from Reading 1. Read the sentences. Circle the answer that best matches the meaning of each bold word.

1. The seeds of each plant carry all of the **genetic** information necessary to transfer characteristics from a parent plant to a new plant.

   a. related to nutrition or ingredients   b. related to development or origin

2. There are so few members of some plant species left that they are in danger of becoming **extinct**.

   a. gone forever   b. overgrown

3. The Global Seed Vault in Norway is trying to **consolidate** many smaller collections of rare plant seeds and shoots from all over the world.

    a. bring together in a single place   b. sell for a large amount of money

4. Some scientists worry that the loss of plants and animals all around the world is **inevitable** because of global warming and human activity.

    a. faster   b. unavoidable

5. Fears of rapid climate change give many scientists a sense of **urgency** about gathering rare seeds and shoots while there is still time.

    a. immediate importance   b. value

6. Natural disasters, as well as the effects of **erosion** over time, can lead to the loss of a plant's natural habitat.

    a. human activities   b. destruction and wearing away

7. The Global Seed Vault will play a **crucial** role in protecting the world's food crops from weather disasters and climate change.

    a. small   b. very important

8. Plants have even more **vulnerability** to climate change and natural disasters than animals do because plants cannot move to other areas.

    a. ability to protect oneself   b. openness to attack or damage

9. Seeds are stored in many different locations, but the Global Seed Vault is a **plan B** in case of disasters at other storage sites.

    a. an alternative solution in case the first idea or arrangement does not succeed

    b. a single, obvious best solution to a problem

10. Food crops are always in danger from **devastating** diseases and natural disasters.

    a. extremely destructive and damaging

    b. minor and easy to stop

11. It is important to **conserve** seeds and shoots so that future generations can enjoy and use the same plants we have today.

    a. plant   b. look after and save

12. Many of the challenges **confronting** the world can be solved only through global cooperation.

    a. facing or threatening   b. hiding from or tricking

iQ PRACTICE Go online for more practice with the vocabulary.
Practice > Unit 4 > Activity 3

C. RESTATE Based on the information in Reading 1, each of the following statements is false. Correct the statements to make them true.

1. Plant species are disappearing quickly, but scientists and governments are not doing much to save them.

2. The Global Seed Vault has the goal of storing seeds from North America and Europe in case an emergency destroys any of them.

3. The United Nations International Treaty on Plant Genetic Resources created a global network for banking and sharing seeds, but it ignored the need to study their genetic traits.

4. The Intergovernmental Panel on Climate Change decided that plants will be affected by global warming, but not by extreme weather events.

5. The Global Seed Vault is located in a dangerous place that is too cold to protect seeds and plant sprouts.

6. Preserving plant genes in the Global Seed Vault won't protect the world's food supply from changing climate conditions or new plant diseases.

D. IDENTIFY Match each detail with the country it is associated with.

_____ 1. Norway

_____ 2. Belgium

_____ 3. France

_____ 4. Mexico

_____ 5. Nigeria

_____ 6. the United States

_____ 7. Afghanistan

_____ 8. the Philippines

_____ 9. the United Kingdom

_____ 10. Ireland

a. This country is the location of the Global Seed Vault.

b. This country was the location of a potato famine in the nineteenth century.

c. This nation donated $20 million to the Global Seed Vault.

d. Ninety-four percent of peas are no longer grown here.

e. Scientists in this country are searching the world for banana samples and preserving their shoots.

f. A typhoon hit a seed bank here, destroying many samples.

g. Scientists in this country are searching for and preserving coffee plant samples.

h. Labs here banked cassava.

i. Seed banks in this country were destroyed in conflicts.

j. Labs here banked corn species.

E. IDENTIFY Look back at Reading 1 and match each paragraph to the most appropriate title.

Paragraphs:

2   4   10   12   13   14   15   19   20   23

1. Seventy-five Percent of Plant Varieties Already Lost   Paragraph ____

2. Organizing Previously Uncoordinated Efforts   Paragraph ____

3. Finding Out More about Plant Genes   Paragraph ____

4. Funding from Around the World   Paragraph ____

5. Global Seed Vault Begins Operations   Paragraph ____

6. Geographical Motivation for an Alternative Plan   Paragraph ____

7. Many Seed Banks Exposed to Conflicts and Disasters   Paragraph ____

8. Safeguarding Against Negative Climate Changes   Paragraph ____

9. Previous Seed Banks Not Focused on Survival   Paragraph ____

10. Farmers Growing Fewer, More Vulnerable Crops   Paragraph ____

F. EXPLAIN Based on the information in Reading 1, write five reasons for the creation of the Global Seed Vault. Then check (✓) the reason you think is the most important. Explain to a partner why you think that reason is the most important.

iQ PRACTICE Go online for additional reading and comprehension.
Practice > Unit 4 > Activity 4

WRITE WHAT YOU THINK

A. DISCUSS Discuss these questions in a group.

1. Will the global partnerships formed while working on the Global Seed Vault help the world in other ways? Why or why not?

2. Do you think the scientists and governments in the article will be successful in preserving seeds and shoots from around the world? What are the consequences for humanity if the Global Seed Vault project is not successful?

3. Does your home country have any unique plants or crops that aren't found anywhere else? Should they be preserved in the Global Seed Vault? Why or why not?

WRITING TIP

In Unit 3, you learned about writing with unity. As you write your response in Activity B, be sure to maintain unity by checking that each of your sentences supports your main idea.

B. COMPOSE Choose one question and write a paragraph in response. Look back at your Quick Write on page 96 as you think about what you learned.

Writers often use facts and opinions to suggest ideas rather than giving the ideas to the reader directly. The reader has to determine, or **infer**, what the writer is saying. Making an inference is making a logical conclusion about something based on the information that is given. Making inferences while reading a text can improve your overall comprehension and help you become a more critical reader.

This excerpt is taken from Reading 1:

⌐ Bored into the middle of a snow-topped Arctic mountain, the seed vault . . .

The text doesn't need to say exactly what kind of place is best for preserving the world's seeds and shoots. From the information in the excerpt, you can infer that it is a place that needs to be safe and secure, as well as cold and far away. You come to this conclusion because of clues such as *bored, snow-topped, Arctic,* and *middle of a . . . mountain.*

A. **EVALUATE** Match each excerpt from Reading 1 with the correct inference on page 104.

Excerpts

____ 1. With plant species disappearing at an alarming rate, scientists and governments are creating a global network of plant banks to store seeds and sprouts—precious genetic resources that may be needed for man to adapt the world's food supply to climate change. (Paragraph 1)

____ 2. In Leuven, Belgium, scientists are scouring the world for banana samples and cryo-preserving their shoots in liquid nitrogen before they become extinct. (Paragraph 3)

____ 3. Those [seed banks] in Nigeria banked cassava. (Paragraph 4)

____ 4. Collectively they [seeds from many different countries] harbor a vast range of characteristics, including the ability to withstand a drier, warmer climate. (Paragraph 10)

____ 5. Eighty percent of corn varieties that existed in the 1930s no longer exist today, for example. In the United States, 94 percent of peas are no longer grown. (Paragraph 12)

____ 6. Seeds must be stored at minus 20 degrees Celsius (minus 4 Fahrenheit), and plant sprouts that rely on cryo-preservation must be far colder. (Paragraph 16)

Inferences

a. These seeds are important because the genetic information they contain will help grow food despite climate change and global warming.

b. Some food crops are more important in certain countries than others.

c. The world's food supply is in danger.

d. Some rare varieties of important food crops are hard to find, and they are in danger of disappearing soon.

e. Cold areas of the globe, such as the Arctic, are excellent locations for seed banks.

f. Farmers are growing fewer varieties of crops compared to the past.

B. INTERPRET Read each statement. What can you infer from the information in the statement? Write your inferences. Then compare your inferences with a partner.

1. **Statement:** Bored into the middle of a snow-topped Arctic mountain, the seed vault has as its goal the storing of every kind of seed from every collection on the planet.

   Inference: _As many of the world's seeds as possible need to be stored in_ _a safe place that is cold and far away._

2. **Statement:** Mexico is the perfect place for corn seeds to be banked.

   Inference: _____

   _____

   _____

3. **Statement:** Scientists cheered when the United Nations International Treaty on Plant Genetic Resources finally created a formal global network for banking seeds and studying their genetic traits.

   Inference: _____

   _____

   _____

4. **Statement:** In the Philippines, a typhoon demolished the wall of a seed bank, destroying many valuable samples.

   Inference: _____

   _____

   _____

iQ PRACTICE Go online for more practice making inferences.
Practice > Unit 4 > Activity 5

READING 2

Building the Perfect Spaceman

OBJECTIVE ▶

You are going to read an article from the weekly news magazine *Maclean's* about preparing to become an astronaut aboard the International Space Station. Use the article to gather information and ideas for your Unit Assignment.

PREVIEW THE READING

A. PREVIEW Look ahead to quickly read only the first sentences of paragraphs 2, 4, 6, 8, 10, and 12. Then discuss with a partner what examples of international cooperation you might find in this article. As you read, check to confirm if your ideas are included in the article.

WRITING TIP
Receiving feedback from a peer can be a valuable part of the writing process.

B. QUICK WRITE What kinds of international cooperation do you think are necessary for successful space exploration? Write for 5–10 minutes in response. When you are finished, exchange your Quick Write with a partner. Give your partner advice on how to improve his or her ideas. Remember to use this section for your Unit Assignment.

C. VOCABULARY Check (✓) the words you know. Then work with a partner to locate each word in the reading. Use clues to help define the words you don't know. Check your definitions in the dictionary.

daunting *(adj.)*	**intensively** *(adv.)*	**navigate** *(v.)*
devote *(v.)* ⦙+	**mediator** *(n.)*	**orbit** *(n.)*
dominate *(v.)* ⦙+ OPAL	**mission** *(n.)* ⦙+	**quarantine** *(v.)*
inhabit *(v.)*	**mundane** *(adj.)*	**reassemble** *(v.)*

⦙+ Oxford 5000™ words   OPAL Oxford Phrasal Academic Lexicon

iQ PRACTICE Go online to listen and practice your pronunciation.
Practice ⟩ Unit 4 ⟩ Activity 6

A. INVESTIGATE Read the article and gather information about why international cooperation is important.

BUILDING THE PERFECT SPACEMAN

Inside NASA's training facility that turns mortals[1] into astronauts, and one into spaceship commander

by Kate Lunau

Canadian astronaut Chris Hadfield

1   FROM THE OUTSIDE, Building 9 at the NASA Johnson Space Center, a sprawling complex on the outskirts of Houston, is nondescript[2]. Inside, it's like Willy Wonka's factory, if Willy were a rocket scientist. The hangar-like facility is filled with robots, moon buggies, and spaceship mock-ups. Robonaut, a humanoid robot with a golden head, sits next to Spidernaut, a robot prototype with eight arched legs. There's an Orion capsule and a Russian Soyuz spacecraft. But what **dominates** the vast room is a full-size mock-up of the International Space Station (ISS), an Earth-orbiting spaceship built by 15 countries, including Canada.

2   One recent Monday morning, astronaut trainer Gwenn Sandoz waited there for Chris Hadfield, who will blast off from Kazakhstan aboard the Soyuz in December and soon after will become the first Canadian to take command of the ISS. Canada has invested heavily in the station, which has been **inhabited** by a rotating crew since 2000, but Canada only gets to send so many astronauts there. For 20 years, Hadfield has worked tirelessly to prove himself in an astronaut corps dominated by the U.S. and Russia. Canada has paid its dues

by contributing the robotics systems that built and maintain the ISS, finally earning a spot for one of its own at the controls of what Hadfield calls "the world's spaceship."

3   Sandoz knew her time with Hadfield was limited; this was his last week of training in Houston before the launch. At 10:15 a.m., right on time, he breezed in[3] wearing a neatly tucked-in polo shirt—the unofficial uniform at Johnson—with the crew patch of Expedition 35, which portrays a moonlit view of Earth from the ISS as the sun peeks from behind it. Assigned to Expedition 34/35 in September 2010, he's been training **intensively** in the U.S., Russia, and elsewhere for the **mission**. It isn't his first space flight, but it will be the longest he's spent off the ground. Hadfield will be on the ISS until May,

---

[1] **mortals:** ordinary people with little power or influence
[2] **nondescript:** having no unusual features
[3] **breeze in:** to arrive in a cheerful and confident way

making him only the second Canadian (after Robert Thirsk) to do a long-duration mission.

4   The list of skills to master is **daunting**. Hadfield has to be a scientist, a plumber, an electrician, trilingual, a spokesperson, a **mediator**, an engineer, and now, of course, a commander. "The entire partnership is trusting the vehicle, and the crew, to his good judgment and command," says Edward Tabarah, deputy director of the astronaut office of the Canadian Space Agency (CSA).

5   On December 19, Hadfield, U.S. astronaut Tom Marshburn, and Russian cosmonaut Roman Romanenko will squeeze themselves into the Soyuz, their knees squished up to their chests. Good weather, bad weather, the Soyuz almost always leaves on schedule. Two days after they blast off, they'll arrive at the ISS, joining a crew of three other astronauts already there. Until March, Hadfield is the mission flight engineer. He then assumes command.

6   As he prepared to leave Houston for a last visit to Canada—then on to Germany for more training—Hadfield was his usual affable[4] self, but with an undercurrent[5] of intensity people around him noticed: he was wearing the weight of command. "I've **devoted** my whole life to being in a position where, at 53 years old, somebody would say, 'We want you to command our spaceship,'" Hadfield remarked one evening, sitting in the giant ISS mock-up after a busy day of training, "and I could say, 'OK. I know what I need to do.'"

7   Hadfield, who was selected as one of four new Canadian astronauts in 1992—beating out about 5,330 hopefuls—has been into space twice. In 1995, he was the first Canadian mission specialist on a NASA space shuttle mission, visiting the Russian space station Mir, and the first Canadian to operate the Canadarm[6] in **orbit**. In 2001, on an 11-day space shuttle flight to the ISS to deliver and install the Canadarm2, Hadfield performed

two spacewalks, another first for Canada. He spent more than 14 hours outside, traveling around Earth 10 times. (The ISS circles the world 16 times per day.)

8   He was also NASA's director of operations at the Yuri Gagarin Cosmonaut Training Center in Star City, Russia, from 2001 to 2003, overseeing ISS crew activities. (Astronauts who travel to the ISS have to speak English and Russian; Hadfield is fluent in both. Canadians must speak French, too.) And he was chief of robotics at the NASA Astronaut Office at Johnson, then chief of ISS operations.

9   In 1992, the CSA assigned Hadfield to the Johnson Space Center, home to NASA's astronaut corps. Active Canadian and Japanese astronauts are based here permanently, and those from the European Space Agency (ESA) and Russia come frequently to train. Fresh recruits spend two years in basic astronaut training. Preparing for a mission to the ISS can take another 2 ½ years.

10   In the years Hadfield has spent training for this mission, mainly split between Russia and Houston, even the most **mundane** aspects of life on the ISS have been endlessly rehearsed. In one five-hour drill, which consumed a recent Tuesday afternoon, Hadfield, Marshburn, and Romanenko convened[7] at Building 9 for a "daily ops" session, essentially a day in the life of the station. Hadfield took apart and **reassembled** the toilet. (Urine on the ISS is recycled into drinking water.) This training is important because life on the ISS is unpredictable. For example, on September 5, American astronaut Sunita Williams and Akihiko Hoshide, from Japan, ventured out on a six-hour spacewalk to fix a failing component, one that carries power from the space station's solar arrays to its systems. The culprit[8], a faulty bolt, seemed to be jammed, so they used an improvised tool— a toothbrush—to clear the blockage.

---

[4] **affable:** pleasant, friendly, and easy to talk to

[5] **undercurrent:** a hidden feeling whose effects are felt

[6] **Canadarm:** a large robotic arm used to move, capture, and release objects in outer space

[7] **convene:** to come together for a formal meeting

[8] **culprit:** a thing responsible for causing a problem

11   Hadfield acknowledged the space program "goes in waves." We're currently in a dip. In 2011, NASA's 30-year space-shuttle program ended, leaving the Russians with the only viable way of getting astronauts to the ISS. (The U.S. has encouraged commercial companies to develop new ways of bringing humans to low-Earth orbit.) The station is scheduled to be decommissioned in 2024, although many expect that to be extended. But while President Obama talked about sending space explorers to asteroids or to Mars, in an age of cutbacks, such missions sound like science fiction. "Saying we'll go to Mars in 15 or 20 years, that's saying some other president, budget, and Congress," says astrophysicist Adam Frank, who blogs about the cosmos and culture for National Public Radio. "We need somebody to say 10 years. That's what Kennedy did with the moon."

12   Two weeks before the launch, Hadfield, Marshburn, and Romanenko will arrive in Kazakhstan and be **quarantined** with a small entourage of others, including Tabarah. Four days before departure, the astronauts' families will arrive with Jeremy Hansen, the crew support astronaut, whose job is to escort them to the launch site and help them **navigate** the process. After a thorough health screening, Hadfield's immediate family will be allowed a short visit. Extended family can see him through a glass divider. Then he's gone, off to the International Space Station.

13   When asked what he'll miss most aboard the ISS, Hadfield cites the basics, like being able to drive out for a slice of pizza on a whim. Then he becomes more somber. "The contact," he says. "This is a scientific monastery. It's not normal human life where you hug somebody, or can be with your family. I'll miss that." He shrugs. "But for me, it's all part of the same life."

B. VOCABULARY Complete each sentence with one of the vocabulary words from Reading 2. You may need to change the form of the word to make the sentence grammatically correct.

daunting *(adj.)*	inhabit *(v.)*	mission *(n.)*	orbit *(n.)*
devote *(v.)*	intensively *(adv.)*	mundane *(adj.)*	quarantine *(v.)*
dominate *(v.)*	mediator *(n.)*	navigate *(v.)*	reassemble *(v.)*

1. Space station commanders must _____ themselves to the welfare of their crews. As a result, safety has to be their number one concern.

2. Astronauts have to know how to take apart and _____ equipment on the International Space Station in case it needs to be repaired.

3. The International Space Station is usually _____ by a crew of six people.

4. While many people are attracted to the idea of becoming an astronaut, there are many dangers involved, and the idea of spending so many days in space can be _____.

5. Crew members preparing to travel to the International Space Station are _____ so that they don't become sick before the big journey.

6. When people are working together in a small space like the International Space Station, it is important to have someone acting as a _____ who can help the crew avoid arguments.

7. One of the future _____ to the International Space Station might include the international recording artist Sarah Brightman.

8. Having an astronaut as part of the family can be very complicated, but NASA provides support to help families _____ the situation.

9. People who want to become astronauts have to study _____ in order to master the necessary science, math, and languages.

10. Although life on the International Space Station seems adventurous, there are still many _____ tasks that have to be performed, such as cooking and cleaning.

11. The training facility was _____ by a huge pool that took up all the space in the building.

12. The International Space Station is located in low-Earth _____, and it circles the planet about 16 times per day.

iQ PRACTICE Go online for more practice with the vocabulary.
Practice > Unit 4 > Activity 7

C. IDENTIFY Number the main ideas in the order they are presented in Reading 2.

_____ a. The space program has good times and bad times.

_____ b. Boring duties on the International Space Station must be practiced many times.

_____ c. Canada has contributed much to the International Space Station.

_____ d. While the exterior of the NASA Johnson Space Center is quite plain, the interior resembles a fictional fantasy place made up of many strange-looking things.

_____ e. There are many skills that have to be learned in order for someone to become an International Space Station commander.

_____ f. Hadfield's experience makes him ready to command and know what to do in almost any situation.

D. IDENTIFY Match each detail with the main idea (a–f in Activity C) that it supports. There are two supporting details for each main idea.

____ 1. The mission depends on Hadfield's sound decisions and ability to lead.

____ 2. The plan is to stop using the International Space Station after the year 2024.

____ 3. The Robonaut looks like a human with a golden head.

____ 4. Canada contributed to the International Space Station mainly in the field of robotics.

____ 5. Hadfield has many abilities, including being a scientist, plumber, electrician, and more.

____ 6. Hadfield has operated the Canadarm in space.

____ 7. Canada can send only a limited number of astronauts to the International Space Station.

____ 8. Hadfield put a toilet back together after taking it apart.

____ 9. The room is filled by a life-size model of the International Space Station.

____ 10. Sunita Williams and Akihiko Hoshide fixed part of the International Space Station with a toothbrush.

____ 11. Hadfield has been on spacewalks.

____ 12. The space shuttle program has ended, and Russians control the only way to get to the International Space Station.

E. EXPLAIN Based on the information in Reading 2, what has each of the following countries contributed to the International Space Station? You may have to infer one of the countries' contribution. Include as many ideas as you can.

1. The United States: _____

2. Russia: _____

3. Canada: _____

4. Kazakhstan: _____

5. Germany: _____

6. Japan: _____

F. IDENTIFY Match the following people in Reading 2 with the statements that best describe them.

a. Chris Hadfield   c. Roman Romanenko   e. Edward Tabarah

b. Akihiko Hoshide   d. Gwenn Sandoz   f. Robert Thirsk

_____ 1. An official in the Canadian Space Agency who comments on Hadfield's command and is together with Hadfield just before his mission.

_____ 2. The first Canadian to spend a long time in space on a mission.

_____ 3. An astronaut trainer who worked with Hadfield to help prepare him for his mission.

_____ 4. A Canadian astronaut with many years of experience preparing to become the commander of Expedition 35 to the International Space Station.

_____ 5. A Russian cosmonaut who is going to the ISS with Hadfield.

_____ 6. An astronaut who fixed a broken part of the ISS with a toothbrush during a six-hour spacewalk.

CRITICAL THINKING STRATEGY

Forming opinions based on a text

Readers can use information in a text to make inferences and then form their own opinions based on what they have read. When you form an opinion, you can use separate details as clues or evidence to support a conclusion. This analytical process shows a deeper understanding of the material. For example, readers can interpret the information in Reading 1 to form the opinion that the world is now better prepared for disasters that could affect the world's supply of seeds. Details in the text that support this opinion include:

> … global network of plant banks to store seeds … (paragraph 1)
>
> … form a backup in case natural disaster or human error … (paragraph 2)
>
> … few [seed banks] are as technologically advanced or secure as the Global Seed Vault. (paragraph 13)

Opinions can also be more personal views or judgements. For example, a reader might form the opinion from Reading 2 that being an astronaut is a difficult and unpleasant job that they would not like to do. Details from the text that could inform this opinion include:

> The list of skills to master is daunting. (paragraph 4)
>
> Urine on the ISS is recycled into drinking water. (paragraph 10)
>
> It's not normal human life where you hug somebody, or can be with your family. I'll miss that. (paragraph 13)

iQ PRACTICE Go online to watch the Critical Thinking Video and check your comprehension. *Practice > Unit 4 > Activity 8*

G. EXPLAIN Answer each of the following questions with your opinion. Provide specific evidence from the reading to support your opinion.

1. Why does Hadfield call the International Space Station "the world's spaceship"?

2. Why do astronauts have to master so many skills?

3. Is it important for astronauts to know more than one language? Why or why not?

4. Why do the astronauts and cosmonauts come from different countries?

5. Do you think space explorers will travel to Mars? Why or why not?

H. DISCUSS Discuss the questions in a group. Look back at your Quick Write on page 105 as you think about what you have learned.

1. What kinds of challenges do you think you would face if you were working on a collaborative global project like the International Space Station? Would you be successful working on a project like this?

2. Is global cooperation necessary for a project like the International Space Station to be successful? Why or why not?

3. Could the resources being used for the International Space Station be put to better use? In your opinion, what projects are more important than the International Space Station? Why?

WORK WITH THE VIDEO

A. PREVIEW Why do you think countries need to trade with each other?

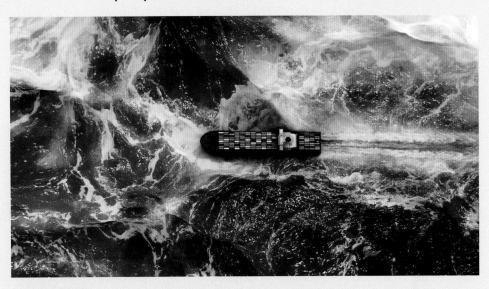

VIDEO VOCABULARY

transform (v.) to change the form of something; make it into something different

import (v.) to bring a product or service into one country from another

export (v.) to sell and send goods to another country

international trade (n.) the activity of buying and selling or of exchanging goods or services between countries

iQ RESOURCES Go online to watch the video about international trade.
Resources > Video > Unit 4 > Unit Video

B. IDENTIFY Watch the video two or three times. Match each country with the role it plays in the international trade of the metal tantalum. There is one extra country that you do not need. Then answer the two questions that follow.

Australia	China	Kazakhstan
Canada	Ethiopia	Korea

_____ 1. Rock containing tantalum metal is mined.

_____ 2. Tantalum rock is processed and refined.

_____ 3. Tantalum is manufactured into a computer chip.

_____ 4. A computer chip with tantalum is put into a smartphone.

_____ 5. The smartphone is sold to a customer.

6. Why do countries trade with each other?

7. How do countries make money through international trade?

C. EXTEND Why is global cooperation important for international trade? Use the information in the video, as well as your own knowledge and ideas, to support your response.

WRITE WHAT YOU THINK

SYNTHESIZE Think about Reading 1, Reading 2, and the video as you discuss the questions. Then choose one question and write a paragraph in response.

1. Which do you think is a better example of global cooperation—the Global Seed Vault, the International Space Station, or international trade? Why?

2. Do you think the importance of international trade will increase or decrease in the future? Why?

VOCABULARY SKILL Prefixes

TIP FOR SUCCESS

Apply new ideas to information you have already learned. For example, while studying prefixes, remember what you learned about Latin and Greek roots in Unit 3.

Understanding the meanings of the different parts of a word is an important way to build vocabulary. A **prefix** can be added to the beginning of a word to change or add meaning, or to create an entirely new word. For instance, the *un-* in *unhappy* changes the root word, *happy*, to mean its opposite. Another example is *tele-* (over a long distance; far) and the word *vision* (the ability to see). They combine to create the word for a piece of equipment with a screen to watch moving pictures sent from another, distant place (*television*).

Use a dictionary to learn more about various prefixes. For example, in this dictionary entry for *co-*, you learn that it can be used with a variety of root words and in different parts of speech. It adds the meaning of "together with" to the root word.

> **co-** /koʊ/ *prefix* (used in adjectives, adverbs, nouns, and verbs) together with: *co-produced* ♦ *cooperatively* ♦ *co-author* ♦ *coexist*

In this dictionary entry for *mal-*, you learn that this prefix can also be used with a variety of root words and in different parts of speech.

> **mal-** /mæl/ *combining form* (in nouns, verbs, and adjectives) bad or badly; not correct or correctly: *malpractice* ♦ *malodorous* ♦ *malfunction*

All dictionary entries are from the *Oxford Advanced American Dictionary for learners of English* © Oxford University Press 2011.

A. APPLY Write the correct prefix from the box next to its definition below. Then write as many words as you know that can use each prefix and their parts of speech. Check your answers in a dictionary and add to the chart if possible.

bio-   dis-   im-   mal-   non-   cryo-   geo-   inter-   multi-   re-

Prefix	Definition	Possible words	Possible parts of speech
1. multi-	more than one; many	multicolored, multimillionaire	nouns, adjectives
2.	not		
3.	involving the use of very low temperatures		
4.	(also *il- / in- / ir-*) not; the opposite of		
5.	of the earth		
6.	again		
7.	between; from one to another		
8.	bad or badly; not correct or correctly		
9.	not; the opposite of		
10.	connected with living things or human life		

B. APPLY Complete each sentence with the correct prefix from the box on page 115.

1. When parts of the Soyuz spacecraft break down, they need to be

   _____replaced before the Soyuz can travel to the International Space Station.

2. Some scientists use _____-preservation to store banana plant shoots.

3. The design of the Soyuz spacecraft is so strong that even if there are a couple of

   _____functions, the crew will most likely land safely on Earth.

4. One of the main goals of the Global Seed Vault is to preserve the

   _____diversity of the world's edible plant species.

5. The scientists working on the International Space Station don't worry about

   _____politics because their job is to solve engineering problems.

6. The Global Seed Vault is run by a(n) _____profit group.

7. The space station was built by a(n) _____national partnership.

8. The _____governmental panel came to the conclusion that extreme weather

   events were going to increase in the future.

9. The age of the Soyuz spacecraft is _____material because its design is robust.

10. Plant species are _____appearing at a very fast rate all around the world.

iQ PRACTICE Go online for more practice with prefixes.
Practice > Unit 4 > Activity 9

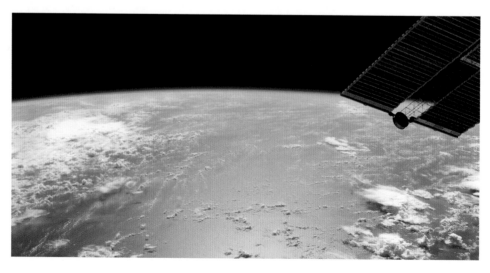

WRITING

OBJECTIVE ▶

At the end of this unit, you will write an essay discussing the importance of global cooperation. This essay will include information from the readings, the unit video, and your own ideas.

WRITING SKILL Organizing supporting ideas

A piece of writing is **coherent** when the ideas are organized in a logical way. The order of main ideas and supporting ideas depends on the writer's subject and purpose. Three of the most common methods of organization are explained below.

TIP FOR SUCCESS

Expository writing fully explains and describes an author's ideas on a subject. **Classification writing** puts people, things, or ideas into groups.

Specificity

Specificity works well with descriptive essays, expository writing, and classification essays.

- Organize your ideas from the more general to the more specific.

- Give one or more general ideas with increasingly specific supporting ideas, facts, and examples.

Emphasis

This form of organization works well with persuasive essays, comparison and contrast essays, and business letters.

- Organize your ideas from the least to the most important. Readers tend to remember best what they read last. This organization strengthens your argument by building up to the strongest ideas.

Time

Time organization works well with process essays, narrative essays, cause and effect essays, case studies, biographies, book reports, and short stories.

- Follow a chronological order.

- Organize your information from the past to the present or from the present to the past.

- Organize a process from the beginning to the end or from the end to the beginning.

A. IDENTIFY Look at the brief outlines for short paragraphs answering the question: "What is a good example of global cooperation?" Decide if the ideas have been organized according to specificity, emphasis, or time.

1. Type of organization: _____
   Global Polio Eradication Initiative

   a. In 1988, the World Health Assembly passed a resolution to eradicate polio.

   b. Nelson Mandela started the Kick Polio Out of Africa campaign in 1996.

   c. The service club Rotary International had raised $500 million in the fight against polio by 2003.

   d. In 2004, 23 countries in west and central Africa immunized more than 80 million children.

2. Type of organization: _____
   The World Health Organization (WHO)

   a. The WHO works toward the highest possible levels of health for people around the world.

   b. It supports the development and strengthening of health systems in every country.

   c. It sets health standards for health systems to follow.

   d. It carries out worldwide campaigns for people to eat healthier food.

3. Type of organization: _____
   International Migratory Bird Day

   a. International Migratory Bird Day is celebrated in Canada, the United States, Mexico, Central and South America, and the Caribbean.

   b. This day can involve bird walks and presentations.

   c. People learn about threats to migratory birds on this day.

   d. By raising public awareness of migratory birds, people can save them from danger and extinction.

B. WRITING MODEL Read this response to an essay question on a political science test. Then answer the questions with a partner.

1. What is the main idea of this essay?

2. What are the supporting ideas for the main idea?

3. How are the supporting ideas organized?

4. Is the organization of the supporting ideas effective? Why or why not?

5. Is there another way the supporting ideas could have been organized? If so, what is it?

What is a good example of global cooperation?

International peace parks are a good example of global cooperation. These parks are protected areas that are located on the borders of two or more countries. There are no fences between the countries in the parks, and animals are free to move wherever they want. An increasing number of international peace parks can be found all over the world, and three of them in particular illustrate how these types of global initiatives can bring different countries closer together.

The first peace park in the world, Waterton-Glacier International Peace Park, was established in 1932. It lies on the border between the United States and Canada, and it was created as a symbol of friendship and peace between these two countries. The United Nations Educational, Scientific and Cultural Organization (UNESCO) recognizes this park as a biosphere reserve and a World Heritage Site.

Another peace park that is also a UNESCO World Heritage Site is located in Central America. La Amistad International Park is shared by Costa Rica and Panama, and it was created in 1988. It is very remote, and the two countries work together to manage the park and maintain its fragile tropical environment.

Finally, the first peace park in Africa, Kgalagadi Transfrontier Park, was founded on May 12, 2000, between Botswana and South Africa. These two countries currently work together to manage the park as a single ecological unit. Kgalagadi is a large wildlife reserve in which people are also able to move freely across the international borders.

International peace parks such as Waterton-Glacier, La Amistad, and Kgalagadi show that global cooperation is possible. Because of these successful examples, the number of international peace parks is sure to increase in the future. It is hoped that people and organizations around the world will continue to promote the collaboration of different governments in the creation of more transfrontier parks like these.

TIP FOR SUCCESS

When answering an essay question on a test, write out your thesis statement first. This will help you organize your ideas and ensure you are happy with the most important sentence of your essay.

C. COMPOSE Complete these steps to write a brief outline for a paragraph on the topic "What is a good example of global cooperation?"

1. Decide on a good example of global cooperation that you are familiar with.

2. Brainstorm a list of five to six ideas that support your choice as a good example of global cooperation.

3. Check (✓) the three or four ideas that you are going to use in your outline.

4. Decide if you are going to organize your ideas according to specificity, emphasis, or time.

5. Number your ideas in the order that you want to include them in your outline.

D. WRITING MODEL During an essay exam, a student wrote the following response to the question: "Why is global cooperation important?" Read the essay. Then answer the questions that follow.

ACADEMIC LANGUAGE
The corpus shows that *importance of* and *benefits of* are often used in academic writing to draw attention to or emphasize points to consider.

_____ OPAL
Oxford Phrasal Academic Lexicon

The Importance of Global Cooperation

Because of globalization, it is now easier than ever to share information and trade goods all around the world. Rapid advances in information and communications technology have resulted in what seems to be a much smaller world. One of the main benefits of a shrinking world is that global cooperation is now much easier. Global cooperation is very important because it can help countries solve problems that cannot be solved by one country alone, and it can promote peace and understanding between different nations.

Global cooperation is vital because many of the world's problems cannot be solved without help from other countries. Take, for example, the environment. There are, unfortunately, many environmental problems that affect the entire planet today. However, countries can work together to solve these environmental problems. At the worldwide level, the United Nations Environmental Programme (UNEP) coordinates international efforts that affect the land, sea, and air for the 192 member states of the United Nations. The UNEP promotes sustainability for the entire planet's environment. At a more regional level, the United States and Canada are working together to fight the air pollution that leads to acid rain. These two countries are members of an international joint commission that has agreed to work on air quality. They do this in a number of ways, including exchanging information and conducting research. These countries have been very successful in reducing the harmful elements that cause acid rain. For example, according to Environment Canada, sulphur dioxide emissions that cause acid rain have been reduced by 57% in Canada and 67% in the United States since 1990. By working together, Canada and the U.S. are protecting the environment on both sides of the border.

Global cooperation does not just help to preserve the environment. It can also promote peace among different countries. The European Union provides a good example of former enemies now working together. This cooperation started in the 1950s, when six European countries, including France and Germany, created the European Coal and Steel Community, which fostered economic cooperation in those industries. Soon, another agreement was signed, in 1957, to create a common market in Europe. Countries in the common market stopped charging customs duties when trading with other member countries. Agricultural cooperation also began around this time. The success of the European Common Market encouraged more countries to join, and in 1973 there were a total of nine members, including the United Kingdom. By 1979 there was a European Parliament, whose members were elected directly by the citizens of the member countries. More countries continued to join in the 1980s, and by 1993 there was a single market for all members. The cooperation continued with the introduction of the euro, with 12 countries using this currency in 2002. Now, people and money can move freely throughout the European Union, and former World War II enemies now live in peace.

Major world problems such as air pollution and acid rain are best solved through global cooperation. Peaceful coexistence is also promoted through countries working together. These two examples demonstrate the importance of global cooperation. The planet is sure to face more challenges in the future, but if countries can collaborate on the solutions, the problems are sure to be overcome.

1. What is the main idea introduced in the introductory paragraph? _____

   _____

2. What is the main idea of the second paragraph? _____

   _____

3. What supporting ideas are included in the second paragraph? _____

   _____

4. Have the supporting ideas in the second paragraph been organized according to specificity, emphasis, or time? _____

5. What is the main idea of the third paragraph? _____

   _____

6. What supporting ideas are included in the third paragraph? _____

   _____

7. Have the supporting ideas in the third paragraph been organized according to specificity, emphasis, or time? _____

8. What is the conclusion in the last paragraph? _____

   _____

iQ PRACTICE Go online for more practice with organizing supporting ideas.
Practice > Unit 4 > Activity 10

When words, phrases, and clauses are used in a series in the same sentence, they should have **parallel structure**. That is, they should have the same grammatical pattern. Using parallel structure makes it easier for the reader to understand a text, especially when a sentence is more complex or contains several supporting points.

Noun
<u>Dedication</u> and <u>tolerance</u> are two things people need if they want to cooperate.

Adjective + noun
Those who work side by side with their Russian counterparts say that <u>strong relationships</u> and <u>mutual respect</u> have resulted from the many years of collaboration.

When you use parallel structure, you often omit words that are repeated in a phrase or sentence. This is called **ellipsis**. You can use ellipsis with modals or verb forms that have auxiliary verbs, such as the present continuous or present perfect. In parallel structure, the auxiliary verbs are usually omitted.

Modal *could*
A collaborative space program <u>could build</u> greater understanding, <u>promote</u> world peace, and <u>improve</u> scientific knowledge.

Present perfect auxiliary verb *have*
Scientists <u>have identified</u> and <u>solved</u> several problems related to the Global Seed Vault.

iQ RESOURCES Go online to watch the Grammar Skill Video.
Resources > Video > Unit 4 > Grammar Skill Video

A. APPLY Read each sentence. Underline and correct each error in parallel structure.

1. The French scientists are taking part in an expedition to the Amazon rain forest, a conference in Rio de Janeiro, and <u>discussing</u> with Brazilian coffee farmers.   *a discussion*

2. Russian cosmonauts and American astronauts are working on experiments, build new space station modules, and learning together.

3. The scientists cataloged the seeds, cryo-preserved the shoots, and have sent them to the Global Seed Vault.

4. Global warming has many people worried, feeling concerned, and frustrated about the future.

5. The rusty launch site, abandoned buildings, and uneven sidewalks are surprising to Americans because of the dependability, famous, and prestige of the Russian space program.

B. **EXTEND** Complete the sentences with your own ideas. Use parallel structure.

1. The Global Seed Vault is an important resource that could save many plants,

    _____.

2. Future global collaborations should focus on promoting peace, _____

    _____.

3. Peace parks encourage global cooperation, _____

    _____.

4. The World Health Organization has monitored health problems, _____

    _____.

5. Global cooperation is important in order to fight poverty, _____

    _____.

iQ PRACTICE Go online for more practice with parallel structure and ellipsis.
Practice > Unit 4 > Activities 11–12

UNIT ASSIGNMENT Write an essay

OBJECTIVE ▶

In this assignment, you will write an essay that answers the Unit Question, "Why is global cooperation important?" Use information from Reading 1, Reading 2, the unit video, and your work in this unit to support your ideas. Refer to the Self-Assessment checklist on page 124.

iQ PRACTICE Go online to the Writing Tutor to read a model essay.
Practice > Unit 4 > Activity 13

PLAN AND WRITE

A. **BRAINSTORM** Based on the readings and your own personal knowledge, think about why global cooperation is important or why international cooperation is not important. Record your best two or three main ideas. Provide two or three supporting ideas or details for each main idea.

B. **PLAN** Review Activity A and decide which information you want to include in your answer. Then complete these tasks to organize your ideas.

1. Choose the method of organizing your ideas that fits best with the information you plan to include in your essay: specificity, emphasis, or time.

2. Download and complete the outline of the essay based on the method you have chosen. Plan a four- or five-paragraph essay, depending on the number of main ideas you have to support your thesis statement.

iQ RESOURCES Go online to download and complete the outline for your essay. *Resources > Writing Tools > Unit 4 > Outline*

C. WRITE Use your planning notes to write your essay.

1. Write an essay answering the Unit Question, "Why is global cooperation important?"

2. Look at the Self-Assessment checklist to guide your writing.

iQ PRACTICE Go online to the Writing Tutor to write your assignment. *Practice > Unit 4 > Activity 14*

REVISE AND EDIT

iQ RESOURCES Go online to download the peer review worksheet. *Resources > Writing Tools > Unit 4 > Peer Review Worksheet*

A. PEER REVIEW Read your partner's essay. Then use the peer review worksheet. Discuss the review with your partner.

B. REWRITE Based on your partner's review, revise and rewrite your essay.

C. EDIT Complete the Self-Assessment checklist as you prepare to write the final draft of your essay. Be prepared to hand in your work or discuss it in class.

SELF-ASSESSMENT	Yes	No
Is there a logical order to the main ideas?	☐	☐
Is there a logical order to the supporting ideas?	☐	☐
Are parallel structure and ellipsis used correctly?	☐	☐
Are there words with prefixes?	☐	☐
Does the essay include vocabulary from the unit?	☐	☐
Did you check the essay for punctuation, spelling, and grammar?	☐	☐

D. REFLECT Discuss these questions with a partner or group.

1. What is something new you learned in this unit?

2. Look back at the Unit Question—Why is global cooperation important? Is your answer different now than when you started the unit? If yes, how is it different? Why?

iQ PRACTICE Go to the online discussion board to discuss the questions. *Practice > Unit 4 > Activity 15*

TRACK YOUR SUCCESS

iQ PRACTICE Go online to check the words and phrases you have learned in this unit. *Practice > Unit 4 > Activity 16*

Check (✓) the skills you learned. If you need more work on a skill, refer to the page(s) in parentheses.

READING	☐ I can make inferences. (p. 103)
CRITICAL THINKING	☐ I can form opinions based on a text. (p. 111)
VOCABULARY	☐ I can use prefixes. (p. 114)
WRITING	☐ I can organize supporting ideas. (p. 117)
GRAMMAR	☐ I can use parallel structure and ellipsis. (p. 122)

OBJECTIVE ▶ ☐ I can gather information and ideas to write an essay about the importance of global cooperation.

5

Urban
Planning

What makes a public place appealing?

A. Discuss these questions with your classmates.

1. What public places do you spend time in (for example, parks, libraries, airports, or malls)?

2. Does your hometown or the town where you are living now have many public places you can walk to? What are they?

3. Look at the photo. How can art affect a public place like a subway station? Why would a city plan a station like this?

B. Listen to *The Q Classroom* online. Then answer these questions.

1. How did the students answer the question?

2. Do you agree with their ideas? Why or why not?

iQ PRACTICE   Go to the online discussion board to discuss the Unit Question with your classmates. *Practice > Unit 5 > Activity 1*

UNIT OBJECTIVE ▶ Read an article from *The Economist* and an article from *The New York Times* about the design of public spaces. Gather information and ideas to write an analysis of a public place and suggest how it may be improved.

READING

READING 1   The New Oases

OBJECTIVE ▶   You are going to read an article from the news magazine *The Economist* that describes a change in the design of public places caused by modern technology and lifestyles. Use the article to gather information and ideas for your Unit Assignment.

READING SKILL   Following ideas

When you read longer texts from newspapers, magazines, and books, you often have to follow complicated ideas and understand how the ideas develop. It is important not just to recognize these ideas, but also to understand how they connect to present a story or argument. Here are some tips that can help you follow ideas through a text:

When you see a pronoun (*it, they, them, her, who, which*, etc.), make sure you know the **referent** (the noun that the pronoun replaces). Find the referent by scanning back in the text.

> **The new library** is a beautiful building. **It** is light, open, and welcoming.

Demonstrative pronouns such as *this* and *these* usually refer to the last idea, not just the last noun (for example, the last sentence or the entire last paragraph). Stop and ask yourself this question: What was the idea?

> **Many students rely on their laptops. This** means that they can work anywhere.

A sentence or paragraph might begin with a word or phrase that acts as a summary of the previous idea. Often, the word is a different part of speech (for example, a noun instead of a verb).

When you see a summary word or phrase, check that you understood the last idea and expect examples, supporting details, or a new topic to come next. In this example, "This shift" refers to the change in the design of public buildings. Details regarding the change follow.

> The design of public buildings **has changed. This shift** can be seen everywhere, from university libraries to public parks.

iQ RESOURCES   Go online to watch the Reading Skill Video.
Resources ⟩ Video ⟩ Unit 5 ⟩ Reading Skill Video

A. IDENTIFY Read the paragraph about an urban sociologist named Ray Oldenburg. Write the referent below each bold word or phrase.

Ray Oldenburg is an urban sociologist from Florida **who** has studied the
1
Ray Oldenburg

importance of informal public gathering places. In **his** book *The Great Good*
2
_____

Place, Oldenburg demonstrates why **these places** are essential to
3
_____

community and public life. **The book** argues that coffee shops, general
4
_____

stores, and other "third places" (in contrast to the first and second places of

home and work) are central to improving communities. By exploring how

these places work and what roles **they** serve, Oldenburg offers tools and
5   6
_____   _____

insight for individuals and communities everywhere.

Adapted from Ray Oldenburg. *Project for Public Spaces*. Retrieved October 12, 2010, from http://www.pps.org/roldenburg.

B. IDENTIFY Complete each second sentence with a noun from the box. Your choices should reflect the meaning of the phrases in bold in the first sentence.

concept   spaces   problem   shift   term

1. In recent years, more effort has gone into the design of **public places**. These _____ function as an alternative to the home and the office.

2. Today, more people **are using smart phones and tablet computers for business**. This _____ makes the traditional office seem old-fashioned.

3. It has been over three decades since Oldenburg first used **the expression** *third places*. Since then, many companies have used the _____ to describe their stores and restaurants.

4. Oldenburg believes that **third places could strengthen a community.** This _____ has been a powerful motivation for many urban planners.

5. Sometimes **people in third places interact with just their devices, not other people.** Some cafe owners are trying to solve this _____.

iQ PRACTICE Go online for more practice following ideas.
Practice > Unit 5 > Activity 2

PREVIEW THE READING

A. PREVIEW Look at the photograph on page 132. It shows the Stata Center at the Massachusetts Institute of Technology (MIT), a university in the U.S. What do you think people do in this building? Write three predictions. After you have read the article, check if your predictions were correct.

1. _____

2. _____

3. _____

B. QUICK WRITE What makes public places like university buildings and libraries attractive and functional for you? Write for 5–10 minutes in response. Remember to use this section for your Unit Assignment.

C. VOCABULARY Check (✓) the words and phrases you know. Use a dictionary to define any unknown words or phrases. Then discuss with a partner how the words and phrases will relate to the unit.

controversy *(n.)* ꭾ+	in decline *(prep. phr.)*	neutral *(adj.)* ꭾ+ OPAL
encounter *(v.)* ꭾ+ OPAL	intentionally *(adv.)*	nomadic *(adj.)*
form bonds *(v. phr.)*	isolated *(adj.)* ꭾ+	pop up *(v. phr.)*
hybrid *(adj.)*	mingle *(v.)*	specialized *(adj.)* ꭾ+ OPAL

ꭾ+ Oxford 5000™ words   OPAL Oxford Phrasal Academic Lexicon

iQ PRACTICE Go online to listen and practice your pronunciation.
Practice > Unit 5 > Activity 3

WORK WITH THE READING

 A. INVESTIGATE Read the article and gather information on what makes a public place appealing.

The New Oases

1   Frank Gehry, a celebrity architect, likes to cause aesthetic **controversy**, and his Stata Center at the Massachusetts Institute of Technology (MIT) did the trick. Opened in 2004 and housing MIT's computer-science and philosophy departments behind its façade[1] of bizarre angles and windows, it has become a new landmark. But the building's most radical innovation is on the inside. The entire structure was conceived with the **nomadic** lifestyles of modern students and faculty in mind. Stata, says William Mitchell, a professor of architecture and computer science at MIT who worked with Mr. Gehry on the center's design, was conceived as a new kind of "**hybrid** space."

2   This is best seen in the building's "student street," an interior passage that twists and meanders through the complex and is open to the public 24 hours a day. It is dotted with nooks and crannies[2]. Cafes and lounges are interspersed with work desks and whiteboards, and there is free Wi-Fi everywhere. Students, teachers, and visitors are cramming for exams, napping, instant-messaging, researching, reading, and discussing. No part of the student street is physically **specialized** for any of these activities. Instead, every bit of it can instantaneously become the venue for a seminar, a snack, or relaxation.

3   The fact that people are no longer tied to specific places for functions such as studying or learning, says Mr. Mitchell, means that there is "a huge drop in demand for traditional, private, enclosed spaces" such as offices or classrooms, and simultaneously "a huge rise in demand for semi-public spaces that can be informally appropriated to ad hoc[3] workspaces." This shift, he thinks, amounts to the biggest change in architecture in this century. In the twentieth century, architecture was about specialized structures—offices for working, cafeterias for eating, and so forth. This was necessary because workers needed to be near things such as landline phones, fax machines, and filing cabinets.

4   The new architecture, says Mr. Mitchell, will "make spaces **intentionally** multifunctional." Architects are thinking about light, air, trees, and gardens, all in the service of human connections. Buildings will have much more varied shapes than before. For instance, people working on laptops and tablets find it comforting to have their backs to a wall, so hybrid spaces may become curvier, with more nooks, in order to maximize the surface area of their inner walls.

> " **Flexibility is what separates successful spaces and cities from unsuccessful ones.** "

5   This "flexibility is what separates successful spaces and cities from unsuccessful ones," says Anthony Townsend, an urban planner at the Institute for the Future. Almost any public space can assume some of these features. For example, a not-for-profit organization in New York has turned Bryant Park, a once-derelict[4] but charming garden in front of the city's public library, into a hybrid space popular with office workers. The

---

[1] **façade:** the front of a building

[2] **nooks and crannies:** small, quiet places that are sheltered or hidden from other people

[3] **ad hoc:** arranged or happening when necessary and not planned in advance

[4] **derelict:** not used or cared for and in bad condition

park's managers noticed that a lot of visitors were using mobile phones and laptops in the park, so they installed Wi-Fi and added some chairs with foldable lecture desks. The idea was not to distract people from the flowers but to let them customize their little bit of the park.

6   The academic name for such spaces is *third places*, a term originally coined by the sociologist Ray Oldenburg in his 1989 book *The Great Good Place*. At the time, long before mobile technologies became widespread, Mr. Oldenburg wanted to distinguish between the sociological functions of people's first places (their homes), their second places (offices), and the public spaces that serve as safe, **neutral**, and informal meeting points. As Mr. Oldenburg saw it, a good third place makes admission free or cheap—the price of a cup of coffee, say—offers creature comforts[5], is within walking distance for a particular neighborhood, and draws a group of regulars.

7   Mr. Oldenburg's thesis was that third places were **in** general **decline**. More and more people, especially in suburban societies such as America's, were moving only between their first and second places, making extra stops only at alienating[6] and anonymous locations such as malls, which in Mr. Oldenburg's opinion fail as third places. Society, Mr. Oldenburg feared, was at risk of coming unstuck without these venues for spreading ideas and **forming bonds**.

8   No sooner was the term coined than big business queued up to claim that it was building new third places. The most prominent was Starbucks, a chain of coffee houses that started in Seattle and is now hard to avoid anywhere. Starbucks admits that as it went global, it lost its ambiance[7] of a "home away from home." However, it has also spotted a new opportunity in catering to nomads. Its branches offer not only sofas but also desks with convenient electricity sockets.

Interior "student street" of the Stata Center of MIT

Bookshops are also offering "more coffee and crumbs," as Mr. Oldenburg puts it, as are YMCAs[8] and public libraries.

9   But do these oases for nomads actually play the social role of third places? James Katz at Rutgers University fears that cyber-nomads are "hollowing them out." It is becoming commonplace for a cafe to be full of people with headphones on, speaking on their mobile phones or laptops and hacking away at their keyboards, more engaged with their email inbox than with the people touching their elbows. These places are "physically inhabited but psychologically evacuated," says Mr. Katz, which leaves people feeling "more **isolated** than they would be if the cafe were merely empty."

---

[5] **creature comforts:** things that make life, or a particular place, comfortable, such as good food, comfortable furniture, or modern equipment

[6] **alienating:** making you feel as if you do not belong

[7] **ambiance:** the character and atmosphere of a place (also *ambience*)

[8] **YMCA (The Young Men's Christian Association):** an international organization that provides accommodation and social and sports activities

A Third Place . . .

- is not expensive, or is free;
- usually offers food or drink;
- is easily accessible to many people;
- has "regulars" (people who go there often);
- has a friendly atmosphere; and
- is a good place to meet old friends and new people.

10   Many cafe owners are trying to deal with this problem. Christopher Waters, the owner of the Nomad Cafe in Oakland, regularly hosts poetry readings, and he actually turns off the Wi-Fi at those times so that people **mingle** more. He is also planning to turn his cafe into an online social network so that patrons opening their browsers to connect **encounter** a welcome page that asks them to fill out a short profile and then see information about the people at the other tables.

11   As more third places **pop up** and spread, they also change entire cities. Just as buildings during the twentieth century were specialized by function, towns were as well, says Mr. Mitchell. Suburbs were for living, downtowns for working, and other areas for playing. But urban nomads make districts, like buildings, multifunctional. Parts of town that were monocultures, he says, gradually become "fine-grained mixed-use neighborhoods" more akin[9] in human terms to pre-industrial villages than to modern suburbs.

[9] **akin:** similar to

B. VOCABULARY Here are some words and phrases from Reading 1. Read the sentences. Circle the answer that best matches the meaning of each bold word or phrase.

VOCABULARY SKILL REVIEW

In Unit 4, you learned about prefixes that change the meaning of words. Which words in Activity B can you modify with a prefix to give them the opposite meaning?

1. Frank Gehry likes to create **controversy** to get people discussing his challenging, modern style of architecture.

    a. fun   b. disagreement   c. harmony

2. College students lead a **nomadic** lifestyle; every day they move among dormitories, classroom buildings, and libraries.

    a. traveling often   b. being busy   c. working hard

3. The new building is a **hybrid** space suitable for both work and play.

    a. different   b. mixed-use   c. beautiful

4. The building's design is not **specialized**, so it can easily be adapted to different purposes.

    a. unusual   b. finished   c. made for a particular use

5. To create a sense of community, city officials **intentionally** created a place where people could sit and work during their lunch hour.

    a. then   b. accidentally   c. deliberately

6. A good public space should be safe, **neutral**, and informal.

    a. brightly colored   b. open for all people   c. open only for some people

7. The city needs to spend more money downtown because many older buildings are **in decline**.

   a. getting worse   b. being used   c. being offered for sale

8. A community is stronger when people care about each other and **form bonds**.

   a. work together   b. play sports   c. develop relationships

9. Customers in many coffee shops never talk to other people there, so they feel **isolated**.

   a. alone   b. intelligent   c. private

10. In good public places, people can **mingle**, getting to know each other if they want.

    a. sit together   b. make noise   c. mix and chat

11. If possible, architects should design places so that visitors **encounter** a welcoming atmosphere in any public space.

    a. meet with   b. hope for   c. appreciate

12. New public places **pop up** all the time in growing cities.

    a. get larger   b. appear suddenly   c. fail

Helsinki Central Library Oodi

iQ PRACTICE Go online for more practice with the vocabulary.
Practice > Unit 5 > Activity 4

C. RESTATE Complete this outline of the main ideas in the article. Use the Reading Skill (Following ideas, page 128) to help you.

Stata Center in Cambridge, Massachusetts

Bryant Park in New York City

Example 1: Stata Center

A _____ space
           1

Used for _____
           2

Example 2: _____
                3

A customizable space

Not only a park but also

_____
           4

Academic term: _____
                5

Definition: _____
                6

Oldenburg thought they were _____ .
                7

New third places were built by _____ .
                8

Problem: _____
                9

Solution: _____
                10

Conclusion: Third places change cities.

Districts become _____ (like the Stata Center).
                11

D. IDENTIFY Read the statements. Write *T* (true), *F* (false), or *I* (impossible to know from the article). Write the number of the paragraph that helped you. Correct the false statements.

_____ 1. Gehry's design is popular with everyone. (Paragraph: ____)

_____ 2. There is no need to make a formal appointment to use an area in the "student street" for a meeting. (Paragraph: ____)

_____ 3. Buildings in the twentieth century followed a limited number of forms. (Paragraph: ____)

_____ 4. Curved walls will become more common because they increase the amount of possible meeting space. (Paragraph: ____)

_____ 5. Future construction will use more color inside buildings. (Paragraph: ____)

_____ 6. The term *third places* was first created by an architect. (Paragraph: ____)

_____ 7. Oldenburg blamed technology for the lack of third places. (Paragraph: ____)

_____ 8. At Christopher Waters's cafe, customers cannot use Wi-Fi at any time. (Paragraph: ____)

E. RESTATE The article describes three reactions to three modern problems. Complete the chart with details from the article. Write the numbers of the paragraphs where you found the information.

	Problem	Solution	Paragraph(s)
1. Classrooms and office buildings	Spaces were specialized because workers needed access to landline phones and other equipment.		
2. Bryant Park			
3. Starbucks			

F. INTERPRET Circle the correct answers. Write a reason for your answer using information from the article.

1. Why does the "student street" in the Stata Center have twists and curves?

   a. to look inventive

   b. because there are no landline telephones

   c. to create controversy and something to discuss

   d. to create space that is comfortable for different uses

   Reason: _____

2. According to Oldenburg's definition, which is a third place?

   a. a bookstore that holds free weekly discussion groups for local residents

   b. a coffee shop with Internet access

   c. a suburban shopping mall

   d. a museum that charges people to attend public lectures

   Reason: _____

3. What can you infer from Reading 1 about people who live in the suburbs?

   a. They work longer hours than other people.

   b. They don't have much contact with other people outside work.

   c. They dislike shopping in urban centers.

   d. They do not have access to coffee shops.

   Reason: _____

4. What is causing the shift to multifunctional districts, according to paragraph 11?

   a. third places   c. modern architecture

   b. the Internet   d. changes in lifestyle

   Reason: _____

G. APPLY Use your understanding of Reading 1 to define these terms.

1. "hybrid space" (paragraph 1): _____

2. "semi-public spaces" (paragraph 3): _____

3. "coffee and crumbs" (paragraph 8): _____

4. "cyber-nomads" (paragraph 9): _____

5. "monocultures" (paragraph 11): _____

iQ PRACTICE Go online for additional reading and comprehension.
Practice > Unit 5 > Activity 5

WRITE WHAT YOU THINK

A. DISCUSS Discuss these questions in a group.

1. Do you know a building like the Stata Center or a place like Bryant Park that is multifunctional or has a hybrid purpose? Describe it and explain whether it is appealing to you.

2. Do you agree with the view that technology such as smartphones and tablet computers can have an alienating effect? Do you like the ideas that Christopher Waters had to encourage customers to mingle more?

3. Do you think third places differ from country to country? Why might some third places in your country be less appealing elsewhere?

ACADEMIC LANGUAGE
The phrase *the view that* is common in academic writing.

⎦ OPAL
Oxford Phrasal Academic Lexicon

B. EXTEND Choose one question and write a paragraph in response. Look back at your Quick Write on page 130 as you think about what you learned.

READING 2

OBJECTIVE ▶

A Path to Road Safety with No Signposts

You are going to read a profile from *The New York Times* about Dutch traffic engineer Hans Monderman. Although he died in 2008, Monderman's ideas about cars, pedestrians, and cyclists sharing roads are still popular today. Use the article to gather information and ideas for your Unit Assignment.

PREVIEW THE READING

A. PREVIEW Read the title, subheadings, and caption in the article. What do you think Monderman did to make roads safer? Make three predictions.

B. QUICK WRITE How do you think urban planners can make towns and cities friendly for motorists, cyclists, and pedestrians? Write for 5–10 minutes in response. Remember to use this section for your Unit Assignment.

C. VOCABULARY Check (✓) the words you know. Use a dictionary to define any new or unknown words. Then discuss with a partner how the words will relate to the unit.

accommodate (v.) 🔑+	counterintuitive (adj.)	negotiate (v.) 🔑+
anticipate (v.) 🔑+	criteria (pl. n.) 🔑+ OPAL	proponent (n.)
appealing (adj.) 🔑+	division (n.) 🔑+ OPAL	regulated (adj.) 🔑+
concede (v.) 🔑+	fatal (adj.) 🔑+	reinforce (v.) 🔑+ OPAL

🔑+ Oxford 5000™ words   **OPAL** Oxford Phrasal Academic Lexicon

WORK WITH THE READING

 A. INVESTIGATE Read the article and gather information on what makes a public place appealing.

A Path to Road Safety with No Signposts

BY SARAH LYALL

1   DRACHTEN, The Netherlands. "I want to take you on a walk," said Hans Monderman, abruptly stopping his car and striding—hatless, and nearly hairless—into the freezing rain.

Pedestrians, bicycles, and cars all share this intersection in Drachten without the need for traffic lights or road signs.

2   Like a naturalist conducting a tour of the jungle, he led the way to a busy intersection in the center of town, where several odd things immediately became clear. Not only was it virtually naked, stripped of all lights, signs, and road markings, but there was no **division** between road and sidewalk. It was, basically, a bare brick square.

3   But in spite of the apparently anarchical[1] layout, the traffic, a steady stream of trucks, cars, buses, motorcycles, bicycles, and pedestrians, moved along fluidly and easily, as if directed by an invisible conductor. When Mr. Monderman, a traffic engineer and the intersection's proud designer, deliberately failed to check for oncoming traffic before crossing the street, the drivers slowed for him. No one honked or shouted rude words out of the window.

4   "Who has the right of way?" he asked rhetorically[2]. "I don't care. People here have to find their own way, **negotiate** for themselves, use their own brains."

5   Used by some 20,000 drivers a day, the intersection is part of a road-design revolution pioneered by the 59-year-old Mr. Monderman. His work in Friesland, the district in northern Holland that takes in Drachten, is increasingly seen as the way of the future in Europe.

6   His philosophy is simple, if **counterintuitive**.

7   To make communities safer and more **appealing**, Mr. Monderman argues, you should first remove the traditional paraphernalia[3] of their roads—the traffic lights and speed signs; the signs exhorting[4] drivers to stop, slow down and merge; the center lines separating lanes from one another; even the speed bumps, speed-limit signs, bicycle lanes, and pedestrian crossings. In his view, it is only when the road is made more dangerous, when drivers stop looking at signs and start looking at other people, that driving becomes safer.

[1] **anarchical:** without order
[2] **rhetorically:** asked only to make a statement or to produce an effect rather than to get an answer
[3] **paraphernalia:** a large number of different objects, especially the equipment that you need for a particular activity
[4] **exhort:** to try hard to persuade someone to do something

8   "All those signs are saying to cars, 'This is your space, and we have organized your behavior so that as long as you behave this way, nothing can happen to you,'" Mr. Monderman said. "That is the wrong story."

9   The Drachten intersection is an example of the concept of "shared space," a street where cars and pedestrians are equal, and the design tells the driver what to do.

10   "It's a moving away from **regulated**, legislated[5] traffic toward space which, by the way it's designed and configured, makes it clear what sort of behavior is **anticipated**," said Ben Hamilton-Baillie, a British specialist in urban design and movement and a **proponent** of many of the same concepts.

11   Highways, where the car is naturally king, are part of the "traffic world" and another matter altogether. In Mr. Monderman's view, shared-space schemes thrive only in conjunction with well-organized, well-regulated highway systems.

12   Variations on the shared-space theme are being tried in Spain, Denmark, Austria, Sweden, and Britain, among other places. The European Union has appointed a committee of experts, including Mr. Monderman, for a Europe-wide study.

SOCIAL SPACE

13   Mr. Monderman is a man on a mission. On a daylong automotive tour of Friesland, he pointed out places he had improved, including a town where he ripped out the sidewalks, signs, and crossings and put in brick paving on the central shopping street. An elderly woman crossed slowly in front of him.

14   "This is social space, so when Grandma is coming, you stop, because that's what normal, courteous human beings do," he said.

15   Planners and curious journalists are increasingly making pilgrimages[6] to meet Mr. Monderman, considered one of the field's great innovators, although until a few years ago he was virtually unknown outside Holland. Mr. Hamilton-Baillie, whose writings have helped bring Mr. Monderman's work to wider attention, remembers with fondness his own first visit.

16   Mr. Monderman drove him to a small country road with cows in every direction. Their presence was unnecessarily **reinforced** by a large, standard-issue European traffic sign with a picture of a cow on it.

17   "He said: 'What do you expect to find here? Wallabies[7]?'" Mr. Hamilton-Baillie recalled. "'They're treating you like you're a complete idiot, and if people treat you like a complete idiot, you'll act like one.'

18   "Here was someone who had rethought a lot of issues from complete scratch[8]. Essentially, what it means is a transfer of power and responsibility from the state to the individual and the community."

19   Dressed in a beige jacket and patterned shirt, with scruffy facial hair and a stocky build, Mr. Monderman has the appearance of a football hooligan[9] but the temperament of an engineer, which indeed he trained to be. His father was the headmaster of the primary school in their small village; Hans liked to fiddle with machines. "I was always the guy who repaired the TV sets in our village," he said.

20   He was working as a civil engineer building highways in the 1970s when the Dutch government, alarmed at a sharp increase in traffic accidents, set up a network of traffic safety offices. Mr. Monderman was appointed Friesland's traffic safety officer.

21   In residential communities, Mr. Monderman began narrowing the roads and putting in design features like trees and flowers, red

[5] **legislated:** controlled by law
[6] **pilgrimage:** a journey to a place that is connected with someone or something that you admire
[7] **wallaby:** an Australian animal like a small kangaroo
[8] **from scratch:** from the beginning
[9] **hooligan:** someone who behaves in an extremely noisy, and sometimes aggressive, way in public

brick paving stones, and even fountains to discourage people from speeding, following the principle now known as psychological traffic calming, where behavior follows design.

22 He made his first nervous foray into[10] shared space in a small village whose residents were upset at its being used as a daily thoroughfare for 6,000 speeding cars. When he took away the signs, lights, and sidewalks, people drove more carefully. Within two weeks, speeds on the road had dropped by more than half.

23 In fact, he said, there has never been a **fatal** accident on any of his roads.

24 Several early studies bear out his contention that shared spaces are safer. In England, the district of Wiltshire found that removing the center line from a stretch of road reduced drivers' speed without any increase in accidents.

LIMITS OF SHARED SPACE

25 [. . .] Mr. Monderman **concedes** that road design can do only so much. It does not change the behavior, for instance, of the 15 percent of drivers who will behave badly no matter what the rules are. Nor are shared-space designs appropriate everywhere, like major urban centers, but only in neighborhoods that meet particular **criteria**.

26 Recently a group of well-to-do parents asked him to widen the two-lane road leading to their children's school, saying it was too small to **accommodate** what he derisively[11] calls "their huge cars."

27 He refused, saying the fault was not with the road, but with the cars. "They can't wait for each other to pass?" he asked. [. . .]

From "A Path to Road Safety with No Signposts" by Sarah Lyall from *The New York Times*, January 22, 2005. © 2005 The New York Times. All rights reserved. Used by permission and protected by the Copyright Laws of the United States. The printing, copying, redistribution, or retransmission of this Content without express written permission is prohibited.

[10] **make a foray into:** to attempt to become involved in (a new activity)
[11] **derisively:** in an unkind way that shows that you think something/someone is ridiculous

B. VOCABULARY Here are some words from Reading 2. Read the sentences. Then write each bold word next to the correct list of synonyms on page 142.

a. In most countries, driving is a **regulated** activity.

b. Drivers learn traffic laws when they get their licenses, but signs **reinforce** the laws in case drivers forget them.

c. Urban planners try to **anticipate** conflict between cars and pedestrians when they design streets.

d. Most street planners try to create a strict **division** between the road and the sidewalk.

e. Whenever possible, roads are built to **accommodate** all the vehicles that are likely to use them.

f. Streets can be hard to **negotiate** if rules are complicated or there is a lot of traffic.

g. Despite many safety measures, sometimes there are **fatal** accidents on the roads.

h. Many home buyers think houses on large, busy streets are less **appealing** than those on small, quiet streets.

i. One street designer is a **proponent** of a planned shared-space movement and is trying to convince other people of the plan's value.

j. The shared-space approach is **counterintuitive** to traditional street design because it removes the traditional traffic signs and signals.

k. Shared-space designers **concede** that the idea does not work everywhere.

l. There are several **criteria** for a successful shared space; only streets that meet these guidelines are likely to succeed.

1. _____ *(v.)* admit • acknowledge • recognize

2. _____ *(v.)* expect • await • look for

3. _____ *(v.)* clear • get around • get past • pass

4. _____ *(v.)* adapt • fit • suit • receive • shelter • work with

5. _____ *(v.)* strengthen • cement • make stronger • repeat

6. _____ *(adj.)* surprising • unexpected • contrary to usual thinking

7. _____ *(adj.)* deadly • lethal

8. _____ *(adj.)* popular • attractive • desirable

9. _____ *(adj.)* overseen • policed • supervised • governed

10. _____ *(pl. n.)* standards • measures • guides

11. _____ *(n.)* separation • split • partition

12. _____ *(n.)* advocate • champion • supporter • promoter

iQ PRACTICE   Go online for more practice with the vocabulary.
Practice > Unit 5 > Activity 7

C. IDENTIFY Check (✓) the techniques that Monderman used for improving intersections. Then discuss with a partner why he did or did not use each method.

☐ 1. adding more road signs

☐ 2. forcing cars, bikes, and pedestrians to share the same space

☐ 3. removing lane divisions

☐ 4. making roads wider

☐ 5. adding more pedestrian crossings

☐ 6. reducing the speed limit on highways

☐ 7. letting people negotiate their own behavior

☐ 8. changing roads in major cities

☐ 9. planting trees and flowers

☐ 10. making road surfaces look the same as sidewalks

D. EXPLAIN Answer these questions. Then highlight the information in the article that supports your answers.

1. Why are intersections like the one in Drachten safe?

   _____

2. In Monderman's view, why are roads with road signs, speed limits, and lane markings more dangerous?

   _____

3. Why don't shared-space ideas apply to highways?

   _____

4. Why does Monderman find road signs and other traditional ways of regulating traffic to be insulting?

   _____

5. Why did Monderman refuse to widen a road leading to a school?

   _____

E. CATEGORIZE Read the statements. Write *T* (true), *F* (false), or *I* (impossible to know from the article). Write the number of the paragraph that helped you. Correct the false statements.

_____ 1. Monderman is compared to a naturalist in a jungle because people are out of place in his intersections. (Paragraph: ____)

_____ 2. Someone is directing traffic in the intersection in Drachten that the reporter visits. (Paragraph: ____)

_____ 3. There has been an increase in deadly car accidents since Monderman redesigned the roads in Drachten. (Paragraph: ____)

_____ 4. In the "traffic world," drivers do not respond to the design of the roads; they respond to road signs. (Paragraph: ____)

_____ 5. Hamilton-Baillie met Monderman because the Dutchman's work was famous in Britain. (Paragraph: ____)

_____ 6. Monderman suggested that the Dutch government hired traffic safety officers in response to increasing car accidents. (Paragraph: ____)

_____ 7. Monderman's experiment with psychological traffic calming was unsuccessful. (Paragraph: ____)

_____ 8. Monderman believed that even the worst drivers would respond positively to shared spaces. (Paragraph: ____)

CRITICAL THINKING STRATEGY

Analyzing verb tense to understand a text

As you saw in the Reading Skill, you can use grammatical clues to follow ideas in complex texts. Verb tenses contain important information that can help your comprehension.

The **simple present** is used for facts, principles, and other ideas that are not expected to change.

> The academic name for such spaces **is** *third places*.

The **simple past** indicates that the event took place in the past or is completed.

> They **installed** Wi-Fi and **added** some chairs.

This tense can also indicate that something is no longer true today.

> In the twentieth century, architecture **was** about specialized structures.

The **present perfect** connects a past event to the present time, or indicates a change.

> a not-for-profit organization in New York **has turned** Bryant Park . . . into a hybrid space.

The **present progressive** emphasizes an activity or change that is ongoing now.

> It **is becoming** commonplace for a cafe to be full of people with headphones on.

This tense also sometimes indicates future time.

> He **is** also **planning** to turn his cafe into an online social network.

iQ PRACTICE Go online to watch the Critical Thinking Video and check your comprehension. *Practice > Unit 5 > Activity 8*

F. **EXPLAIN** Read the sentences and choose the best explanation for the choice of verb tense.

1. Libraries **have** always **been** important community resources.

   a. Libraries are not important community resources today.

   b. Libraries were only important community resources in the past.

   c. Libraries were important community resources in the past, and they still are today.

2. Recently, however, many libraries **have become** spaces for small-business consulting, chess clubs, and art projects.

   a. Using libraries for these purposes is a new idea.

   b. Libraries were always used for these purposes.

   c. Libraries will start to create these functions in the future.

3. Some libraries **are** even **opening** cafes.

   a. Library cafes existed only in the past.

   b. Library cafes existed in the past and they still exist today.

   c. Library cafes did not exist in the past.

4. In the past, libraries **were** just places to borrow books and read magazines.

   a. It is a fact that libraries are always places to borrow books and read magazines.

   b. It is not true today that libraries are only places to borrow books and read magazines.

   c. Libraries are now starting to let users borrow books and read magazines.

5. E-books and online databases **have changed** the mission of public libraries.

   a. The mission of public libraries has always been the same.

   b. The mission of public libraries will be different in the future.

   c. The mission of public libraries is now different from the past.

6. The library **is** a good example of a third place.

   a. This is a fact about third places.

   b. This is a new idea about third places.

   c. This is about the history of third places.

7. Most libraries **do not allow** food and drink in the reading rooms.

   a. In the past, you could not eat or drink in libraries.

   b. Generally, you cannot eat or drink in libraries.

   c. In the future, you will not be able to eat or drink in libraries.

8. However, some university libraries **are relaxing** their rules to fit students' nomadic lifestyles.

   a. The rules were relaxed in the past but are stricter today.

   b. The rules are as strict today as they were in the past.

   c. The rules have started to become less strict recently.

WORK WITH THE VIDEO

A. PREVIEW What problems does traffic congestion cause?

VIDEO VOCABULARY

congestion (n.) the state of being crowded and full of traffic

smog (n.) a form of air pollution that is or looks like a mixture of smoke and fog

respiratory (adj.) connected with breathing

gridlock (n.) a situation in which there are so many cars in the streets of a town that the traffic cannot move at all

gear up (v.) to prepare to do something

iQ RESOURCES Go online to watch the video about traffic congestion.
Resources > Video > Unit 5 > Unit Video

B. CATEGORIZE Watch the video two or three times. Take notes in the chart.

Causes	Effects	Solutions
increased car ownership	air and noise pollution	build new roads

C. EXTEND What are other causes, effects, and solutions for traffic congestion? Use Reading 2 and your own ideas to add information to the chart.

WRITE WHAT YOU THINK

SYNTHESIZE Think about Reading 1, Reading 2, and the video as you discuss these questions. Then choose one question and write a paragraph in response.

1. Should the design of public spaces change to better suit our behavior (as in Reading 1), or should we change our behavior to meet the expectations of the design (as in Reading 2)? Use suggestions from the video in your answer.

2. As you saw in the video, some cities have regulated or banned cars in the city center. However, Hans Monderman recommended fewer regulations as a solution. Which idea do you agree with, and why?

VOCABULARY SKILL Using the dictionary: verb complements

The main verb controls the pattern of a clause or sentence. Knowing the **verb complements**, or the types of words and phrases allowed with the verb, is important in improving your writing and speaking. For example, some verbs can be followed by a direct object (transitive verbs), but others cannot (intransitive verbs). The dictionary can help you write better sentences by telling you which complements are possible or required with each verb: objects, prepositional phrases, noun clauses, infinitives, or gerunds.

[I] means *intransitive*. The verb can be used without an object.

~**what** means the verb is followed by a *wh-* noun clause. A *that* noun clause is not possible here.

This additional note explains the difference in meaning between two complements.

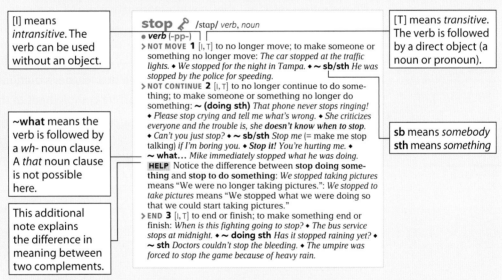

[T] means *transitive*. The verb is followed by a direct object (a noun or pronoun).

sb means *somebody*
sth means *something*

When a verb can be followed by a prepositional phrase, it is especially important to use a dictionary because it is very difficult to guess the correct preposition.

~**(with sb):** This use of *negotiate* is intransitive, so it does not take a direct object. Use *with* to add the person you are negotiating with.

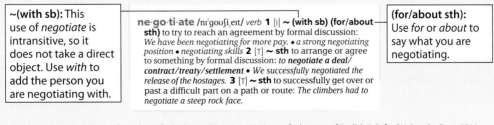

(for/about sth): Use *for* or *about* to say what you are negotiating.

All dictionary entries adapted from the *Oxford Advanced American Dictionary for learners of English* © Oxford University Press 2011.

A. CATEGORIZE Are the bold verbs transitive or intransitive? Write *T* (transitive) or *I* (intransitive). Check your answers in a learner's dictionary.

_____ 1. The "student street" twists and **meanders** through the complex.

_____ 2. Architects **are thinking** about light, air, trees, and gardens.

_____ 3. He **led** the way to a busy intersection.

_____ 4. The drivers **slowed** for him.

_____ 5. Mr. Hamilton-Baillie's writings **have helped** bring Mr. Monderman's work to wider attention.

_____ 6. Mr. Monderman **began** narrowing the roads.

B. ANALYZE Four of the bold words in the paragraph below have verb complement errors. Read the paragraph. Then complete the tasks below.

> The design of my high school did not **appeal** me. It was built to **accommodate** 1,000 students. However, more than 1,500 students **occupied** the building. The designers did not **anticipate**. Every day, we had to **negotiate** with the crowded corridors and staircases to **go** to class. The principal **told** that they could not **improve** the situation. However, he **conceded** that a better system was necessary.

1. Look up each bold verb from the paragraph in a learner's dictionary. Find the meaning that fits the context. Write the correct complement in the chart.

Verb	Complement	Correct in paragraph? Yes	Correct in paragraph? No
a. appeal	verb + to somebody	☐	☐
b. accommodate		☐	☐
c. occupy		☐	☐
d. anticipate		☐	☐
e. negotiate		☐	☐
f. go		☐	☐
g. tell		☐	☐
h. improve		☐	☐
i. concede		☐	☐

2. Is the complement of each verb correct in the paragraph? Check (✓) *Yes* or *No*.

3. For each complement that is incorrect, write the correct sentence.

iQ PRACTICE Go online for more practice using the dictionary to identify verb complements. *Practice > Unit 5 > Activity 9*

WRITING

OBJECTIVE ▶ At the end of this unit, you will write an analysis of a place you know. This analysis will include information from the readings, the unit video, and your own ideas.

GRAMMAR Passive voice to focus information

Forming the passive

In most **active** sentences, the subject of the verb is also the **agent**: that is, it does the action of the verb.

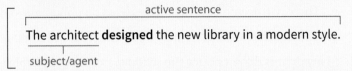

active sentence
The architect **designed** the new library in a modern style.
subject/agent

In a **passive** sentence, the agent of the verb is not the subject. The passive voice is formed with a form of *be* + the past participle of a transitive verb.

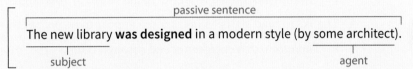

passive sentence
The new library **was designed** in a modern style (by some architect).
subject   agent

The *by* phrase containing the agent is often omitted in academic writing.

Focusing information

The passive is used when you want to focus on the result or receiver of the action instead of the agent of the action.

> The entire structure **was conceived** with the nomadic lifestyles of modern students and faculty in mind.

The focus is on *the entire structure*, not the architect who conceived it.

The passive also allows writers to report opinions without saying whose they are.

> His work in Friesland . . . **is** increasingly **seen** as the way of the future in Europe.

The focus is on Monderman's work, and the sentence emphasizes his reputation; it is not important who specifically has this opinion.

Two other forms of the passive, the *passive infinitive* and the *passive gerund*, can also help make sentences more logical and focused because they avoid introducing a new grammatical subject into the sentence.

> ? The road needs someone to widen it.
> ✓ The road needs **to be widened**.
> ? Customers like coffee shop owners treating them as members of a community.
> ✓ Customers like **being treated** as members of a community.

Remember that only transitive verbs can be used in the passive voice.

Active voice is more common than passive voice. The passive should not be used in contexts where active sentences are more direct and easier to understand. However, the passive voice can be useful in academic and other formal writing.

A. EVALUATE Read each sentence. Circle the best sentence to follow it. Then explain your choice to a partner.

1. Monderman distinguished the "social world" of the town from the "traffic world" of the highway.

    a. Engineers design the traffic world for cars.

    (b.) The traffic world is designed for cars.

    The first sentence ends with "the traffic world," so the traffic world should be the focus of the next sentence. The engineers are not important.

2. Small towns and villages are examples of the social world.

    a. There, we decide how to behave based on politeness and human contact.

    b. There, behavior is determined by politeness and human contact.

3. Many drivers do not notice the schools, stores, and people that they pass.

    a. Road signs distract them from the social world.

    b. They are distracted from the social world by road signs.

4. Thanks to road signs, villages often appear to be part of the traffic world.

    a. Therefore, drivers often speed through them.

    b. Therefore, they are often driven through too fast.

5. Traditional traffic-calming techniques, such as stop signs, are ineffective.

    a. Drivers simply speed up between the stop signs.

    b. Cars are simply driven faster between the stop signs.

Activity text adapted from Vanderbilt, Tom. *Traffic: Why We Drive the Way We Do (and What It Says About Us)* (2008). New York: Knopf, 189–190.

B. CATEGORIZE Read the paragraph. Complete each sentence with the correct passive or active form of the verb.

Online social media sites ___are considered___ (consider) third places. According
                                    1
to some experts, these websites _____ (need) because they fit our
                                              2
nomadic lifestyle better than traditional third places. For example, social media
can _____ (access) from any computer or smartphone anywhere
           3
in the world. However, some users _____ (encounter) unexpected
                                              4
problems. One study found that family time _____ (decrease)
                                                        5
because of increased use of the Internet. Ironically, we _____
                                                                   6
(isolate) by technology that _____ (design) to connect us.
                                      7
Proponents of online social media _____ (concede) that these sites
                                              8
should be used responsibly. Children's use of such sites, for example, should
_____ (regulate) by their parents.
        9

C. CATEGORIZE Complete each sentence with a passive infinitive or a passive gerund. Use your dictionary if you are not sure if the preceding verb uses an infinitive or a gerund as complement.

1. The architect agreed _____to be interviewed_____ (interview) for this story.

2. The building seems _____ (design) for modern student life.

3. I appreciate _____ (tell) about the problem, and I will try to find a solution.

4. Cyclists keep _____ (hit) by drivers at this intersection.

5. The Internet has started _____ (see) as an obstacle to human interaction.

iQ PRACTICE Go online for more practice with the passive voice.
Practice > Unit 5 > Activities 10–11

WRITING SKILL Connecting information Part 1

Good paragraphs have unity and are written in a logical order (see the Writing Skills in Units 3 and 4). They contain clues to help readers follow the main ideas. To achieve this, most clauses and sentences follow a regular pattern of information: old information followed by new information. Often, the new information in one sentence becomes the old information—and, therefore, the beginning—of the next sentence.

The old-new pattern allows writers to connect sentences logically while developing ideas.

old (third place)   new
No sooner was **the term** coined than big business queued up to claim that it was building new third places.

old   new
The most prominent **was** Starbucks.

old   new
Starbucks admits that as it went global, it lost its ambiance.

This is called **linear information structure** because the logic flows in a straight line. The new information in one sentence becomes the old information in the next. You can use this pattern to create smooth, logical connections between the sentences in your paragraphs.

A. WRITING MODEL Read the first two paragraphs in a description of another third place. Then complete the tasks below.

"The Third Place" Coffeehouse

"The Third Place" is the name of a coffeehouse in Raleigh, North Carolina. (Raleigh) is the home of the state capitol and many businesses. However, many workers have not had options for spending their time in locations other than their first places (homes in the suburbs) and second places (downtown offices). The Third Place is a friendly cafe that fills this gap.

When you walk into The Third Place, you first see cozy, inviting chairs. Behind them, on the walls, are colorful rugs, suggesting an international theme. Between the rugs, you will see pictures taken by local photographers. The photos are changed monthly and really help develop a sense of community. This feeling of community is enhanced by the customers, who represent the range of Raleigh's inhabitants. Businesspeople, students, and families can be found at The Third Place on any day of the week.

1. If a sentence contains old information, circle the old information.

2. Connect each circled phrase to the new information in the previous sentence.

3. Discuss with a partner how the last sentence in paragraph 1 is linked to the previous sentence.

4. Underline the three passive verbs in the second paragraph. Explain why the passive voice is used in each case.

WRITING SKILL Connecting information **Part 2**

In Activity A, you saw an example of linear information structure, in which the new information in one sentence becomes the old information at the start of the next. An alternative organization is **constant information structure**. In this pattern, the same old information is used at the start of several sentences, and each sentence adds new information on the topic. Use constant information structure to define or explain a complex topic.

> The new architecture . . . will make spaces intentionally multifunctional.
>
> Architects are thinking about light, air, trees, and gardens, all in the service of human connections.
>
> Buildings will have much more varied shapes than before.

Synonyms and pronouns help you avoid repetition and make a smooth flow of information.

B. WRITING MODEL Read the next paragraph in the description of The Third Place coffeehouse. Then complete the tasks below.

(1) The menu at The Third Place is varied. (2) It is available from 11 a.m. to 7 p.m. (3) Much of the food is homemade and includes creative sandwiches, delicious soups, and fresh salads. (4) All the meals are vegetarian and use local ingredients. (5) Weekly specials offer something new even to regular customers. (6) And, of course, good coffee is served all day and evening! (7) _____ will keep you coming back.

1. Discuss with a partner how the first words in sentences 2–6 are related to *The menu* in sentence 1.

2. With your partner, complete sentence 7 with the appropriate information.

C. WRITING MODEL Read the model of a student's analysis of a third place.

A Third Way for Modern Libraries

1   Because of the rapid growth in e-books and e-readers, some have questioned the need for libraries, with their shelves of dusty books and outdated technology. Libraries have responded to the challenges and opportunities of digital reading in many different ways. One solution can be found at my local public library in Kirkwood, which is a good example of a relevant modern library that mostly succeeds in accommodating the needs of both traditional and digital users.

2   The overall design of the Kirkwood Library is fresh and appealing. Large picture windows look out over a children's playground and the woods beyond, giving the building an open and welcoming atmosphere. These windows also reduce the need for artificial lighting, which, in addition to the installation of solar panels and a rooftop garden, make this an environmentally friendly library. No barriers obstruct the entrance to the library from the lobby, and an information desk is positioned close by the entrance, but not so close that it might intimidate first-time visitors. Flat-screen TVs announce library events and community activities, which users can learn more about by scanning special codes on their smartphones or tablets. Most noticeably, visitors are greeted, not by stacks of books, but by a large reading room with comfortable chairs and tables that can be moved together for small-group discussions or separated for more isolated reading and studying.

3   In addition to these design features, the library's resources have also been updated. In fact, Kirkwood could be considered a hybrid library because of its commitment to both digital and print media. The library's e-book collection has been vastly expanded, and digital books can be borrowed in the library or by logging in at home. Databases of newspapers and academic articles are also available. E-readers and other technology can even be borrowed for a week at a time.

Proponents of good old-fashioned books should also be satisfied at the library. To make room for the new seating, many of the books have been moved to the basement, but librarians promise to retrieve them in less than an hour. Furthermore, as a good example of Kirkwood's hybrid strategy, books can be requested online or by a smartphone app. The books will then be waiting at the information desk on the patron's arrival at the library.

4   Kirkwood Library meets most of the criteria for a successful modern-day library. It provides easy access to print and digital materials, and its flexible seating makes the space useful for multiple purposes. However, users may encounter two problems. One small difficulty is that the electric outlets in the reading area are all located along the walls, meaning that most users cannot charge their tablets, phones, and laptops from their seats. Patrons who are not yet familiar with digital resources may also encounter problems using the new technology, and there is currently little support available for them.

5   Both criticisms can easily be solved. Additional electric outlets can be provided around the building, with the possibility of new wireless charging mats on the armrests of chairs in the future. Librarians could also do more to anticipate the needs of patrons who are new to digital libraries. They could offer workshops and provide written instructions for using the e-books and databases. With these improvements, Kirkwood should be in a strong position to be a sustainable library of the future.

WRITING TIP

In Units 3 and 4, you learned about unity and coherence. Notice how paragraphs that use these types of information structure have unity and form a coherent essay.

D. IDENTIFY Highlight examples of these writing techniques in the essay.

1. linear information structure

2. constant information structure

3. passive voice to organize information

4. descriptive language

5. evaluative language

E. EVALUATE Answer these questions. Then decide whether the paragraphs below have linear (L) or constant (C) information structure.

_L_ 1. In paragraph 1, what old information does *one solution* (in the third sentence) refer to?

___ 2. In paragraph 2, what do you notice about the subjects of the first five sentences?

___ 3. In paragraph 3, what is the connection between the second and third sentences?

___ 4. In paragraph 3, what is the old information in the last sentence?

___ 5. In paragraph 4, what synonym is used for *problem*?

___ 6. In paragraph 5, what does the phrase *these improvements* in the last sentence refer to?

iQ PRACTICE Go online for more practice connecting information.
Practice > Unit 5 > Activity 12

Write an analysis

In this assignment, you will write an analysis of a particular public place and suggest ways to make it more appealing. As you prepare your analysis, think about the Unit Question, "What makes a public place appealing?" Use information from Reading 1, Reading 2, the unit video, and your work in this unit to support your ideas. Refer to the Self-Assessment checklist on page 156.

iQ PRACTICE Go online to the Writing Tutor to read a model analysis. *Practice > Unit 5 > Activity 13*

PLAN AND WRITE

A. BRAINSTORM Choose a public place that you know well. Follow the steps below to brainstorm ideas about the place.

1. List descriptions of the place, its design, the people who use it, and the activities that happen there.

2. Make a chart to evaluate the place. Write a list of criteria that make a public place appealing in the first column. Explain why your place does or does not meet those criteria in the second column.

TIP FOR SUCCESS

When comparing and contrasting, it is important to develop strong criteria to support your conclusions.

Criteria	Evaluation + Reasons
easy to meet with others	yes: well-maintained tables with three or four comfortable chairs

3. Make a list of suggestions for improving the public place based on your negative evaluations. Use ideas from Readings 1 and 2 to help you.

B. PLAN Work with a partner to add to your list of suggestions for improving the public place for your analysis.

iQ RESOURCES Go online to download and complete the outline for your analysis. *Resources > Writing Tools > Unit 5 > Outline*

C. WRITE Use your planing notes to write your analysis.

1. Write your analysis essay to describe and evaluate a public place. Connect information using clear information structures.

2. Look at the Self-Assessment checklist to guide your writing.

iQ PRACTICE Go online to the Writing Tutor to write your assignment.
Practice > Unit 5 > Activity 14

REVISE AND EDIT

iQ PRACTICE Go online to download the peer review worksheet.
Resources > Writing Tools > Unit 5 > Peer Review Worksheet

A. PEER REVIEW Read your partner's essay. Then use the peer review worksheet. Discuss the review with your partner.

B. REWRITE Based on your partner's review, revise and rewrite your analysis.

C. EDIT Complete the Self-Assessment checklist as you prepare to write the final draft of your analysis. Be prepared to hand in your work or discuss it in class.

SELF-ASSESSMENT	Yes	No
Did you use linear and/or constant information structure clearly?	☐	☐
Are your evaluation criteria clear?	☐	☐
Is the passive voice used appropriately?	☐	☐
Did you use the correct verb complements?	☐	☐
Does the essay include vocabulary from the unit?	☐	☐
Did you check the essay for punctuation, spelling, and grammar?	☐	☐

D. REFLECT Discuss these questions with a partner or group.

1. What is something new you learned in this unit?

2. Look back at the Unit Question—What makes a public place appealing? Is your answer different now than when you started the unit? If yes, how is it different? Why?

iQ PRACTICE Go to the online discussion board to discuss the questions.
Practice > Unit 5 > Activity 15

TRACK YOUR SUCCESS

iQ PRACTICE Go online to check the words and phrases you have learned in this unit. *Practice > Unit 5 > Activity 16*

Check (✓) the skills you learned. If you need more work on a skill, refer to the page(s) in parentheses.

READING	☐ I can follow ideas. (p. 128)
CRITICAL THINKING	☐ I can analyze verb tenses to understand a text. (p. 144)
VOCABULARY	☐ I can use the dictionary for help with verb complements. (p. 147)
GRAMMAR	☐ I can use the passive voice to focus information. (p. 149)
WRITING	☐ I can connect information. (pp. 151 and 152)

OBJECTIVE ▶ ☐ I can gather information and ideas to write an analysis of a public place and suggest how it may be improved.

Ecology

6

READING	anticipating content through questions
VOCABULARY	suffixes
WRITING	paraphrasing
CRITICAL THINKING	synthesizing Information
GRAMMAR	modals of possibility

How can we turn trash into treasure?

A. Discuss these questions with your classmates.

1. What do you do with things you no longer use? What do you throw away? What do you recycle?

2. Do you think society is wasteful? How could people decrease the amount of garbage they throw away?

3. Look at the photo. What materials were used to make this sculpture? What message do you think the artist is trying to convey?

B. Listen to *The Q Classroom* online. Then answer these questions.

1. Why does Marcus think we should turn trash into treasure? Do you agree or disagree? Why?

2. How do Yuna, Felix, and Sophy answer the Unit Question? Whose ideas do you agree with the most? Why?

iQ PRACTICE Go to the online discussion board to discuss the Unit Question with your classmates. *Practice > Unit 6 > Activity 1*

UNIT OBJECTIVE ▶ Read an article from *New Scientist* and an article from *The Atlantic* news magazine on ways to recycle or avoid waste. Gather information and ideas to prepare a business plan that describes a new recycling company to potential investors.

READING 1

Garbage of Eden

You are going to read an article from *New Scientist* magazine that examines the unique way that Singapore is dealing with its garbage. Use the article to gather information and ideas for your Unit Assignment.

READING SKILL Anticipating content through questions

Being an active reader is the key to becoming a better reader. One way to be an active reader is to think about the topic of a text and form questions before you begin reading. Base your questions on the information or content you think will be in the reading. Use question words (*who, what, where, when, why,* and *how*). Then, while you read, keep your questions in mind and look for the answers.

For example, this title, subtitle, and photo are from a news article.

Stop! I'm Full

No more room in local landfill; it will close at the end of this year.

These are possible questions to ask before reading the article:

Who is in charge of this landfill?

What kinds of garbage are in this landfill?

Where is this landfill?

When was the landfill opened?

Why is the landfill full?

How will this landfill be cleaned up so that it doesn't harm the environment?

While reading the article, note any answers to your questions. After you finish reading, use the answers to your questions to help you identify the main ideas of the text.

A. CREATE Read the title and subtitle of Reading 1 on page 162. Also look at the photos and landfill plan that accompany the article. Use the *wh*-word question chart to write six questions you think the reading should answer.

Question	Answer
Who	
What	
Where	
When	
Why	
How	

B. IDENTIFY As you read the article "Garbage of Eden," look for the answers to your questions. Annotate your text to remind you where you found the answers. Do not complete the chart yet.

iQ PRACTICE Go online for more practice anticipating content through questions. *Practice > Unit 6 > Activity 2*

PREVIEW THE READING

A. PREVIEW What are three possible ways Singapore could get rid of its waste in an environmentally friendly way? As you read, check to see if your ideas are similar to the ideas presented in the article.

1. _____

2. _____

3. _____

WRITING TIP
Using transitions between ideas can improve the smooth flow of information in your writing. Think of appropriate transitions to insert between your ideas.

B. QUICK WRITE How can a landfill site become a place of natural beauty? Write for 5–10 minutes in response. Remember to use this section for your Unit Assignment.

C. VOCABULARY Check (✓) the words you know. Use a dictionary to define any new or unknown words. Then discuss with a partner how the words will relate to the unit.

abundant *(adj.)*	contaminated *(adj.)*	incinerate *(v.)*
anticipate *(v.)* 🔑+	disposal *(n.)* 🔑+	obsolete *(adj.)*
conservation *(n.)* 🔑+ OPAL	dubious *(adj.)*	sustainable *(adj.)* 🔑+
constraint *(n.)* 🔑+ OPAL	elimination *(n.)*	thrive *(v.)* 🔑+

🔑+ Oxford 5000™ words   OPAL Oxford Phrasal Academic Lexicon

iQ PRACTICE Go online to listen and practice your pronunciation.
Practice › Unit 6 › Activity 3

WORK WITH THE READING

 A. INVESTIGATE Read the article and gather information on how we can turn trash into treasure.

GARBAGE OF EDEN

Want to be at one with nature? Take a stroll around Singapore's island of trash.

By Eric Bland

Ecotourists on Pulau Semakau

1   SINGAPORE'S only landfill is a 20-minute ferry ride south from the main island. On Pulau Semakau, coconut trees and banyan bushes line an asphalt road. Wide-bladed grass, short and soft, forms a threadbare[1] carpet. The only visible trash is a bit of driftwood on the rocky shore, marking high tide in an artificial bay. Water rushes out of the bay through a small opening, making waves in the Singapore Strait. The smell of rain is in the air.

2   You would never know that all the trash from Singapore's 4.4 million residents is being dumped here 24 hours a day, seven days a week—as it will be for the next 40 years. This is no ordinary landfill: the island doubles as a biodiversity hotspot, of all things, attracting rare species of plants and animals. It even attracts ecotourists on specially arranged guided tours. Eight years in the making, the

---

[1] **threadbare:** thin due to use or age

artificial island is setting an example for the future of **conservation** and urban planning.

3   Pulau Semakau, which is Malay for Mangrove[2] Island, is not the first isle of trash to rise from the sea. That **dubious** honor goes to a dump belonging to another island nation, the Maldives, off the southern coast of India. In 1992, the Maldives began dumping its trash wholesale into a lagoon on one of its small islands. As the island grew, it was named Thilafushi; its industries include a concrete manufacturing plant[3], a shipyard, and a methane bottler.

4   What distinguishes Semakau from Thilafushi—and most any other landfill—is that its trash has been **incinerated** and sealed off from its surroundings. Singapore burns more than 90 percent of its garbage, for reasons of space. Since its independence from Malaysia in 1965, Singapore has grown to become one of the world's 50 wealthiest nations. Not bad for a city-state little more than one-quarter the size of the smallest U.S. state, Rhode Island. Its rapid rise, however, created a huge waste problem. In the early 1990s, the government began to heavily promote a national recycling program and to campaign for industry and residents to produce less waste.

FROM TRASH TO ASH

5   Since 1999, garbage **disposal** companies have been recycling what they can—glass, plastic, electronics, even concrete—and incinerating the rest. The Tuas South incineration plant, the largest and newest of four plants run by the Singapore government, is tucked away in the southwest part of the main island. A recent visit by *New Scientist* found it surprisingly clean and fresh. The incinerator creates a weak vacuum that sucks the foul air from the trash-receiving room into the combustion[4] chamber.

6   Not that incineration is problem-free. When Singapore began burning garbage, its carbon emissions into the atmosphere rose sharply while its solid carbon deposits dropped, according to data gathered by the Oak Ridge National Laboratory in Tennessee. During the last couple of years, however, its emissions have stabilized. "Our recycling program has been more effective than we **anticipated**," says Poh Soon Hoong, general manager of the Tuas South plant.

7   Once they started burning trash, the big question was where to put the ash. In 1998, the government built a seven-kilometer-long rock bund[5] to connect two offshore islands, Semakau and Sekang, and named the new island Pulau Semakau. The complex cost about 610 million Singapore dollars (US $400 million). The first trash was dumped there in April 1999, the day after the last landfill on the main island closed. "We weren't trying to design an island that would attract tourists," says Semakau's manager, Loo Eng Por. "Disposing of the waste was a matter of survival."

8   How they do that is key to the island's success. At the receiving station, cranes[6] unload the ash from barges[7] into dumptrucks, which drive out to one of 11 interconnected bays, called *cells*, where they dump their

---

[2] **mangrove:** a tropical tree that grows in mud or at the edge of rivers
[3] **plant:** a factory
[4] **combustion:** the process of burning
[5] **bund:** a wall or embankment; a road or path across water or wet ground that is higher than the area around it
[6] **crane:** a tall machine with long arms, used to lift and move heavy objects
[7] **barge:** a large boat with a flat bottom, used to carry goods

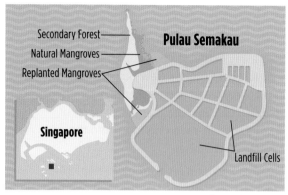

Semakau Island plan

debris (see Plan). The seawater is first pumped out of a cell, which is then lined with a layer of thick plastic to seal in the trash and prevent any leakage. Materials that can't be burned or recycled, such as asbestos, are wrapped in plastic and buried with dirt. Each month, samples are tested from the water surrounding a working cell, and so far there is no sign of any **contaminated** water seeping into the ocean. Four of the 11 cells have been filled to about two meters above sea level, then topped off with dirt and seeded with grass. A few trees dot the landscape. "Gifts from the birds," says Loo. "We plant the grass, but not the trees." Once all the cells are filled, which will be in 2030 or so, workers will start over again, dumping burnt trash onto the plots and covering it with earth, gradually forming taller hills. The government predicts that by 2045 its recycling and waste **elimination** programs will make its landfills **obsolete**.

9   One complaint about Pulau Semakau was that it called for the destruction of mangroves on part of the original island. Singapore's National Environmental Agency saw to it that the mangroves were replanted in areas adjoining the landfill. "We expected some of the new mangroves to die off," says Poh. "But they all survived. Now we have to trim them back." The island now has more than 13 hectares[8] of mangroves, which serve as a habitat for numerous species.

10   "Pulau Semakau is quite a success," says Wang Luan Keng of the Raffles Museum of Biodiversity Research at the National University of Singapore, and by all accounts the ecosystem is **thriving**—so much so that since July 2005, the island has been open for guided tours. "Visitors are stunned and amazed to see the rich biodiversity," says Ria Tan, an expert in ecology who runs wildsingapore.com, a website on nature-related activities in the area. At low tide, nature groups walk the intertidal zone, where they can see starfish, snails, and flatworms. Coral reefs are **abundant** off the western shore, and dolphins, otters, and green turtles have been spotted. Fishing groups come to catch and release grouper, barracuda, and queenfish. Birdwatchers look for the island's most famous resident, a great billed heron named Jimmy, as well as brahminy kites and mangrove whistlers[9]. In 2006, the island logged more than 6,000 visitors, and that number is expected to rise.

11   The island is crucial to Singapore's future. "People may say the Semakau landfill is bad," Tan says. "What is the alternative? Toss it to some other country? Kill off some other habitat on the mainland? The garbage has to go somewhere. I see the Semakau landfill as an example of one aspect of successful, **sustainable** urbanization." Tan shares the concerns of city planners. "The resource **constraints** that Singapore faces today will be those the rest of the world will face eventually," she says.

12   That is why the rest of the world should be watching: time will tell whether Semakau is a useful model for conservation. Meanwhile, the island's managers would like to see it become a permanent nature reserve where people can come to hike, relax, and learn about nature, without a guide. As Loo says, "It's a great place to get away from the boss."

[8] **hectare:** a measurement equal to 10,000 square meters; 2,471 acres
[9] **heron, kite, and whistler:** types of birds that live near water

B. VOCABULARY Here are some words from Reading 1. Read the sentences. Then match each bold word with its definition.

_____ 1. Many people are interested in the **conservation** of Earth's resources so that future generations will benefit from them.

_____ 2. Some countries **incinerate** their garbage before it is put into a landfill. However, this often contributes to pollution in the atmosphere.

_____ 3. The safe **disposal** of garbage is very important in order to protect the environment.

_____ 4. The government **anticipates** that local landfills will become full in the next five years.

a. *(v.)* to expect and prepare for the fact

b. *(v.)* to burn

c. *(n.)* the protection of the natural world

d. *(n.)* the process of throwing away and removing

_____ 5. The local water supply became **contaminated** because someone dumped toxic waste into the river.

_____ 6. The **elimination** of recyclable materials from people's garbage reduces the amount of trash that goes to landfills.

_____ 7. Environmental activists hope that one day everything will be recycled and landfills will become **obsolete**.

_____ 8. The Maldives has the **dubious** honor of having the first island of trash to rise from the sea.

e. *(adj.)* dirty and unsafe

f. *(adj.)* no longer used because they are out of date

g. *(adj.)* that you cannot be sure about; that is probably not good

h. *(n.)* the process of taking away

_____ 9. Although there are only a few trees on the island, they can **thrive** because they have enough sunshine and fresh water.

_____ 10. Fish are **abundant** in this lake. They are everywhere you look!

_____ 11. Many countries want long-term, **sustainable** economic growth that preserves their resources.

_____ 12. Putting **constraints** on the amount of garbage we can throw away stops us from making more trash than the environment can handle.

i. *(adj.)* plentiful and existing in large numbers

j. *(n.)* a limit

k. *(adj.)* that can be continued and is environmentally friendly

l. *(v.)* to grow and develop well

iQ PRACTICE Go online for more practice with the vocabulary.
Practice > Unit 6 > Activity 4

C. IDENTIFY Look at the questions you wrote in the Reading Skill activity on page 161. Complete the chart with the answers you were able to find in the reading.

D. EXPLAIN Write short answers to these questions. Then tell a partner or group which of your questions from the chart on page 161 helped you.

1. What kind of landfill does Singapore have?

_____

_____

2. What does Singapore do with its trash?

_____

_____

3. How is trash disposed of in Singapore's landfill?

_____

_____

4. What is the state of the environment on and around the island?

_____

_____

5. What can the rest of the world learn from the Semakau landfill?

_____

_____

E. CATEGORIZE Read the statements. Write *T* (true) or *F* (false). Then correct each false statement to make it true.

_____ 1. The landfill is located 20 minutes by car from the main island.

_____ 2. The landfill took eight years to make.

_____ 3. Singapore incinerates less than 20 percent of its garbage.

_____ 4. Garbage disposal companies incinerate glass, plastic, electronics, and concrete.

_____ 5. Singapore has four incineration plants.

_____ 6. The rock wall that created the artificial island is 17 kilometers long.

_____ 7. The landfill is made up of 11 cells, which are being filled with waste.

___ 8. Four of the eleven cells have been filled to about two meters above sea level.

___ 9. The government of Singapore plants trees on each filled cell.

___ 10. Singapore's National Environmental Agency destroyed all of the mangroves on the original island.

F. CATEGORIZE Write the number of each true and corrected statement from Activity E next to the main idea it supports.

Main ideas of Reading 1	Supporting details
1. Singapore has an environmentally friendly and unique landfill.	
2. Singapore is able to reduce a large amount of the waste going into its landfill.	
3. Singapore has carefully planned the building of its island landfill.	
4. Singapore has done a lot to maintain the natural environment on and around its landfill.	

Pulau Semakau: no ordinary landfill

G. EXPLAIN Based on the information in Reading 1, number the following events in the most logical order for creating an island out of trash. Compare your order with a partner and explain why you think your order is the most correct.

_____ a. Full landfill cells are covered with dirt and planted with grass seeds.

_____ b. Interconnected empty landfill cells are built.

_____ c. Landfill cells are full once they reach about two meters above sea level.

_____ d. Ash and debris arrive on barges and are loaded onto dump trucks by cranes.

_____ e. Once the cells are filled, workers start again by adding waste to make taller hills.

_____ f. A thick plastic liner is inserted in each empty landfill cell.

_____ g. Trucks drive to a working landfill cell to dump their loads of incinerated trash.

_____ h. Trash is burned in an incineration plant and taken to the island.

_____ i. Monthly seawater samples are taken near working cells to check for contamination.

_____ j. Seawater is pumped out of a landfill cell.

iQ PRACTICE Go online for additional reading and comprehension.
Practice › Unit 6 › Activity 5

WRITE WHAT YOU THINK

A. DISCUSS Discuss these questions in a group.

1. How did Singapore turn its trash into treasure? Is this project worth 610 million Singapore dollars (about $400 million U.S. dollars)? Why or why not?

2. Would Singapore's solution to its garbage problem work in other countries? Why or why not?

B. COMPOSE Choose one question and write a paragraph in response. Look back at your Quick Write on page 161 as you think about what you learned.

The Glorious Feeling of Fixing Something Yourself

OBJECTIVE ▶

You are going to read an article from the news magazine *The Atlantic* about repairing broken things so that they can be used again. Use the article to gather information and ideas for your Unit Assignment.

PREVIEW THE READING

A. PREVIEW Look ahead at the pictures accompanying Reading 2. Then write three or four questions that might be answered by this article.

B. QUICK WRITE Can old or broken items be repaired so that they can be used again? Write for 5–10 minutes in response. Remember to use this section for your Unit Assignment.

C. VOCABULARY Work with a partner to find these words in the reading. Circle clues in the text that help you understand the meaning of each word. Then use a dictionary to define any unknown words.

adjust *(v.)* ઈ+ OPAL	device *(n.)* ઈ+ OPAL
appliance *(n.)*	founder *(n.)* ઈ+
aptitude *(n.)*	participant *(n.)* ઈ+ OPAL
consequence *(n.)* ઈ+ OPAL	permeate *(v.)*
convene *(v.)*	the concept of *(n. phr.)* OPAL
craftsmanship *(n.)*	tinker *(v.)*

ઈ+ Oxford 5000™ words   OPAL Oxford Phrasal Academic Lexicon

iQ PRACTICE   Go online to listen and practice your pronunciation.
Practice > Unit 6 > Activity 6

WORK WITH THE READING

 A. INVESTIGATE Read the article and gather information on how we can turn trash into treasure.

THE GLORIOUS FEELING OF FIXING SOMETHING YOURSELF

When I mended my lamp at one of Portland's repair cafes, it was no longer "just" a lamp to me; I felt a fierce sense of attachment to it.

By Christina Cooke

1 Along with his broken toaster, Steve Vegdahl brought a slice of bread with him to Portland's repair cafe one day last month. By the time he left, his toaster was working again—and the sweet smell of toasted wheat **permeated** the room.

2 "This is the highlight of my day," Vegdahl said as he waited for the chrome Sunbeam, probably a 1950s model, to cool off so he could take it home. "I'm a software person; I don't have a lot of mechanical **aptitude**. I'm not good at taking things apart."

3 Since a woman named Martine Postma established the first repair cafe in Amsterdam in 2009, **the concept of** free events at which volunteers with repair skills assist **participants** with broken furniture, **appliances**, bicycles, clothing, and toys has spread far and wide.

4 More than 50 cafes operate throughout the Netherlands, France, Germany, and the United Kingdom, and, in the U.S., people have begun **convening** regularly at coffee shops and event spaces in New York, Chicago, Palo Alto, Los Angeles, Seattle, and—as of earlier this year—my hometown of Portland, Oregon, to fix busted items.

5 Repair PDX **founder** Lauren Gross, 33, says the Portland events attract people philosophically opposed to waste as well as those who simply want a favorite item to work again. Around 50 people attended the first gathering, held last May in a large,

Repair PDX volunteer Bryce Jacobson tries to twist the knob to my broken floor lamp.

airy coffee shop, she said, and about 35 have shown up to the monthly gatherings since.

6 "We're going back to some of the old values our grandparents held and moving away from mainstream consumption," said Cindy Correll, one of the cafe's other organizers. "By reusing, we're keeping things out of the waste stream and eliminating the need to make another product." Plus, she said, reusing requires fewer resources than its more publicized counterpart recycling.

7 Correll attributes the success of fix-it ventures like Repair PDX in part to the recent economic downturn. When money was tight, she said, "people started looking at things differently."

8 When I carried my broken floor lamp into Portland's December gathering, held in a historic firehouse on the north side of town, numerous repairs were already underway.

9 At one table, Stan Jones shaved rotten foam from around a stereo speaker with a thin blade, preparing

the surface for a new foam cover. At another, Brett Stern tackled an electric stand mixer, eventually offering to take the contraption home for further inspection. Laurie Sugahbeare fixed a necklace a woman had snagged on her sweater earlier that day.

10   And Bryce Jacobson wrapped plumber tape around the center rod of a broken coffee grinder to compensate for the stripped threads. "We're just buying a little time from the landfill," he said, acknowledging the jankiness[1] of the solution.

11   Jacobson, who works as a regional solid waste planner by day, said he's always liked to **tinker**. Even as a kid, he would take home appliances he found in dumpsters, and he'd disassemble and rebuild them. As a Repair PDX volunteer, Jacobson wants to instill a repair ethic in participants—and teach them the practical skills to back up the ideal.

"I just have to admire the fixing of something— I love it!" says a woman looking on as Repair PDX volunteers Bryce Jacobson (left) and Randy Greb (right) tackle a broken coffee grinder.

12   "One of the most powerful things to realize is that you can actually fix your stuff when it's not working," he said. "I like seeing people make that connection."

13   Despite recent efforts by people like Repair PDX volunteers, repair culture stands counter to the dominant[2], disposable mentality. While products like disposable diapers and paper plates are unabashedly[3] designed for the dump, many other objects—radios, televisions, microwaves, etc.—are made to be tossed as well (though they're slightly less blatant[4] about it).

14   Last month, when my washing machine began skipping the spin cycle, for example, my landlord's first response was to have a brand-new machine delivered to the house. Replacing the washer, he reasoned, would be cheaper and easier than diagnosing the problem, finding new parts, and paying a handyman to install them.

15   While I saw his point, I also regretted that the entire appliance would rust away in the landfill when probably just a small component had malfunctioned.

16   Though they're a determined bunch, Portland's fix-it volunteers say they often encounter objects that are not only impractical to repair, but impossible too.

17   "An old appliance makes it easy, because you can unscrew the bolts and take it apart," said volunteer Randy Greb, the man who revived[5] Vegdahl's toaster. "Newer stuff, you can sometimes get it apart, but it's often hard to get back together."

18   Across the board, tinkering is a challenge these days. Unlike the radios of generations past, it's hard to get inside an iPod, and once you do, you face a battery and computer chip rather than moveable components that can be tweaked and **adjusted**.

19   Even the businesses that supply the repair industry have become increasingly scarce: in an attempt to boost plunging profits, RadioShack switched in 2009 from selling cables, connectors, and widgets for garage and basement hobbyists to selling smartphones and other wireless **devices**.

20   The societal shift toward products that are untouchable, robotic, and useless when single parts break has given rise to a number of unfortunate **consequences**. First off, our landfills have swollen: the average American throws away 4.4 pounds

of trash per day, compared to 2.68 pounds in 1960, according to the U.S. Environmental Protection Agency.

21   Additionally, we've been forced into shallow relationships with our material possessions and have become increasingly dependent on manufacturers. And finally, overall **craftsmanship** has declined, and we possess fewer objects worth taking pride in and passing to the next generation. (No one's going to inherit my $32 athletic watch.)

22   Back on the Repair PDX floor, I set my damaged lamp beside Jacobson's table and explained the problem: the on/off knob had become too stiff to turn, and though I'd been able to control the light by screwing and unscrewing the bulb, that strategy had stopped working as well.

23   Jacobson removed the shade, disconnected the socket, and tried cleaning the device with a solvent. When the knob still did not rotate easily, he advised me to install a new electrical connector and showed me how I'd fasten the lamp's wires to the new piece once I'd obtained it.

24   The next day, I visited the hardware store up the road: four dollars and a few at-home adjustments later, the bulb lit up. I felt a surge of pride—and a sudden, fierce attachment to the lamp.

25   While repairing rather than replacing may have become a rebellious action over the last few decades, Jacobson sees room for the concept to grow. From coffee grinders to speakers to lawnmowers to furniture, Repair PDX alone has endowed[6] a multitude of objects with new life.

26   "It might be a fringe activity, but so was stuff like Craigslist[7] at first," he said. "It's got to start with the curious ones, the people willing to take a risk."

---

[6] **endow:** to give something
[7] **Craigslist:** a popular classified advertisements website

B. VOCABULARY Here are some words from Reading 2. Complete each sentence with a vocabulary word from the box. You may need to change the form of the word to make the sentence grammatically correct.

ACADEMIC LANGUAGE
The corpus shows that *the concept of* is often used in academic writing to specify topics and relations between ideas.

_____| OPAL
Oxford Phrasal Academic Lexicon

adjust *(v.)*	convene *(v.)*	participant *(n.)*
appliance *(n.)*	craftsmanship *(n.)*	permeate *(v.)*
aptitude *(n.)*	device *(n.)*	the concept of *(n. phr.)*
consequence *(n.)*	founder *(n.)*	tinker *(v.)*

1. After the coffeemaker was fixed, the smell of freshly brewed coffee _____ the room.

2. Although many people may think they don't have a(n) _____ for fixing broken items, with a little help and patience, they can learn to repair many different kinds of things.

3. _____ a repair cafe where volunteers help people fix things is becoming more and more popular around the world.

4. There were over 50 _____ at the repair cafe event last Saturday, and most of them were able to fix the items they brought along.

5. Instead of being thrown away when they are broken, _____ like toasters, coffeemakers, blenders, and electric kettles can easily be fixed and used again.

6. The university recycling club _____ every week in the student union building.

7. The _____ of the repair club started the organization about three years ago.

8. Many people enjoy _____ with broken appliances because fixing them results in a great sense of satisfaction.

9. The toast was popping out of the toaster too quickly. It was fixed by _____ the timer so that the bread stayed in the toaster for a longer period of time.

10. Many electronic _____, such as smartphones and tablets, are difficult for the average person to repair because they have so many complicated parts.

11. Fixing items instead of throwing them away can lead to a lot of positive _____, such as saving money and helping the environment.

12. Because of the high-quality _____, my father's wristwatch will last for many years.

iQ PRACTICE Go online for more practice with the vocabulary.
Practice > Unit 6 > Activity 7

C. IDENTIFY Match each subheading with the paragraphs it best describes.

Paragraphs	Subheadings
_____ 1. Paragraphs 1–2	a. Values of Repairing and Saving
_____ 2. Paragraphs 3–4	b. Serious Consequences of Modern Products
_____ 3. Paragraphs 5–7	c. Repair Cafes around the World
_____ 4. Paragraphs 8–9	d. Opposition to a Disposable Society
_____ 5. Paragraphs 10–12	e. Predict Future Growth
_____ 6. Paragraphs 13–15	f. Power of Tinkering
_____ 7. Paragraphs 16–19	g. Toaster Success
_____ 8. Paragraphs 20–21	h. Some Stuff Too Hard to Fix
_____ 9. Paragraphs 22–24	i. Old Lamp Fixed
_____ 10. Paragraphs 25–26	j. Variety of Items Being Repaired

D. IDENTIFY Circle the answer that best completes each statement.

1. Steve Vegdahl brought a slice of bread with him to Portland's repair cafe because ____.

    a. he wanted to test his toaster after it was repaired to make sure it worked

    b. he wanted to make the entire room smell like toast

    c. he wanted to give the Repair PDX volunteer something to eat

    d. he wanted to highlight how delicious toast could be

2. More than ____ repair cafes can be found in the Netherlands, France, Germany, and the United Kingdom.

    a. 50   b. 33   c. 35   d. 20

3. Every month, about ____ people come to the repair events in Portland.

    a. 33   b. 35   c. 50   d. 20

4. Stan Jones, Brett Stern, and Laurie Sugahbeare were fixing a ____.

    a. toaster, coffee grinder, and a necklace

    b. stereo speaker, toaster, and a lamp

    c. stereo speaker, electric stand mixer, and a necklace

    d. coffee grinder, lamp, and an athletic watch

5. Bryce Jacobson is a ____.

    a. software person   c. founder

    b. reporter   d. volunteer

6. In 2009, RadioShack stopped selling ____.

    a. smartphones and other wireless devices

    b. lamps and stereo equipment

    c. cables, connectors, and widgets

    d. toasters and coffee grinders

7. People in the United States today throw away ____ trash per day than people in the 1960s.

    a. 1.72 pounds more   c. 2.68 pounds more

    b. 6.4 pounds less   d. 4.4 pounds less

8. Christina Cooke's athletic watch is an example of ____.

    a. an object worth taking pride in

    b. something she inherited

    c. something inexpensive

    d. high-quality craftsmanship

E. IDENTIFY Match each of the following people with the information that best describes them.

____ 1. Steve Vegdahl   ____ 5. Stan Jones

____ 2. Martine Postma   ____ 6. Bryce Jacobson

____ 3. Lauren Gross   ____ 7. Randy Greb

____ 4. Cindy Correll   ____ 8. Christina Cooke

a. A person fixing an old coffee grinder with plumber tape

b. The owner of a toaster that was repaired at Repair PDX

c. A person who fixed a broken lamp by following the advice of a Repair PDX volunteer

d. A person who said that older items are easier to repair

e. The person who started the first repair cafe in Amsterdam

f. A person fixing a stereo speaker

g. The founder of the repair cafe in Portland

h. A repair cafe organizer who feels people are returning to the values of their grandparents

F. EXPLAIN Based on Reading 2, what answers can you infer to the following questions?

1. Why was getting his toaster repaired the highlight of Steve Vegdahl's day?

2. Why have repair cafes become so popular around the world?

3. How would you describe the "old values our grandparents held" that Cindy Correll talks about?

4. Why would an economic downturn contribute to the success of repair cafes?

5. Why does Jacobson want to instill a repair ethic in people?

6. Why are products such as radios, televisions, and microwaves designed to be thrown away?

7. Why did the author's landlord want to replace the broken washer instead of fixing it?

8. Why did RadioShack switch from selling cables, connectors, and widgets to smartphones and other wireless devices?

9. Why isn't anyone going to inherit the author's athletic watch?

10. Why did the author feel such a sense of pride and fierce attachment to her lamp?

G. **DISCUSS** Discuss these questions in a group. Look back at your Quick Write on page 169 as you think about what you have learned.

1. Which item fixed at the repair cafe do you think was the most valuable? Is this an item that you would fix if it ever became broken?

2. Why do you think Martine Postma started the first repair cafe?

3. Do you think that repair cafes will still be around in 10 years? Why or why not?

WORK WITH THE VIDEO

A. **PREVIEW** What can we do with old cooking oil?

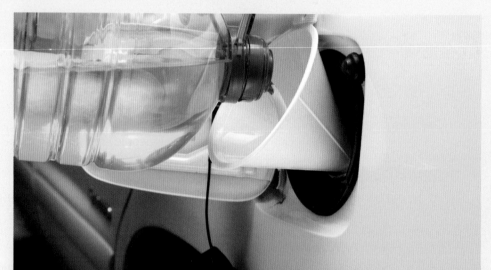

iQ RESOURCES Go online to watch the video about using vegetable oils as fuel. *Resources > Video > Unit 6 > Unit Video*

B. **EXPLAIN** Watch the video two or three times. Then answer the questions based on the information in the video.

1. How does the video describe the molecular structure of vegetable oil?

2. What is the main problem with using old vegetable oils as fuels?

3. What is a solution to the main problem with using old vegetable oils as fuels?

4. How does the video describe the process for releasing energy from diesel and vegetable oil?

C. **EXTEND** What are the benefits of using old vegetable oil as a fuel? Use the information in the video, as well as your own knowledge and ideas, to support your response.

WRITE WHAT YOU THINK

WRITING TIP
In Unit 5, you learned about connecting information. Use linear information structure or constant information structure in your response.

SYNTHESIZE Think about Reading 1, Reading 2, and the video as you discuss these questions. Then choose one question and write a paragraph in response.

1. Three different methods of turning trash into treasure were presented by the readings and video in this unit: (1) incinerating waste and creating an artificial island, (2) fixing broken items so they can be used again, and (3) using old cooking oil as engine fuel. What are some positive and negative aspects for each of these options? Which one do you think is the best?

2. Who do you think is the most effective at disposing of trash or finding ways to turn it into treasure—governments, individuals, or large companies? Why?

VOCABULARY SKILL Suffixes

A **suffix** is an ending that is added to a root word. There are several **suffixes that form nouns**. Some of them indicate people or concrete objects or things, and others indicate more abstract nouns. The *Oxford Advanced American Dictionary for learners of English* has a list of suffixes with their meanings and uses. Understanding the meaning of suffixes will help you build your vocabulary by giving you clues to the meaning and function of new words.

Noun suffixes	Suffix meaning	Examples
-ation / -tion	an action or process, or the result of it	conservation, production
-er / -or	a person or thing that	manufacturer, editor
-ist	a person who does or believes in something	ecotourist
-ty / -ity	the quality or state of	biodiversity, clarity
-ment	the action or result of	agreement

A. APPLY Complete the chart with the correct form of each noun by using the most appropriate suffix from the skill box. Use your dictionary to help you.

Verb	Not a person / Abstract idea	Person or thing
1. incinerate	incineration	incinerator
2. present		
3. fertilize		
4. invest		
5. invent		

B. APPLY Read the paragraph. Write the correct noun form of each word to complete the sentence.

Waste disposal is a big issue all around the world. Many countries have created new _____regulations_____ (regulate) about recycling that encourage

_____ (retail) and _____ (manufacture)
       2   3

to recycle their waste. This recycling keeps waste materials from being

burned in _____ (incinerate) or dumped into landfills. The
                              4

_____ (eliminate) of a large amount of garbage helps protect the
          5

environment and the _____ (pure) of nearby lakes and rivers.
                              6

Many of these retail and manufacturing companies have now started working

with people such as _____ (environmental) to think of more
                        7

ways to lower the amount of waste they produce. Also, _____
                                            8

(invest) are putting their money into recycling companies. With the increase in

environmental awareness around the world, their _____ (invest)
                                          9

are starting to make a profit. As greater numbers of _____
                                          10

(corporate) become aware of the importance of recycling, recycling programs

are sure to become more popular.

iQ PRACTICE Go online for more practice with suffixes.
Practice > Unit 6 > Activity 8

WRITING

OBJECTIVE ▶ At the end of this unit, you will write a business plan. This business plan will include information from the readings, the unit video, and your own ideas.

WRITING SKILL Paraphrasing

Paraphrasing means putting someone else's words into your own words. A good paraphrase keeps the same meaning and is about the same length as the original text. Paraphrasing is a useful skill for both studying and integrating other people's ideas into your writing. However, it is important to cite the sources for other people's ideas that you use in your writing, even when you are paraphrasing.

Here are some tips for effective paraphrasing.

- Read over the text you want to paraphrase several times in order to completely understand it.

- Take notes in your own words.

- Find good synonyms for some of the key vocabulary in the text.

  Around 50 people **attended** the first **gathering**.
  Approximately 50 people **went to** the first **meeting**.

- Write the paraphrase using your own notes without looking at the original.

- Change the grammatical structure of your paraphrase by:

  Changing the order of the clauses
  Since its independence from Malaysia, Singapore has become wealthy.
  Singapore has become wealthy **since its independence from Malaysia**.

  Changing to active or passive voice
  Martine Postma **established** the first repair cafe in Amsterdam in 2009.
  The first repair cafe **was established** by Martine Postma in 2009.

  Changing the word forms
  Pulau Semakau is quite a **success**.
  Pulau Semakau is quite **successful**.

Check your paraphrases against the original texts to make sure that they are similar in content, but different in terms of vocabulary and grammar.

A. RESTATE Rewrite each sentence according to the instructions. (Read each sentence carefully in order to fully understand the meaning.)

1. Find synonyms for the underlined words. Change the order of the clauses.

   Despite recent <u>efforts</u> by people like Repair PDX volunteers, repair culture stands counter to the <u>dominant</u>, <u>disposable mentality</u> (Cooke, 2014).

2. Find synonyms for the underlined words. Change from the active to the passive voice. Move the prepositional phrase "in the future" to the end of the paraphrased sentence.

   In the future, ecotourists will <u>visit</u> the island of Pulau Semakau on <u>specially arranged</u> guided <u>tours</u> (Bland, 2007).

3. Find a synonym for the underlined word. Change from active to passive voice. Move the final clause to the beginning of the sentence. Think of a different way of stating "according to the U.S. Environmental Protection Agency."

   The <u>average</u> American throws away 4.4 pounds of <u>trash</u> per day, compared to 2.68 pounds in 1960, according to the U.S. Environmental Protection Agency (Cooke, 2014).

TIP FOR SUCCESS

When paraphrasing someone else's words or ideas in your writing, you should always reference the source, or tell the reader where the ideas came from. This will help you avoid plagiarism.

B. RESTATE Paraphrase each pair of sentences. Begin by reading the sentences carefully and taking notes. Then write the paraphrase without looking at the original. Use a variety of techniques as appropriate.

1. All the trash from Singapore's 4.4 million residents is dumped on an artificial island. This island could become one of Singapore's main tourist attractions in the near future (Bland, 2007).

   According to Bland, Singapore dumps the garbage from its 4.4 million citizens on an artificial island. In the near future, this island could become one of Singapore's main tourist spots.

2. Singapore burns more than 90 percent of its garbage for reasons of space. Singapore will need to recycle more of its garbage to lower carbon emissions in the atmosphere (Bland, 2007).

3. Along with his broken toaster, Steve Vegdahl brought a slice of bread with him to Portland's repair cafe one day last month. By the time he left, his toaster was working again—and the sweet smell of toasted wheat permeated the room (Cooke, 2014).

4. While repairing rather than replacing may have become a rebellious action over the last few decades, Jacobson sees room for the concept to grow. From coffee grinders to speakers to lawnmowers to furniture, Repair PDX alone has endowed a multitude of objects with new life (Cooke, 2014).

References

Bland, E. (2007, April 11). Garbage of Eden. *New Scientist*.

Cooke, C. (2014, January 10). The glorious feeling of fixing something yourself. *The Atlantic*. Retrieved from http://www.theatlantic.com

C. WRITING MODEL Read the model business plan, noting the underlined paraphrased ideas taken from Reading 1 and an article found on the Internet. Look back at Reading 1 on pages 162–164 to find the original wording of phrases 1–3, and record the original quotes on the lines that follow the business plan (on page 183). Then analyze with a partner how the quotes were turned into paraphrases.

The Clever Compost Company:
Small Compost Bins for People Who Love the Environment

Introduction

The Clever Compost Company is an exciting new environmentally friendly company that manufactures small compost bins made of 100% recycled plastic. Compost bins are containers into which people can put their everyday kitchen scraps, such as vegetable peels, coffee grounds, and many other things, rather than throwing them away. This food waste will soon turn into valuable compost that can be used as soil for growing plants.

The Clever Compost Company believes in the motto that garbage can be turned into gold. This approach has been inspired by what has been done in Singapore with its garbage. Singapore has created a nature-filled island out of incinerated trash. (1) This island is an important place for many different kinds of natural life, and it is surprisingly appealing to infrequently seen types of animals and plants (Bland, 2007). Just like in Singapore, the Clever Compost Company wants to help people create a little natural oasis out of unwanted trash.

Business Description

With the goal of diverting garbage from local landfills and creating high-quality compost, the Clever Compost Company makes compost bins that are a conveniently small size for individuals living in apartments and townhouses with no gardens. The compost bins are made of 100% recycled plastic from old yogurt containers, margarine tubs, and other similar plastics. This product has been inspired by the success of TerraCycle. At TerraCycle, boxes of Capri Sun drink pouches, old computer components, and cookie packages have been recycled into pencil cases, picture frames, and kites, respectively (Feldman, 2009). However, TerraCycle does not make compost bins, and the Clever Compost Company fills this gap.

With landfills all around the world reaching their capacity, people everywhere need to start throwing away less. As a result, businesses that come up with a solution to prevent trash from being thrown away are going to be an excellent investment. A good example of what the future may look like can be found in Singapore, where (2) the limits on resources now are the same problems that other places around the globe will have to deal with soon (Bland, 2007). However, one of the drawbacks of Singapore's solution is that they burn their garbage. (3) When Singapore started to incinerate its trash, the amount of carbon it released into the air increased rapidly (Bland, 2007). In an age of global warming, it is not a good idea to release too many greenhouse gases into the atmosphere. The Clever Compost Company has one solution—the carbon in household kitchen waste is kept in solid form as compost that can be used to grow plants, which remove carbon dioxide from the atmosphere.

Finally, the creativity of this idea, coupled with its environmental goals, is sure to make money. Although TerraCycle has struggled from time to time, since 2004, Tom Szaky has made money: inventive recycling has contributed to TerraCycle's income annually increasing twofold (Feldman, 2009). The industry as a whole appears ready to break into consistent profitability. More importantly, the Clever Compost Company will avoid mistakes such as when the head of TerraCycle, instead of making a recycled tote bag in-house, choose to make them with a local producer that billed him $20 for each bag (Feldman, 2009).

Sales and Marketing

The potential customers for this product are environmentally conscious individuals living in apartments and townhouses with only a small amount of outdoor space, such as a balcony. In the first year of production, the compost bins will be available in hardware stores and garden centers across North America, but there are plans for global distribution.

Conclusion

The Clever Compost Company is set to create a highly successful product made of 100% recycled plastic that produces compost, instead of garbage headed toward a landfill. The small size of these compost bins makes them convenient for the majority of people living in city apartments today, and they help to fight global warming by keeping carbon in its solid form and avoiding incineration. All of these factors, plus the need for environmentally conscious companies, combine to create a financially solid investment in a product that will be a big seller in North America, and eventually around the world.

References

Bland, E. (2007, April 11). Garbage of Eden. *New Scientist*.

Feldman, L. (2009, March 25). Garbage mogul makes millions from trash. *CNN Money*. Retrieved from http://money.cnn.com

Quote 1: _____

_____

_____

Quote 2: _____

_____

_____

Quote 3: _____

_____

_____

D. RESTATE Choose three of the paraphrases in the model business plan, and rewrite them once more into your own words.

1. _____

_____

_____

2. _____

_____

_____

3. _____

_____

_____

iQ PRACTICE Go online for more practice with paraphrasing.
Practice > Unit 6 > Activity 9

⚙ CRITICAL THINKING STRATEGY

Synthesizing information

The Unit Assignment asks you to develop a business plan for an innovative new company. In order to do this, you will synthesize information from the unit with your own ideas and prior knowledge to create something new.

This critical thinking skill involves putting together, reorganizing, and rearranging information from a variety of sources to support your own ideas. For example, you could synthesize information from the readings and video in this unit as well as what you already know to create an effective business plan for a recycling company. As you are synthesizing information, you may have to infer the relationships between your sources of information. By synthesizing information in this manner, you can draw stronger conclusions because your information is coming from a variety of sources and you are making connections between different ideas.

Consider the following example that synthesizes information from Readings 1 and 2 in this unit to support the idea that trash can be turned into treasure:

Turning Trash into Treasure

Trash can be turned into treasure. For example, in Singapore, the country's garbage is being turned into an artificial island. This island is a beautiful place with plants and animals. Instead of an ugly landfill that no one wants to visit, it is a thriving environment that attracts tourists (Bland, 2007). Repair cafes are another example of places where trash can become treasure. At these cafes, people fix broken items, such as speakers, lawnmowers, and furniture, with the help of volunteers. Instead of going into a landfill, these items can be used again (Cooke, 2014). It seems like good things can be made out of old trash.

References

Bland, E. (2007, April 11). Garbage of Eden. *New Scientist.*

Cooke, C. (2014, January 10). The glorious feeling of fixing something yourself. *The Atlantic.*

iQ PRACTICE Go online to watch the Critical Thinking Video and check your comprehension. *Practice > Unit 6 > Activity 10*

E. SYNTHESIZE Write a short paragraph on the benefits of turning trash into treasure. To support the main idea of your paragraph, think of examples from your own experiences and knowledge. Then synthesize these examples with information from the unit readings, video, or other sources to create a well-developed paragraph. You may include some of the rewritten paraphrases you created for Activity D on page 183.

We use modals to talk about possibilities in the future and to make predictions. The choice of modal depends on how certain you are about the possibility of something happening in the future.

Absolutely certain	The local landfill **will** be full in ten years. People **won't** be able to get free bags in grocery stores anymore. We **cannot** keep making more trash without hurting the environment. With the building of the new nature reserve, the environmentalists **couldn't** be happier.
Very certain	With the new laws, people **should** recycle their garbage. The fertilizer company **should not** go bankrupt because new investors have been found. People are very concerned about the environment, so our new company **ought to** make a lot of money on our green products.
Somewhat certain	More people **may** start buying reusable bags if they become cheaper. Students **may not** buy our new recycled paper products because they are more expensive than regular paper products.
Less certain	The business **could** be making bracelets out of recycled toothbrushes by next year. Unrecyclable plastic **might** be banned in the next few years. Consumers **might not** buy nonrecyclable products in the future.

iQ RESOURCES **Go online to watch the Grammar Skill Video.**
Resources › Video › Unit 6 › Grammar Skill Video

A. APPLY Check (✓) the most appropriate level of certainty for each prediction.

	Absolutely	Very	Somewhat	Less
1. The environment cannot be saved unless everyone starts recycling waste.	☐	☐	☐	☐
2. A lot of recyclable products might be banned from landfills soon.	☐	☐	☐	☐
3. Old-fashioned incandescent lightbulbs won't be sold in stores by 2050.	☐	☐	☐	☐
4. The city should start seeing the benefits of its new recycling program soon.	☐	☐	☐	☐
5. If something isn't done soon, the landfill ought to fill up quickly.	☐	☐	☐	☐
6. Consumers may be more interested in buying recycled products if they become less expensive.	☐	☐	☐	☐
7. The recycling program is a big success, and the mayor couldn't be happier.	☐	☐	☐	☐
8. A recycling depot could be built in the neighborhood if more people wanted one.	☐	☐	☐	☐

B. INTERPRET Read each green business idea and write a prediction about the success or failure of the business. Then write a reason for your prediction. Use modals of possibility in your predictions and reasons.

1. Recycle used toothbrushes into fashion bracelets for women.

   Prediction: _This idea might not be successful._

   Reason: _People may not want to wear somebody else's old toothbrush_
   around their wrists.

2. Make umbrellas out of recycled newspapers.

   Prediction: _____

   Reason: _____

3. Pay people to recycle their garbage (a garbage recycling company).

   Prediction: _____

   Reason: _____

4. Collect used coffee grounds from cafes and sell them to gardeners as fertilizer.

   Prediction: _____

   Reason: _____

5. Turn used cooking oil into gasoline for cars.

   Prediction: _____

   Reason: _____

C. COMPOSE You live in a large city, and the only landfill in the area is almost full. What is the future going to be like in this city? Write five sentences predicting the future. Use a different modal of possibility in each sentence.

A new landfill might be built on a farm outside of the city.

iQ PRACTICE Go online for more practice with modals of possibility.
Practice > Unit 6 > Activities 11–12

UNIT ASSIGNMENT

OBJECTIVE ▶

Write a business plan

In this assignment, you will pretend to start an innovative new company that reuses or recycles garbage. You must find investors for your company. As you prepare your business plan, think about the Unit Question, "How can we turn trash into treasure?" Use information from Reading 1, Reading 2, the unit video, and your work in this unit to support your ideas. Refer to the Self-Assessment checklist on page 188.

---

iQ PRACTICE Go to the online Writing Tutor to read a model business plan.
Practice > Unit 6 > Activity 13

PLAN AND WRITE

A. BRAINSTORM What kind of businesses turn trash into treasure? In a group or with a partner, discuss these questions. Then use a cluster diagram like the one below to map your ideas for one business.

1. What are three possible businesses that recycle or reuse trash?
2. What kind of services or products would each company provide?
3. Why would each business be attractive to potential investors?
4. Who would the customers be, and how would they buy the product or service?

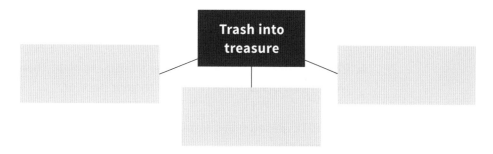

B. PLAN Choose a business from Activity A. Then read these questions, which are commonly asked by investors before they invest in a new business. With a partner, answer each question to prepare to write your business plan for the new company that you want to start.

1. What is the name of your business? _____

2. What kind of business is it? _____

3. What product or service are you going to provide? _____
   _____

4. Why is this business a great idea? _____
   _____

5. What are the main goals for this business? _____
   _____
   _____

6. Who are the customers going to be? _____
   _____

7. Where will you sell the product or service? _____
   _____

iQ RESOURCES Go online to download and complete the outline for your business plan. *Resources > Writing Tools > Unit 6 > Outline*

C. WRITE Use your planning notes to write your business plan.

1. Write a business plan for a company that reuses or recycles garbage. Use examples and paraphrase when necessary.

2. Look at the Self-Assessment checklist below to guide your writing.

iQ PRACTICE Go online to the Writing Tutor to write your assignment.
Practice > Unit 6 > Activity 14

REVISE AND EDIT

iQ RESOURCES Go online to download the peer review worksheet.
Resources > Writing Tools > Unit 6 > Peer Review Worksheet

A. PEER REVIEW Read your partner's business plan. Then use the peer review worksheet. Discuss the review with your partner.

B. REWRITE Based on your partner's review, revise and rewrite your business plan.

C. EDIT Complete the Self-Assessment checklist as you prepare to write the final draft of your business plan. Be prepared to hand in your work or discuss it in class.

SELF-ASSESSMENT	Yes	No
Does the business plan build a convincing argument using facts, reasons, and examples?	☐	☐
Has information from Reading 1 and Reading 2 been paraphrased correctly where appropriate?	☐	☐
Are modals of possibility used correctly to express predictions?	☐	☐
Do nouns have the correct suffixes where appropriate?	☐	☐
Does the business plan include vocabulary from the unit?	☐	☐
Did you check the text for punctuation, spelling, and grammar?	☐	☐

D. REFLECT Discuss these questions with a partner or group.

1. What is something new you learned in this unit?

2. Look back at the Unit Question—How can we turn trash into treasure? Is your answer different now than when you started the unit? If yes, how is it different? Why?

iQ PRACTICE Go to the online discussion board to discuss the questions.
Practice > Unit 6 > Activity 15

TRACK YOUR SUCCESS

iQ PRACTICE   Go online to check the words and phrases you have learned in this unit. *Practice > Unit 6 > Activity 16*

Check (✓) the skills you learned. If you need more work on a skill, refer to the page(s) in parentheses.

READING	☐ I can anticipate content through questions. (p. 160)
VOCABULARY	☐ I can recognize noun suffixes. (p. 177)
WRITING	☐ I can paraphrase. (p. 179)
CRITICAL THINKING	☐ I can synthesize information from a variety of sources. (p. 184)
GRAMMAR	☐ I can recognize and use modals of possibility. (p. 185)

OBJECTIVE ▶   ☐ I can gather information and ideas to prepare a business plan that describes a new recycling company to potential investors.

History

How do new discoveries and inventions change the world?

A. Discuss these questions with your classmates.

1. What was the most important discovery or invention from the last 200 years?

2. How did that discovery or invention change the world?

3. Look at the photo. What discoveries or inventions do you see? How did they impact people's lives?

B. Listen to *The Q Classroom* online. Then answer these questions.

1. How did the students answer the question?

2. Do you agree or disagree with their ideas? Why or why not?

iQ PRACTICE Go to the online discussion board to discuss the Unit Question with your classmates. *Practice ⟩ Unit 7 ⟩ Activity 1*

UNIT OBJECTIVE ▶ Read an article from *The Oxford Encyclopedia of the Modern World* and an article from *The Atlantic* news magazine about inventions and change. Gather information and ideas to develop a summary and response essay based on an informational text.

READING

READING 1

OBJECTIVE ▶

The First Industrial Revolution

You are going to read an entry from *The Oxford Encyclopedia of the Modern World* about the industrial revolution in Great Britain. Use the encyclopedia entry to gather information and ideas for your Unit Assignment.

PREVIEW THE READING

A. PREVIEW What are some of the major events that took place during the Industrial Revolution? For example, James Watt designed a better steam engine. List three more events. As you read, check to see if your events are similar to the examples presented in the reading.

1. _____

2. _____

3. _____

B. QUICK WRITE How do new discoveries and inventions change the world? Write for 5–10 minutes in response. Before you start, spend a couple of minutes planning what you are going to write about. Remember to use this section for your Unit Assignment.

C. VOCABULARY Check (✓) the words or phrases you know. Then work with a partner to locate each word or phrase in the reading. Use clues to help define the words or phrases you don't know. Check your definitions in the dictionary.

breakthrough *(n.)* 🔑+	provision *(n.)* 🔑+
encompass *(v.)* 🔑+	sector *(n.)* 🔑+ OPAL
fundamental *(adj.)* 🔑+ OPAL	sequence *(n.)* 🔑+
impact *(n.)* 🔑+ OPAL	stimulus *(n.)* 🔑+
in particular *(prep. phr.)* OPAL	textile *(n.)*
innovation *(n.)* 🔑+	transition *(n.)* 🔑+ OPAL

🔑+ Oxford 5000™ words   OPAL Oxford Phrasal Academic Lexicon

iQ PRACTICE Go online to listen and practice your pronunciation.
Practice > Unit 7 > Activity 2

A. INVESTIGATE Read the encyclopedia entry and gather information on how new discoveries and inventions change the world.

The First Industrial Revolution

Nineteenth-century steam locomotive

1   The expression *industrial revolution* as a generic term refers to the emergence, during the **transition** from a preindustrial to an industrial society, of modern economic growth. Talking about "revolution" does not mean that this process would necessarily be sudden and fast. It primarily indicates that the process was deep and pervasive. The first industrial nation was Britain. There the transition took roughly from the 1750s to the 1850s. Per capita income really started growing only after the 1840s, when growth rose to more than 1 percent a year.

Phases

2   Industrialization is an ongoing process. One often comes across references to a first, "classic," industrial revolution in Britain, of coal, iron, and cotton, and later of steam and railways; to a second one, from the 1870s onward, in which steel, the chemical industry, and electricity became more prominent; and to a third one, already well into the 20th century, of automobiles and motorization. This article deals only with the first wave of industrialization, **encompassing** various regions in western Europe. Specific references will be to the British case.

3   All preindustrial economies were subject to what have become known as Malthusian constraints. The English economist Thomas Malthus (1766–1834) pointed out that in all known history the **provision** of the basic needs of the population—that is, food, clothing, shelter, and energy—depended almost entirely on the quantity and quality of the available land. For the first three needs, this is obvious. With regard to energy, the bulk of it was provided by human and animal muscle power and by heat produced by burning wood. Besides that, there was the contribution of wind and water power. These were not directly dependent on the land. Considering the technological possibilities of the time and the inherent limits of wind and water power, their contribution could be only relatively minor.

Energy, Power, and Industry

4   With industrialization this changed—first and foremost because of **fundamental** changes in the quantities and the characteristics of the energy that was used. At the heart of this change lay the phenomenal increase in the use of fossil fuel, in this case coal. In Britain, total annual consumption increased from 3 million to more than 200 million tons between 1700 and 1914. Two hundred million tons of coal produce about as much heat as 500 million tons of firewood. That is the annual sustainable production of a forest of 13 times the size of England and Wales.

5   The massive availability of cheap energy allowed for an increase in the production of materials that are quintessential[1] in a modern economy but whose production is extremely energy intensive. British

---

[1] **quintessential:** most typical or representative

output of pig iron, to give only the most important example, between 1700 and 1850, rose from less than 30,000 tons to 2.25 million tons. There were similar increases in the output of glass, brick, and, later, steel. The dependency on land, so crucial in a Malthusian economy, was further reduced by the introduction of new materials like artificial fertilizers and dyes, which were made of minerals, and by the use of gas lighting.

Interior of a nineteenth-century textile factory

6   What opened up an entirely new window of opportunities was the fact that coal also began to provide power as fuel for steam engines. This marked a fundamental **breakthrough** in the history of energy. The **impact** would be enormous. Again, the British case can serve as an illustration. In 1900, stationary steam power alone provided an amount of energy equivalent to that of about 420 million adult men working eight hours per day. Not only did it increase the total amount of power enormously, steam also made possible its concentrated use at a level that in a Malthusian regime simply was unimaginable.

7   Steam engines after some time also were used to move trains and ships. This was to change transport beyond recognition. For the first time in history, a truly global division of labor evolved. Countries that did not industrialize could still become very involved in industrialization by providing industrializing countries with foodstuffs and raw materials or by buying their industrial products.

Production and Transportation

8   The fundamental changes in the way that goods were produced and transported, and in the kinds of goods that were produced, were bound to have consequences for the organization of production. In this respect, probably nothing has come to symbolize industrialization more than the factory. As a site of centralized mass production by means of iron machines that use steam power, it indeed is a telling symbol of a new mode of production. In quantitative terms, however, the number of big factories and the number of people actually working there continued to be quite small during the first three-quarters of the 19th century. Because of the huge size of inputs and outputs, factories nevertheless had a big impact on the rest of the manufacturing **sector**. In agriculture, machinery and fertilizer began to have a major impact only well into the second half of the 19th century. Changes in the transport sector—more than anything else the application of the steam engine—very quickly were consequential for all sectors of the economy.

9   The complex set of changes called *industrialization* triggered a **sequence** of increasing returns and turned growth from the exception into the rule, in this case while population increased faster than ever before. Industrialization led to big societal changes. With the passing of time, industrialization led to increasing urbanization and fundamental changes in the occupational structure of the economy. The relative weight of agriculture in the economy decreased, while that of the modern industrial sector increased.

10   Without a set of technological breakthroughs, industrialization would have been impossible. In that sense, its direct causes have to be sought in the specific history of technology and science in western Europe. Many **innovations** during the very beginning of the process of industrialization may not have been based on science, but the fundamental breakthroughs in the production and use of energy were. The actual technological breakthroughs that are normally associated with

the first Industrial Revolution almost all originated in Britain. The challenge to find solutions for bottlenecks in the supply of energy and in **textile** production was particularly acute there. The rather porous demarcations[2] among the worlds of scientists, engineers, artisans, and entrepreneurs clearly helped in actually finding those solutions.

11   The causes mentioned so far are primarily internal to western Europe. They were the most important ones. Intercontinental trade for most of the industrializing countries in the first three-quarters of the 19th century was still fairly marginal. But in the globalizing economy of the period, international connections, of course, played their part. Nothing can illustrate that better than Britain's biggest industry, the production of cotton textiles. An important **stimulus** behind its expansion lay in the effort to outperform Indian textile producers. All its raw material had to be imported from other continents. About half of its production went abroad, much of it to other continents. Slaves, who were used to produce raw cotton in the southern parts of the United States, originally came from Africa. The cotton-textile industry definitely is one that has to be analyzed in global terms.

Broader Changes

12   Whatever its causes, the impact of the first Industrial Revolution was not confined to Britain or western Europe. It was truly global. **In particular,** Japan and the so-called Four Asian Tigers (Hong Kong, Singapore, South Korea, and Taiwan) have managed to catch up, and some countries, like China and India, now appear to be taking off.

[2] **porous demarcations:** imprecise boundaries, allowing the easy movement of people and ideas

B. **VOCABULARY** Here are some words and phrases from Reading 1. Complete the sentences using each word at least once. You may need to change the form of the word or phrase to make the sentence grammatically correct.

ACADEMIC LANGUAGE
The corpus shows that *the impact of* and *an impact on* are often used in academic writing to show causal and other relationships.

_____| OPAL
Oxford Phrasal Academic Lexicon

breakthrough (n.)	in particular (prep. phr.)	sequence (n.)
encompass (v.)	innovation (n.)	stimulus (n.)
fundamental (adj.)	provision (n.)	textile (n.)
impact (n.)	sector (n.)	transition (n.)

1. The _____ of events during the first Industrial Revolution started with the invention of the steam engine in the early 1700s and ended with a new way of making steel in the mid-1800s.

2. The first Industrial Revolution saw the _____ of Great Britain from a largely agricultural society to an industrial society.

3. The industrial _____ of the economy became more important than agriculture in the years between 1750 and 1850.

4. The large increase in factories and railways brought about _____ changes in people's lives, such as where they worked and how they moved around.

5. During the Industrial Revolution, the _____ of energy no longer depended on the amount of available land to gather wood.

6. The first Industrial Revolution _____ many different industries, such as coal, iron, cotton, and railways.

7. The invention of the spinning jenny was a major _____ during the Industrial Revolution. It helped people spin more wool or cotton than ever before.

8. There were many important inventors who contributed to the Industrial Revolution. _____, James Watt improved the steam engine and made it more efficient.

9. The need for cost effective and efficient transportation during the Industrial Revolution was an important _____ for the building of railways across Great Britain.

10. The production of cotton _____ was a major industry in Great Britain during the Industrial Revolution.

11. The invention of the telegraph, which sent messages over a wire, was an important _____ in communication technology during the Industrial Revolution.

12. The _____ of the Industrial Revolution is still being felt today. Before the Industrial Revolution, most people lived in rural areas. Now most people live in cities.

iQ PRACTICE Go online for more practice with the vocabulary.
Practice > Unit 7 > Activity 3

C. **IDENTIFY** Match each of these paragraphs from the encyclopedia entry with their main idea.

Paragraph 1: ____   Paragraph 4: ____   Paragraph 6: ____   Paragraph 10: ____

Paragraph 3: ____   Paragraph 5: ____   Paragraph 9: ____   Paragraph 11: ____

a. Before the Industrial Revolution, people's basic needs, such as food, clothing, housing, and energy, depended on how much land was available.

b. Technological discoveries and inventions to solve certain problems made the Industrial Revolution possible in Britain.

c. During the Industrial Revolution, people could make a lot more things, such as iron, glass, and brick, because of a large amount of inexpensive energy sources.

d. The Industrial Revolution in Britain was a time of general economic growth from 1750 to 1850 that changed the country into an industrial society.

e. Intercontinental trade played a role in certain industries during the Industrial Revolution, such as in the production of textiles.

f. Faster and bigger growth became normal during the Industrial Revolution.

g. During the Industrial Revolution, people started using a lot more coal.

h. Steam engines using coal provided a lot more power than was possible before the Industrial Revolution.

D. EXPLAIN What is the overall main idea of Reading 1? Write down your ideas in one or two sentences and compare with a partner.

_____

_____

E. EXPLAIN Refer back to the reading as you answer these questions. For each response, indicate the paragraph number(s) where you found your answers.

1. What industries were mainly involved in the first Industrial Revolution? (Paragraph: _____)

_____

2. Before the Industrial Revolution, what were some of the possible sources of power? (Paragraph: _____)

_____

3. What are some examples of materials needed for an industrialized economy that could be produced because of inexpensive energy? (Paragraph: _____)

_____

4. Why was the use of coal to provide power as fuel for steam engines a fundamental breakthrough in the history of energy? (Paragraph: _____)

_____

5. How could countries that were not industrialized still take part in the Industrial Revolution? (Paragraph: _____)

_____

6. Why do factories symbolize industrialization? (Paragraph: _____)

_____

7. What were some societal changes that resulted from the Industrial Revolution? (Paragraph: _____)

_____

8. Why did the technological breakthroughs associated with the Industrial Revolution take place in Britain? (Paragraph: _____)

_____

9. What caused the cotton textile industry in Britain to expand during the Industrial Revolution? (Paragraph: _____)

_____

10. Why does the cotton textile industry in Britain during the Industrial Revolution have to be analyzed in global terms? (Paragraph: _____)

_____

F. EXTEND Look back at your Quick Write on page 192. How do new discoveries and inventions change the world? Add any new ideas or information you learned from the reading.

iQ PRACTICE Go online for additional reading and comprehension.
Practice > Unit 7 > Activity 4

WRITE WHAT YOU THINK

A. DISCUSS Discuss the questions in a group. Think about the Unit Question, "How do new discoveries and inventions change the world?"

1. What do you think was the most important discovery or invention during the first Industrial Revolution? Why?

2. Do you think the societal changes that took place during the Industrial Revolution were positive or negative? Explain your answer.

3. How is the Industrial Revolution still affecting people's lives today?

B. COMPOSE Choose one of the questions from Activity A and write a response. Look back at your Quick Write on page 192 as you think about what you learned.

Question: _____

My response: _____

_____

_____

_____

READING SKILL Identifying the author's intent

Authors can have many different reasons for writing. These reasons are the author's **intent**, or purpose. Everything you read has a purpose, and authors may have more than one purpose for writing something. They may want to inform, persuade, and/or entertain their readers. Authors do this through a combination of their writing style, the inclusion of certain facts and ideas, and their choice of particular words.

This chart gives three basic reasons authors have for writing something. Use the key indicators and examples to help guide you in judging an author's intent. Learning how to identify an author's intent will help you better analyze texts and become a more critical reader.

	Information	Persuasion	Entertainment
Intent	Explains, describes, or informs the reader about something	Tries to make the reader believe a particular idea, think in a certain way, or take action	Entertains the reader
Style	Expository writing	Persuasive writing	Narrative and descriptive writing
Key indicators	Provides mostly factual information or instructions on how to do something	Contains opinions, feelings, and beliefs	Creates an image in the reader's mind that may make the reader feel a strong emotion
Examples	Textbooks, lab reports, directions, cookbooks, some newspaper and magazine articles	Some newspaper and magazine articles, editorials, advertisements, opinion essays, academic essays	Short stories, novels, anecdotes, poems, comics, graphic novels

A. IDENTIFY Read these excerpts from Reading 1. Decide if the author is trying to inform (*I*), persuade (*P*), or entertain (*E*). You may decide that more than one option may be correct. Provide a reason for your choice(s) and a reason for excluding the other option(s), if applicable. Be prepared to defend your answer.

____ 1. The expression *industrial revolution* as a generic term refers to the emergence, during the transition from a preindustrial to an industrial society, of modern economic growth.

____ 2. Considering the technological possibilities of the time and the inherent limits of wind and water power, their contribution could be only relatively minor.

____ 3. British output of pig iron, to give only the most important example, between 1700 and 1850, rose from less than 30,000 tons to 2.25 million tons.

____ 4. The fundamental changes in the way that goods were produced and transported, and in the kinds of goods that were produced, were bound to have consequences for the organization of production.

____ 5. Without a set of technological breakthroughs, industrialization would have been impossible.

____ 6. In particular, Japan and the so-called Four Asian Tigers (Hong Kong, Singapore, South Korea, and Taiwan) have managed to catch up, and some countries, like China and India, now appear to be taking off.

B. DISCUSS Work in a group. Discuss these questions about the author's intent. Be sure to give reasons for your answers.

1. In your opinion, why did the author write this encyclopedia entry about the first Industrial Revolution?

2. Find examples from the encyclopedia entry to support your opinion of the author's purpose(s).

3. How does identifying the author's intent help you become a better reader?

iQ PRACTICE Go online for more practice with identifying the author's intent. *Practice > Unit 7 > Activity 5*

TIP FOR SUCCESS

When you read a newspaper or a magazine, thinking about the author's intent will help you decide on the trustworthiness and reliability of what you are reading.

Glass Is Humankind's Most Important Material

OBJECTIVE ▶

You are going to read an article from the news magazine *The Atlantic* about how glass has changed the world more than any material. Use the article to gather information and ideas for your Unit Assignment.

PREVIEW THE READING

A. PREVIEW How has glass changed the world? List three ways that people use glass. As you read, check to see if the uses you have identified are mentioned in the article.

1. _____

2. _____

3. _____

B. QUICK WRITE Why do you think that glass is humankind's most important material? Write for 5–10 minutes in response. Use ideas and evidence that you already know about to support your argument. Remember to use this section for your Unit Assignment.

C. VOCABULARY Check (✓) the words or phrases you know. Then work with a partner to locate each word or phrase in the reading. Use clues to help define the words or phrases you don't know. Check your definitions in the dictionary.

allegedly *(adv.)* 𝕃+	lens *(n.)* 𝕃+	prior to *(adj. phr.)* OPAL
conceal *(v.)* 𝕃+	magnification *(n.)*	retain *(v.)* 𝕃+
disrupt *(v.)* 𝕃+	ornamental *(adj.)*	substance *(n.)* 𝕃+ OPAL
facilitate *(v.)* 𝕃+ OPAL	presence *(n.)* 𝕃+ OPAL	texture *(n.)* 𝕃+

𝕃+ Oxford 5000™ words   OPAL Oxford Phrasal Academic Lexicon

iQ PRACTICE Go online to listen and practice your pronunciation.
Practice > Unit 7 > Activity 6

WORK WITH THE READING

 A. INVESTIGATE Read the article and gather information on how new discoveries and inventions change the world.

GLASS IS HUMANKIND'S MOST IMPORTANT MATERIAL

1   Without glass, the world would be unrecognizable. It's in the eyeglasses on your face, the lightbulbs in your room, and the windows that let you see outside. But despite its ubiquity[1], there's still some debate within the research community about how to define "glass." Some tend to emphasize its solid qualities, others its liquidity. Unanswered questions abound, like what makes one type of glass stronger than another, or why certain mixtures produce their unique optical or structural properties. Add to this the nearly infinite varieties of glass, and you get a surprisingly large and active field of research that regularly produces astounding new products. Glass has shaped the world more than any other **substance**, and in many sneaky ways, it's the defining material of the human era.

2   Natural volcanic glasses like obsidian were fashioned into tools early in human history. However, glass was probably first manufactured in Mesopotamia[2] more than 4,000 years ago. Likely, it was developed as an offshoot of ceramic-glaze production. The technique soon spread to ancient Egypt. The first glass objects consisted of beads, amulets, and rods, often colored with added minerals to look like other materials, says Karol Wight, the executive director at the Corning Museum of Glass.

3   By early in the second millennium BCE[3], craftsmen began making small vessels like vases. Archaeologists have unearthed cuneiform[4] tablets that spell out the recipe for such materials. Wight adds that these were written in cryptic language meant to **conceal** trade secrets.

4   Glass had already become a serious business by the dawn of the Roman empire. The writer Petronius recounts the tale of a craftsman presenting Emperor Tiberius with a piece of **allegedly** unbreakable glass. Tiberius asked the craftsman, "Does anyone else know how to blow glass like this?" "No," the craftsman replied, thinking he'd made it big. Without warning, Tiberius had the man beheaded. Although Tiberius's motives remain mysterious, one can imagine such an invention would have **disrupted** Rome's important glass industry, the first of its kind.

5   The first big innovation came in the first century BCE, when glassblowing was invented around Jerusalem. Soon the Romans figured out how to make glass relatively clear, and the first glass windows appeared. This was an important shift. Previously the material was valued primarily for its color and **ornamental** properties. Instead of looking at glass, people could now look through it. Within a couple centuries, Romans began producing glass at an industrial scale, and it eventually spread throughout Eurasia.

---

[1] **ubiquity:** the fact that something seems to be everywhere or in several places at the same time; the fact of being very common
[2] **Mesopotamia:** ancient region in the Middle East in the area of present-day Iraq
[3] **BCE:** before the Common Era; before the year 0
[4] **cuneiform:** an ancient system of writing used in Persia and Assyria

6   At this time, the science wasn't well understood. Glass **retained** a magical air. For example, the Romans created a fourth-century goblet known as the Lycurgus cup. It appears jade green when lit from the front but blood red when backlit. Research shows that its incredible properties are due to the **presence** of silver and gold nanoparticles, which change color depending on the observer's location.

7   Though windows had been around since Roman times, they remained expensive and hard to come by. But that began to change after the building of the Crystal Palace for the 1851 Great Exhibition. The Crystal Palace was a massive structure in London. It contained nearly 1 million square feet of glass. (That's more than four times the glazed area of the United Nations headquarters in New York, erected a century later.) The Crystal Palace showed people the power and beauty of windows. It also had an important influence on architecture and consumer demand down the road, says Alan McLenaghan, the CEO of SageGlass, a company that makes tinted windows and other products. The Crystal Palace burned to the ground in 1936, but windows became much more affordable some years later, when the British glass company Pilkington invented the float-glass technique. This technique is a simple way of creating flat planes of glass by floating them atop molten tin.

8   Long before windows became commonplace, unknown inventors in northern Italy created the first spectacles[5] at the end of the thirteenth century. The invention helped spread literacy and paved the way for more advanced **lenses**. These lenses would enable humans to see unfathomable things. Nearby, by the 1400s, Venetians began perfecting the process of making *cristallo*, a very clear glass. The Venetians borrowed techniques developed in the Middle East and Asia Minor. One recipe involved melting carefully selected quartz pebbles with purified ashes from salt-loving plants. These plants, unknown at the time, supplied the right ratio of silica, manganese, and sodium. Secrecy was a matter of life and death. Glassmakers, though they enjoyed a high social status, faced execution if they left the Venetian Republic. The Venetians dominated the glass market for the next 200 years.

9   The Venetians also created the first mirrors made of manufactured glass, which would change the world in untold ways. **Prior to** this, mirrors consisted of polished metal or obsidian. Metal or obsidian mirrors were expensive and didn't reflect nearly as well. The invention paved the way for telescopes and revolutionized art. It allowed the Italian painter Filippo Brunelleschi to discover linear perspective in 1425. They also changed the conception of the self. The writer Ian Mortimer goes so far as to suggest that prior to glass mirrors, the concept of individual identity didn't really exist. Glass mirrors allowed people to see themselves as unique and separate from others.

10   Besides reflection, glass allowed for **magnification**. Around 1590, the father-son team Hans and Zacharias Janssen invented a compound microscope. Their microscope had lenses at two ends of a tube, producing a nine-power enlargement. A Dutchman, Antony van Leeuwenhoek, made another leap forward. He was a relatively uneducated apprentice in a dry-goods store, where he counted threads in cloth using magnifying glasses. He developed new ways of polishing and grinding lenses, creating a device that allowed him to magnify images up to 270 times. This allowed him to accidentally discover microorganisms like bacteria and protists, beginning in the 1670s.

---

[5] **spectacles:** a pair of glasses

11   Robert Hooke, an English scientist, reconfirmed these findings and improved upon van Leeuwenhoek's microscope. He made history when he authored *Micrographia*. It was the first book about the microscopic world. It had beautiful sketches of previously invisible sights, such as the **texture** of sponges and tiny creatures like fleas. Peering at cork through a microscope, the honeycomb-like structure therein reminded him of monastery cells. This discovery led him to coin the term *cell*. These advances transformed science and led, amongst other things, to germ theory and microbiology.

12   Elsewhere in the lab, the development of clear glassware and equipment like beakers and pipettes made it possible to measure and mix different materials and subject them to different pressures. These glass tools enabled the development of modern chemistry and medicine. It also led to advances such as the steam engine and internal combustion engine.

13   While some tinkered with microscopes and graduated cylinders, others were searching the stars. Though there is some debate about who invented the telescope, the first records show up in the Netherlands in 1608. They were made famous a year later by Galileo Galilei, who improved upon the design and began observing the heavens. The next year, he observed the moons of Jupiter. Eventually, he realized that the geocentric view that had held sway since Greek times didn't make sense.

14   Glass's influence doesn't show any signs of waning. Looking to the future, researchers hope to make breakthroughs of similar prominence. They want to use glass to bind up nuclear waste, make safer batteries, and fashion biomedical implants. Engineers are also trying to make sophisticated touch screens, self-tinting windows, and truly unbreakable glass.

15   The next time you find yourself before glass of one sort or another, consider how strange it is that this material, born of earth and fire, frozen like the rind of ice on a pond, trapped in atomic purgatory, has **facilitated** so much human activity and progress. Really see it, instead of just looking through. Without it, there are so many truths we could not see.

VOCABULARY SKILL REVIEW

In Unit 1, you learned about using a thesaurus and how learning synonyms and antonyms is a good way to build your vocabulary. How many synonyms and antonyms can you find for the vocabulary words and phrases from Reading 2?

B. VOCABULARY Here are some words and phrases from Reading 2. Read the sentences. Then match each bold word or phrase with its definition.

_____ 1. Some scientists think that glass is the most important **substance** in the world because it is so useful.

_____ 2. In the old days, craftspeople tried to **conceal** the recipe for making glass to protect their business.

_____ 3. An ancient Roman craftsperson **allegedly** made an unbreakable piece of glass around 2,000 years ago.

_____ 4. A new kind of unbreakable glass could **disrupt** the glass industry and change it forever.

a. to hide something or someone

b. a type of solid, liquid, or gas that has particular qualities

c. to make it difficult for something to continue in the normal way

d. stated as a fact but without giving proof

_____ 5. Glass is often admired for its **ornamental** qualities, such as its color and beauty.

_____ 6. Venetian glass is a good purchase because these glass objects usually **retain** their value for many years.

_____ 7. The **presence** of elements such as silver or gold can make glass quite beautiful.

_____ 8. Without **lenses**, we couldn't have important things such as spectacles, microscopes, and telescopes.

e. a curved piece of glass or plastic that makes things look larger, smaller, or clearer when you look through it

f. used as decoration rather than for a practical purpose

g. the fact of being in a particular place or thing

h. to keep something; to continue to have something

_____ 9. **Prior to** the invention of glass mirrors, most people had to use polished metal mirrors.

_____ 10. **Magnification** is much easier with glass, and Antony van Leeuwenhoek was able to count threads in cloth using a magnifying glass.

_____ 11. Blown glass vases often have a very smooth **texture**.

_____ 12. Glass materials **facilitate** many daily activities.

i. the way a surface, substance, or piece of cloth feels when you touch it, for example how rough, smooth, hard, or soft it is

j. before something

k. to make an action or process possible or easier

l. the act of making something look larger

iQ PRACTICE Go online for more practice with the vocabulary.
Practice ˃ Unit 7 ˃ Activity 7

C. RESTATE Answer these questions. Write the paragraph number(s) that contain information to support your answers.

_____ 1. What is the main idea of this article?

_____

_____ 2. Why is there scientific debate about how to define glass?

_____

_____ 3. Why is glass going to continue influencing the world in the future?

_____

D. IDENTIFY Number the events in the history of glass in the order in which they happened, from 1 (earliest) to 10 (most recent). Then add the date or time period when the event happened.

_____ a. Romans began producing glass on an industrial scale. Date: _____

_____ b. Microorganisms like bacteria were discovered. Date: _____

_____ c. The first eyeglasses were created. Date: _____

_____ d. A British glass company invented the float-glass technique to create flat planes of glass. Date: _____

_____ e. Linear perspective (the ability to show depth and distance in flat pictures) was discovered. Date: _____

_____ f. Glassblowing was invented near Jerusalem. Date: _____

_____ g. The compound microscope was invented, with lenses at the two ends of a tube. Date: _____

_____ h. Ancient Egyptians made glass objects such as beads, amulets, and rods. Date: _____

_____ i. Galileo Galilei improved the telescope and observed the moons of Jupiter. Date: _____

_____ j. The Crystal Palace was built for the Great Exhibition. Date: _____

E. CATEGORIZE Read the statements. Write _T_ (true) or _F_ (false). Then correct each false statement to make it true.

_____ 1. Glass manufacturing probably developed from the clear liquid ancient craftspeople put on objects made from clay to give them a hard, shiny surface.

_____ 2. The Roman emperor Tiberius cut off the head of a craftsperson who said he was the only person who could make a delicately clear blown glass.

_____ 3. Clear glass windows were first made by the British for the Crystal Palace in 1851.

_____ 4. The United Nations headquarters, built in New York in the middle of the twentieth century, had four times more glass than the Crystal Palace in London.

_____ 5. Cristallo is a very clear glass that can be made by combining plant ash with quartz pebbles to get the right amounts of sodium, manganese, and silica.

_____ 6. Ancient Romans created the first mirrors made out of manufactured glass.

_____ 7. Clear glass tools, such as beakers and pipettes, made the development of modern chemistry and medicine possible.

_____ 8. There are different opinions about who invented the telescope, but telescopes are mentioned in Dutch records from 1608.

F. IDENTIFY Match the people with the ideas associated with them in the article. Note that there are more names listed than ideas.

a. Filippo Brunelleschi   e. Antony van Leeuwenhoek
b. Galileo Galilei   f. Alan McLenaghan
c. Robert Hooke   g. Ian Mortimer
d. Hans and Zacharias Janssen   h. Petronius

_____ 1. said that the Crystal Palace affected people's opinions about architecture, and it was an example of how powerful and beautiful windows can be.

_____ 2. with the help of telescopes, discovered how to make it seem like a picture had depth.

_____ 3. put forward the idea that people didn't think of themselves as individuals before the invention of glass mirrors.

_____ 4. created a piece of equipment with polished and ground lenses that could magnify things up to 270 times.

_____ 5. used a microscope to look at cork, and called the structures he saw *cells*.

_____ 6. improved telescope design and carefully looked at the moons of the planet Jupiter, realizing that the Earth wasn't at the center of the solar system.

G. EXPLAIN Read the questions. What answers can you infer based on the information in the reading?

1. Why is glass a very common material that is used almost everywhere in the modern world?

_____

2. Why did craftspeople in the second millennium BCE want to hide their secrets for making glass and write their recipes in language not easy to understand?

_____

3. Why does the author suggest that the creation of unbreakable glass could have disrupted Rome's glass industry?

_____

4. Why did people think the Lycurgus cup, which sometimes looks green and sometimes looks red, was magical?

_____

5. Why did the Venetians dominate the glass market for 200 years?

_____

6. How do you think Antony van Leeuwenhoek accidently discovered microorganisms?

_____

WORK WITH THE VIDEO

A. PREVIEW How were the lives of humans changed by the invention of the electric light bulb?

VIDEO VOCABULARY

prehistoric (adj.) connected with the time in history before information was written down

artificial (adj.) made or produced to copy something natural; not real

candle (n.) a round stick of wax with a piece of string through the middle that is lit to give light as it burns

emit (v.) to send out something such as light, heat, gas, etc.

iQ RESOURCES Go online to watch the video about the invention of the electric light bulb. *Resources > Video > Unit 7 > Unit Video*

B. IDENTIFY Watch the video two or three times. Then answer the questions based on the information in the video.

1. In prehistoric times, what did people do after sunset?

_____

2. What are the sources of natural light mentioned in the video?

_____

3. What are the sources of artificial light mentioned in the video?

_____

4. According to the video, how did people's nightlives change after they started using light bulbs?

_____

C. EXTEND How do electric light bulbs impact people's lives? Use the information in the video, as well as your own knowledge and ideas, to support your response.

WRITE WHAT YOU THINK

SYNTHESIZE Think about Reading 1, Reading 2, and the video as you discuss these questions. Then choose one question and write a response.

1. The two readings and the video mention discoveries and inventions that have changed the world, such as steam engines, glass, and the electric light bulb. Which of these do you think has changed the world the most? Why?

2. Is there a discovery or invention not mentioned in the readings or video that you think had a bigger impact on people's lives? How did it change the world?

3. What do you think will be the next new discovery or invention that will change the world?

VOCABULARY SKILL Using the dictionary

It is important to **make appropriate word choices** when you write. The first word that you think of when you are writing isn't always the best word to express your ideas. By looking critically at your vocabulary choices, you can choose words that are the best fit for your writing purpose.

Synonyms

Synonyms may be misleading as no two words are exactly the same. A synonym may be slightly different from the exact meaning you want, or it may be accurate, but inappropriate for the **audience, register,** or **genre** of your writing. If you are not sure of the exact definition or how to use the word, look it up in a dictionary.

Audience

The vocabulary choices you make need to match the audience for your writing. Who is the target audience? American English speakers? British? Academic scholars? The dictionary gives specific information about this sort of usage.

Register and genre

You should always be aware of the level of formality of a word or phrase. Formal and informal writing often require different vocabulary choices. Are you writing an article for a fashion magazine or for an academic journal? Are you posting a comment online? You can check your dictionary to see if the word you are using is appropriate or if a more suitable word exists.

> **ex·ac·er·bate** /ɪgˈzæsərˌbeɪt/ *verb* ~ **sth** (*formal*) to make something worse, especially a disease or problem
> **SYN** AGGRAVATE: *The symptoms may be exacerbated by certain drugs.* ▸ **ex·ac·er·ba·tion** /ɪgˌzæsərˈbeɪʃn/ *noun* [U, C]

From the example, you can see that *exacerbate* is a verb that means "to make something worse" and the noun form is *exacerbation*. You can also see that this word is used in formal language and that it is used when talking about diseases and problems, as in the example sentence. If you are writing or speaking in an informal way, it is more appropriate to say *made worse* than *exacerbated*.

All dictionary entries are from the *Oxford Advanced American Dictionary for learners of English* © Oxford University Press 2011.

A. IDENTIFY Circle the most appropriate italic word or phrase to complete each of these sentences from a formal piece of writing in a magazine. Use your dictionary to help you.

1. Living conditions for workers in large cities during the Industrial Revolution were *made worse / exacerbated* by high levels of air pollution from factories.

2. In some places, workers were *killed / executed* if they shared the secret recipes for making glass.

3. The Industrial Revolution *transformed / changed* the way people lived in Britain during the nineteenth century.

4. Glass has changed the world more than any other kind of *substance / stuff*.

5. Antony van Leeuwenhoek's *thing / device* for magnifying objects helped him discover microorganisms.

6. The *manufacturing / making* of cotton goods in Britain increased a great deal between the years 1700 and 1900.

B. APPLY Replace the words in bold with a more academic vocabulary word or phrase from Reading 1 or Reading 2.

1. Many **new things** during the Industrial Revolution were created to solve problems related to energy supplies and textile production.

2. One of the most **important** changes during the Industrial Revolution was the rapid increase in the use of coal as an energy source.

3. Before the Industrial Revolution, the **supply** of food, clothing, shelter, and energy was almost totally dependent on the amount of land available to produce those necessities of life.

4. In ancient times, craftspeople wrote down the recipes for glass in a secret language to **hide** important information.

5. **Before** the invention of the telescope, most people thought that the Earth was at the center of the solar system.

6. Glass tools have **helped** the development of modern medicine, chemistry, and important fields.

C. COMPOSE Choose ten vocabulary words or phrases from this unit. Write a sentence using each word. Be sure to look up the words in the dictionary to see how they are used.

iQ PRACTICE Go online for more practice with using a dictionary.
Practice > Unit 7 > Activity 8

WRITING

OBJECTIVE ▶

At the end of this unit, you will write a summary and response essay about how new discoveries and inventions change the world. Your essay will include information from the readings, the unit video, and your own ideas.

WRITING SKILL Summarizing

A **summary** is a shortened version of a text such as an article or textbook excerpt. It is an objective piece of writing that does not contain any of your opinions or ideas. To write a summary, determine the main ideas in the original text and write a paragraph about them. Summarizing is a useful study aid to help you remember and understand main ideas when you are taking an exam or doing research.

Here are some steps to help you write a summary.

Before you write: Read the text thoroughly. Use techniques you learned in Unit 1 (Distinguishing main ideas from details, page 11) and Unit 4 (Making inferences, page 103) to determine the main ideas the author is expressing.

As you write: Write a draft of the summary using your own words. Follow these guidelines:

- **Topic sentence:** Introduce the piece by giving the author's name, the title of the piece, the source, and the general topic of the text.

- **Body:** Write the main ideas in the order they appear. Do not include details.

- **Conclusion:** One way you can end a summary is to briefly restate the main ideas found in the reading.

After you write: Ensure that the summary is much shorter than the original text. Read over your summary to see if it makes sense and expresses the main ideas of the reading. Eliminate any unnecessary details. Then revise and edit your work.

- Always use your own words. Never copy the author's words. (See Paraphrasing, page 179, in Unit 6.)

- Do not overuse quotes. Use mostly indirect speech. A short quotation of a key phrase may be included.

- Do not add your own ideas or opinions and do not change the writer's ideas and opinions.

A. INVESTIGATE Read this article from the (fictional) *Canadian Invention Newsletter* about the invention of the egg carton. As you read, annotate the text and underline the main ideas.

A Canadian Invention that Keeps Eggs Safe

BY STANLEY ITOGA

1   There is an expression that says it is dangerous to put all your eggs in one basket. It's a piece of advice that means you shouldn't rely on only one option. After all, if you drop your basket of eggs, they will probably break. However, before the invention of the egg carton, putting eggs in baskets was exactly what people used to do. Unfortunately, these eggs were easily broken. It wasn't until a Canadian came up with an innovative way to protect and transport eggs that people could be sure of being able to use all of theirs. Joseph Coyle changed egg storage and transportation forever with the invention of the egg carton.

2   Eggs carried around in baskets break easily. Farmers used to collect eggs from their chickens and put them in baskets, which were then used to transport the eggs to their customers. The eggs touched each other directly, and because of road conditions and transportation methods at the time, many of them ended up cracked and unusable. Roads were often unpaved, and horse carts or early cars did not provide a particularly smooth ride. Sometimes straw or sawdust was added to the baskets in order to protect the eggs, but there was still a good chance that some of them would break. This breakage could lead to customer dissatisfaction and loss of income for farmers.

3   Joseph Coyle first began thinking about the problem of cracked eggs because of an argument he overheard. Coyle was a journalist in the Bulkley Valley in British Columbia, and his newspaper office was beside a hotel. One day in 1911, when he was about 40 years old, Coyle was listening to a heated conversation between the hotel owner and a farmer. The owner was upset because the farmer often delivered broken eggs to the hotel. Besides working as a journalist, Coyle also liked to invent things. He decided to try and solve the problem of the broken eggs so that customers could be happy and farmers could stop losing money. He wanted to find a simple way to transport eggs safely and inexpensively from a farm to its customers.

4   Coyle soon came up with a solution to the problem of cracked and broken eggs. Using paper, he created a carton with individual spaces for each egg. The eggs no longer touched each other, and the fragile shells were protected from cracking during transportation and storage. The paper carton held two rows of six eggs, and these were safe because the design could absorb shock. Coyle named his new invention the Egg-Safety carton. The new cartons greatly reduced the problem of damaged eggs. In fact, his invention was so good that the eggs were sometimes protected even if a full carton was dropped on the ground.

5   As Coyle improved the manufacturing process for the egg cartons, his design began to spread around the world. Coyle patented his idea in 1918 and, at first, made his invention by hand in Smithers, British Columbia. However, handmade cartons were expensive. He decided to move to Vancouver, where in 1920 he created a machine to make the cartons. The new machine helped to lower the manufacturing costs and make the egg cartons more affordable. Eventually, his Egg-Safety cartons were manufactured in Canada (Toronto and London, Ontario), the United States (Los Angeles, Chicago, Pittsburgh, and New York), South America, and Europe.

6   After World War II, less expensive plastic and Styrofoam egg cartons gained popularity, but they were still based on Coyle's design. And although millions and millions of these cartons have been made, Coyle, who died in 1972, never earned a lot of money from his invention. In fact, other business people and lawyers have managed to become richer than he did from sales of the cartons.

7   Today, egg cartons still use the same basic design that Coyle created and can be found everywhere. Canadians alone use over 300 million egg cartons every year. Such an ingenious idea has helped us save money and avoid wasting food. Coyle's invention changed the way eggs are transported and stored, making life easier and more convenient for millions of people.

References
Canadian Press. (2017, June 28). Canadian tinkerers, inventors, scientists, and engineers have changed the world. *National Post*. Retrieved from https://nationalpost.com

Dhillon, S. (2013, December 28). BC inventor created better way to carry eggs. *The Globe and Mail*. Retrieved from https://www.theglobeandmail.com

Smith, M.G. (2018, September 3). The egg carton invented in BC. *BC Food History Network*. Retrieved from https://www.bcfoodhistory.ca

 CRITICAL THINKING STRATEGY

Evaluating information

Evaluating information involves making a decision about whether a source of information, such as an article or other piece of writing, is useful, accurate, and trustworthy. You should determine the quality of your sources of information before synthesizing them into your writing. Your decision is based on proof you find in the source. This proof helps you decide if the information in the source is appropriate. For example, if you are evaluating information in a summary, you should keep in mind that a summary should not have too many unnecessary details or strong personal opinions that were not present in the original source.

Activity B asks you to assess whether the summary is effective or not. When you assess, you use your own knowledge and opinions to judge another's ideas. People can form different but equally valid assessments. Making judgments based on the information available and your own values and beliefs can help you understand a topic better.

iQ PRACTICE   Go online to watch the Critical Thinking Video and check your comprehension. *Practice ⟩ Unit 7 ⟩ Activity 9*

B. EVALUATE Read the summaries and answer the questions, providing the reasons for your answers. Then discuss your answers with a partner.

> The article "A Canadian Invention that Keeps Eggs Safe," by Stanley Itoga, tells us that eggs used to break a lot because of poor road conditions and old methods of transportation such as horse carts. Joseph Coyle, who was from the Bulkley Valley in British Columbia, was a journalist. He invented the egg carton because a hotel owner and a farmer had an argument. His egg carton could hold 12 eggs in two rows of six. He called his invention the Egg-Safety carton. He patented his idea in 1918 and created a machine to make the cartons. His egg cartons were sold in cities such as Toronto, Los Angeles, Chicago, Pittsburgh, and New York. Joseph Coyle passed away in 1972. He did not make a lot of money.

1. Is this an effective summary? Why or why not? Provide a reason for your answer.

_____

_____

> The article from the *Canadian Invention Newsletter* "A Canadian Invention that Keeps Eggs Safe," by Stanley Itoga, looks at how the invention of the egg carton by Joseph Coyle changed the way eggs were stored and moved around so that they were kept safe. In the old days, eggs were kept in baskets, and they were easily broken. One day, Joseph Coyle heard an argument between a hotel owner and farmer over broken eggs. Coyle solved this problem by creating an egg carton with individual spaces to protect each egg. He soon created a machine to make his egg cartons, and his idea spread to many different countries. Coyle did not make a lot of money from his invention even though millions of egg cartons were made. However, Coyle's design saved many eggs from breaking and changed egg storage and transport for the better.

2. Is this an effective summary? Why or why not? Provide a reason for your answer.

_____

_____

Stanley Itoga, in the article "A Canadian Invention that Keeps Eggs Safe," informs us that Joseph Coyle invented the egg carton. Broken eggs used to cost farmers a lot of money. Coyle probably felt bad when he heard a farmer having an argument with a hotel owner about broken eggs. It probably wasn't even the farmer's fault. Coyle came up with an egg carton to protect the farmer's eggs. Coyle's design was very good because it had 12 compartments, one for each egg. He then created a really great machine to make the egg cartons. Coyle was probably one of the smartest Canadians of all time. However, he did not make much money from his invention. This was terrible. In my opinion, inventors need to make money from their inventions because it will encourage them to create new inventions that will benefit the world.

3. Is this an effective summary? Why or why not? Provide a reason for your answer.

_____

_____

4. Which summary is the best? Why?

_____

_____

C. WRITING MODEL A summary and response essay has two main sections. After the introduction, there is typically a summary section of one or two paragraphs that summarizes the main ideas of a reading text. Next, there is a response section of two to four paragraphs, depending on the number of main ideas that you are responding to. The response section contains your opinions of or personal reaction to the main ideas that you just summarized. The essay then finishes with a conclusion. Read the summary and response essay below. Then answer the questions that follow.

Eggs are a popular food all around the world, and many people buy their eggs at a supermarket, where they are kept in stacks of cartons that keep them safe. However, eggs were not always stored in cartons. In an article in the *Canadian Invention Newsletter*, "A Canadian Invention that Keeps Eggs Safe," Stanley Itoga shares the story of how the invention of the egg carton changed people's lives. This article points out that cracked eggs used to be a big problem. The solution was good design, and the key was creating a machine to manufacture the cartons.

In his article, Stanley Itoga describes how Joseph Coyle's invention of the egg carton stopped large numbers of eggs from breaking by changing the way they were stored and transported. Before the invention of the carton, eggs were easily broken because they were kept in baskets. Coyle found out that this was a big problem when he overheard a farmer and a hotel owner having an argument about broken eggs. To solve this problem, Coyle invented the egg carton, which had individual compartments to protect each egg from breaking. Although he made his cartons by hand in the beginning, within a few years, Coyle built a machine to manufacture them. Soon, the cartons were being used all around the world. Millions of egg cartons have been sold, but Coyle never became a wealthy man. Nevertheless, egg storage and transportation were greatly improved, and many eggs have been saved from breaking.

One of the first things that the author points out in the story of how Joseph Coyle invented the egg carton was the problem of cracked eggs. It is easy to imagine how the hotel owner must have been frustrated when he needed a certain number of eggs but didn't receive all the ones that he had ordered. People who wanted to eat eggs for breakfast must have been disappointed, and it was generally a terrible waste of food. Farmers were also losing an important source of income because putting eggs in baskets certainly wasn't a very safe way to get eggs from the farm to the customer. It was a problem that desperately needed a solution.

The article also mentions that Coyle solved the problem of broken eggs with the invention of his egg carton. His solution involved creating a good design. His idea of keeping each egg separate from the others was a major breakthrough. In addition, the suspension of the eggs in individual pockets was also an innovation that set him apart from other inventors at that time. His design was strong and safe, and people must have been impressed when they first saw it. Less food would be wasted, and egg sellers would be able to make more money. His design was so good that it is almost unchanged since those early days of egg cartons.

Finally, the article talks about the creation of a machine that enabled egg cartons to be manufactured cheaply and easily. Having a good idea is often not enough. At first, Coyle made his cartons by hand. However, he was able to sell many more egg cartons once he improved the manufacturing process. Now, large numbers of cartons could be made in many different countries. The most important thing was increasing production by following through with his idea to the next logical step so that more people could benefit from his discovery.

All in all, the article by Stanley Itoga highlights key events in the story of how Joseph Coyle invented the egg carton, such as the initial problem of too many broken eggs, the development of a good solution, and the final creation of a machine to manufacture large numbers of egg cartons. There are still many other problems in the world, particularly related to wasted and spoiled food. It is hoped that the story of Joseph Coyle will inspire people to think of solutions to these problems and invent products that have the potential to change the world.

WRITING TIP

The thesis statement summarizes the main ideas of the essay and is usually found in the first paragraph.

1. What is the thesis statement for this essay? Restate the thesis statement in your own words.

2. How would you evaluate the summary in this essay? Is it effective? Provide reasons for your evaluation.

3. What is the first main idea that the essay writer responds to?

4. What is the essay writer's reaction to the first main idea?

5. What is the second main idea that the essay writer responds to?

6. What is the essay writer's reaction to the second main idea?

7. What is the third main idea that the essay writer responds to?

8. What is the essay writer's reaction to the third main idea?

iQ PRACTICE Go online for more practice with summarizing.
Practice > Unit 7 > Activity 10

In every sentence, the main subject and verb must agree with each other. Singular subjects agree with singular verbs, and plural subjects agree with plural verbs. To avoid errors when writing, identify the main subject of the sentence and the subjects of any clauses, and check that they each have a verb that agrees. Prepositional phrases, relative clauses, and noun clauses can be tricky.

Prepositional phrases: A plural noun at the end of a prepositional phrase modifying a singular subject can cause writers to make subject-verb agreement errors. The subject, not the noun at the end of the prepositional phrase, determines if the verb is singular or plural.

Poor **health** among factory workers **was** an issue during the Industrial Revolution.
prepositional phrase

Subject relative clauses: The verb in a subject relative clause agrees in number with the noun that the clause modifies. The verb in the main clause of the sentence also agrees with the noun.

Many **inventors** who **create** wonderful things **find** inspiration in small problems.
subject relative clause

Noun clauses: A noun clause can be the subject of a sentence. Use a singular verb in these sentences.

What many inventors have shown is that a simple idea can change the world.
noun clause

Quantifiers: When quantifiers (see Unit 3, pages 89–90) are used, they usually precede a noun. Look at the noun and check that the main verb agrees with it.

Almost **every** <u>inventor</u> **is** a creative person. (singular)

Most of my <u>money</u> **is** spent on interesting gadgets. (noncount)

A lot of my <u>friends</u> **like** to visit museums and **experience** history. (plural)

iQ RESOURCES Go online to watch the Grammar Skill Video.
Resources > Video > Unit 7 > Grammar Skill Video

A. IDENTIFY Underline the main subject in each clause of these sentences. Then choose the correct verb in italic.

1. Many people *uses / use* things that were invented in Canada, and most of these inventions *improves / improve* people's lives.

2. Innovation *is / are* an important part of an inventor's skills, which also *includes / include* perseverance, critical thinking, and creativity.

3. Inventors sometimes *creates / create* new devices for patients in a hospital who *has / have* problems that need solutions.

4. How often people use Canadian inventions *becomes / become* obvious when you realize that insulin, peanut butter, basketball, garbage bags, and electric wheelchairs were all invented by Canadians.

5. Not every new invention *changes / change* people's lives.

6. Recommendations for improving conditions in factories during the Industrial Revolution *was / were* made by reformers such as Robert Owen and Titus Salt.

B. APPLY Read the summary. Underline and correct the twelve subject-verb agreement errors.

The article by *Global News*, "Here's a Look at Famous Inventions Made by Canadians," reveal that Canadians is innovators who create things that changes the world both socially and economically. One major Canadian invention are the smartphone. It began with the development of the Blackberry, and it changed how people communicate with each other. Another invention was the foghorn, which protect ships during fog. A third famous Canadian invention are the snowmobile, which enable people to travel across deep snow. What these examples show are that Canada produce more inventions than the world might expect. Canada's institutions, culture, and safety contributes to an innovative environment. In addition, curiosity among Canadians encourage innovation and lead to improving people's lives.

Reference
Global News. (2017, June 9). Here's a look at famous inventions made by Canadians. *Global News*. Retrieved from https://globalnews.ca

iQ PRACTICE Go online for more practice with subject-verb agreement.
Practice > Unit 7 > Activities 11–12

UNIT ASSIGNMENT Write a summary and response essay

OBJECTIVE ▶

In this assignment, you will write a summary and response essay for Reading 1 or Reading 2. As you prepare your essay, think about the Unit Question, "How do new discoveries and inventions change the world?" Use information from Reading 1, Reading 2, the unit video, and your work in this unit to support your paragraph. Refer to the Self-Assessment checklist on page 222.

---

iQ PRACTICE Go online to the Writing Tutor to read a model summary and response essay. *Practice > Unit 7 > Activity 13*

PLAN AND WRITE

A. BRAINSTORM Keeping the Unit Question in mind ("How do new discoveries and inventions change the world?"), choose Reading 1 or Reading 2 and complete these tasks.

1. Reread the article you chose and annotate it as you read. Use these questions to guide you.

   a. How does the article relate to the Unit Question?

   b. What are the main ideas of the article?

   c. What main ideas in the article do you find most interesting? Why?

   d. What information in the article supports your choice of the most interesting main ideas?

   e. Do you have any personal experience with or prior knowledge of this topic? What facts and examples support or disprove the main ideas in the article?

2. Discuss your answers with a partner who chose the same article.

B. PLAN Follow these steps to plan your summary and response essay.

Choose three main ideas from the article and write them below. Write your personal reaction to each one and how each relates to the Unit Question. You will use your personal reactions and how they relate to the Unit Question in the response part of your essay.

Main idea 1: _____

_____

Personal reaction: _____

_____

Relation to Unit Question: _____

_____

Main idea 2: _____

_____

Personal reaction: _____

_____

Relation to Unit Question: _____

_____

Main idea 3: _____

_____

Personal reaction: _____

_____

Relation to Unit Question: _____

_____

iQ RESOURCES Go online to download and complete the outline for your summary and response essay. *Resources > Writing Tools > Unit 7 > Outline*

C. WRITE Use your planning notes to write your summary and response essay.

1. Write your summary and response essay for the article you chose.

2. Look at the Self-Assessment checklist on page 222 to guide your writing.

iQ PRACTICE Go online to the Writing Tutor to write your assignment. *Practice > Unit 7 > Activity 14*

REVISE AND EDIT

iQ RESOURCES Go online to download the peer review worksheet.
Resources > Writing Tools > Unit 7 > Peer Review Worksheet

A. PEER REVIEW Read your partner's summary and response essay. Then use the peer review worksheet. Discuss the review with your partner.

B. REWRITE Based on your partner's review, revise and rewrite your summary and response essay.

C. EDIT Complete the Self-Assessment checklist as you prepare to write the final draft of your summary and response essay. Be prepared to hand in your work or discuss it in class.

SELF-ASSESSMENT	Yes	No
Does the essay build a convincing argument using facts, reasons, and examples?	☐	☐
Was information from Reading 1 or Reading 2 summarized correctly where appropriate?	☐	☐
Did you check the essay for subject-verb agreement errors?	☐	☐
Did you use the dictionary to make appropriate word choices?	☐	☐
Does the essay include vocabulary from the unit?	☐	☐
Did you check the essay for punctuation, spelling, and grammar?	☐	☐

D. REFLECT Discuss these questions with a partner or group.

1. What is something new you learned in this unit?

2. Look back at the Unit Question—How do new discoveries and inventions change the world? Is your answer different now than when you started the unit? If yes, how is it different? Why?

iQ PRACTICE Go to the online discussion board to discuss the questions.
Practice > Unit 7 > Activity 15

TRACK YOUR SUCCESS

iQ PRACTICE   Go online to check the words and phrases you have learned in this unit. *Practice* > *Unit 7* > *Activity 16*

Check (✓) the skills and strategies you learned. If you need more work on a skill, refer to the page(s) in parentheses.

READING	☐ I can identify the author's intent. (p. 199)
VOCABULARY	☐ I can use the dictionary to make appropriate word choices. (p. 209)
WRITING	☐ I can write a summary. (p. 211)
CRITICAL THINKING	☐ I can evaluate information. (p. 213)
GRAMMAR	☐ I can recognize and correct subject-verb agreement errors. (p. 218)

OBJECTIVE ▶   ☐ I can gather information and ideas to develop a summary and response essay based on an informational text.

Health Sciences

CRITICAL THINKING	applying new learning to problems
READING	organizing notes and annotations in a chart
VOCABULARY	adjective/verb + preposition collocations
WRITING	writing a cause and effect essay
GRAMMAR	cause and effect connectors

What affects people's energy levels?

A. Discuss these questions with your classmates.

1. When do you feel like you have the most and least amounts of energy?

2. What kinds of things give you energy? What makes you feel tired?

3. Look at the photo. What are these people doing to energize themselves? Do you think they all have the same level of energy? Why or why not?

B. Listen to *The Q Classroom* online. Then answer these questions.

1. For Sophy, Marcus, Yuna, and Felix, what affects their energy levels? Are their energy levels affected by the same things?

2. According to Felix, why aren't people getting enough sleep nowadays? What are some other reasons people might not be getting enough sleep in today's society?

iQ PRACTICE Go to the online discussion board to discuss the Unit Question with your classmates. *Practice > Unit 8 > Activity 1*

UNIT OBJECTIVE

Read an article from the website *Medical News Today* and an article from the website *Stack* about energy levels. Gather information and ideas to write a cause and effect essay analyzing two or three factors that affect people's energy levels.

READING

READING 1

OBJECTIVE ▶

How Can You Boost Your Energy Levels?

You are going to read an article from the website *Medical News Today* about how people can increase their energy levels. Use the article to gather information and ideas for your Unit Assignment.

PREVIEW THE READING

A. PREVIEW What gives people more energy? Check (✓) what you think are the three best ways for people to increase their energy levels. What else might give people more energy?

☐ Eating some chocolate   ☐ Running 10 kilometers

☐ Drinking a glass of water   ☐ Doing the dishes

☐ Watching television before bed   ☐ Taking an afternoon nap

B. QUICK WRITE What affects people's energy levels? Write for 5–10 minutes in response. Before you start, spend a couple of minutes planning what you are going to write about. Remember to use this section for your Unit Assignment.

C. VOCABULARY Check (✓) the words or phrases you know. Then work with a partner to locate each word or phrase in the reading. Use clues to help define the words or phrases you don't know. Check your definitions in the dictionary.

alleviate *(v.)*	**depletion** *(n.)*	**immune system** *(n.)*
calorie *(n.)*	**derive from** *(v. phr.)*	**meditation** *(n.)* ⚡+
chronic *(adj.)* ⚡+	**fatigue** *(n.)*	**resilience** *(n.)*
conducive *(adj.)*	**hydrated** *(adj.)*	**sluggish** *(adj.)*

⚡+ Oxford 5000™ words   **OPAL** Oxford Phrasal Academic Lexicon

iQ PRACTICE   Go online to listen and practice your pronunciation.
Practice > Unit 8 > Activity 2

A. INVESTIGATE Read the article and gather information on what affects people's energy levels.

How Can You Boost Your Energy Levels?

To get more energy, integrate whole grains, nuts, fruit, and leafy greens into your diet.

1   Do you often feel tired and wish you could be more energetic and able to take better advantage of your time? The reasons you may feel tired and depleted of energy can vary from simple explanations, such as lack of sleep or dealing with stress at work, to much more complex ones, such as living with a **chronic** condition or following treatment for a chronic disease. While dealing with **fatigue** caused by a chronic condition may be more difficult, forming some good lifestyle habits can help you maximize your energy levels on a day-to-day basis.

1 Pay attention to diet

2   One of our main sources of energy is, of course, the food we eat. So, if we want to keep our energy levels up, we must eat healthfully and try to integrate the most nutritious foods into our diets. We measure the energy that we can **derive from** foods in **calories**. If we don't consume enough calories, our bodies may feel tired, as they don't have enough "fuel" to run on. At the same time, however, if we get too many calories, there's a system overload, and we may end up feeling **sluggish**. So, in order to feel fresh and ready for action, we must learn to maintain a balance in terms of our calorie intake.

3   What are some specific foods that you might want to add into your diet at a time when you feel tired and in urgent need of an energy boost? Harvard specialists advise going for foods "with a low glycemic index"—that is, whose sugar content is broken down by our bodies at a slow rate ("Nine Tips," 2018). This means that energy derived from these foods is released gradually, helping keep us alert for longer. Such foods include whole grains, nuts, and some fruits—particularly grapes, apples, oranges, peaches, pears, and grapefruit—and vegetables and legumes with a high fiber content, including peas, beans, and leafy greens.

4   In addition to food, what people drink, such as water and coffee, also affects energy levels. If you're not feeling at your best, it's important to make sure you stay **hydrated**. Fatigue can be a symptom of dehydration, so making sure that you drink enough

water throughout the day could help **alleviate** the feeling of tiredness. However, for so many of us, coffee is the go-to solution when we don't feel as awake as we'd like. The authors of a Harvard Medical School report explain that caffeine—which naturally occurs in coffee, tea, and cocoa—can help improve concentration and render our brains more alert and receptive (Komaroff, 2016). Caffeine also increases your pulse, which may lend you more physical strength for a while. But, the authors caution, these effects may not be seen in habitual drinkers, whose bodies may have built up tolerance to this substance.

2 Do some light exercise

5   Sometimes, in the middle of the work day, I start to feel sluggish and my brain can "shut down." At those times, I find it useful to get up from my chair, stretch a little, walk around the office, and then continue work at my standing desk. A little movement helps revitalize me.

6   As specialists from the Harvard Medical School explain in their dedicated report (Komaroff, 2016), exercise stimulates your body and mind in some vital ways. First, they write, in any form of exercise, at the cellular level, more energy-producing units form in your muscles so that your body may sustain the activity. Exercise also "increases your body's oxygen-carrying capacity" and boosts circulation, so said oxygen will reach and "feed" all your body parts sooner. Moreover, it stimulates the release of stress hormones—in moderation—which make you feel more energized and alert.

7   "But what type of exercise should you do?" ask the report authors, who then go on to explain that, in short, anything will do—just as long as you engage in some kind of physical activity. "You don't have to spend a lot of time worrying about this. When it comes to exercise and energy, it's hard to go wrong—and you don't have to run for miles or work out to the point of exhaustion to start reaping benefits."

3 Put time aside for yoga and meditation

8   Practicing yoga and **meditation** might also help boost your energy levels. This is because these practices focus on techniques—such as mindful breathing—that aim to promote a state of calm. So, if your fatigue is due—at least in part—to increased stress, taking up yoga or meditation as a routine "self-care" approach can help you become more resistant to stressors.

9   People who practice meditation and yoga often seem to have better **immune systems** and to have developed **resilience** in the face of stress and anxiety. Also, engaging in just 25 minutes of yoga or meditation—compared with 25 minutes of quiet reading—can boost people's moods, as well as their energy levels and executive function[1] (Paddock, 2017). A review of studies investigating the health benefits of yoga also concluded that this practice can improve resilience to stress in people working in fairly high-intensity domains, as well as reduce anxiety and improve the symptoms of depression (Field, 2016).

4 Learn to delegate tasks

10   We might feel stifled by our responsibilities—from the very small daily chores, such as doing the dishes, to the less mundane, such as a vital work project with many ramifications. However, if we don't find a decent strategy to redistribute some of these responsibilities, at least from time to time, it may lead to burnout and a constant sense of fatigue in our day-to-day lives, which is not at all **conducive** to productivity and happiness.

11   Research has shown that people who invest in services that allow them to stop worrying about some of the house chores that they dislike, so that they don't have to deal with the mental and physical overload, have a greater sense of overall well-being (Whillans et al., 2017). "[O]ur research suggests," explains Elizabeth Dunn, a professor in the Department of Psychology at the University of British Columbia in Vancouver, Canada, "people should [...] consider buying their way out of unpleasant experiences" (University of British Columbia, 2017).

[1] **executive function:** the group of complex mental processes and cognitive abilities (e.g., working memory) that control the skills (e.g., remembering details) required for doing tasks

5 Don't underestimate sleep

12   Finally, it's vital to make sure that you get enough good-quality sleep at night to prevent fatigue or recover from the effect of tiring or stressful activity throughout the day. Although this may be the most obvious advice, many of us often underestimate the impact that shortened sleeping time, or disrupted sleep, can have on our energy levels, health, and well-being, in general. Research has associated disrupted sleep with neurodegeneration (Musiek, et al., 2018), mental health problems (Franzen & Buysse, 2008), and increased predisposition to worry (Galbiati, et al., 2017). How much sleep we need largely depends on our age and some other factors. However, on average, adults should sleep for around seven to nine hours per night in order to feel refreshed.

Getting enough sleep should be a top priority

13   The Centers for Disease Control and Prevention (CDC) suggest that, to get a good night's sleep, we should form a healthful routine. This includes going to bed at roughly the same time each night and getting up at roughly the same time every morning. They also advise avoiding exposure to bright screens—such as those of smartphones, laptops, or tablets—just before bed, as this interferes with your natural body clock, leading to a state of alertness that will keep you awake even if you are tired and would like to sleep.

14   In short, if you lack the energy that you think you should have, make sure that you familiarize yourself with your own needs and prioritize them. There are no shortcuts for keeping your energy resources well stocked. So, it's best to form healthful habits that will help you cope with stress and avoid energy **depletion**.

References

Nine tips to boost your energy—naturally. (2018). *Healthbeat*. Retrieved from https://www.health.harvard.edu/energy-and-fatigue/9-tips-to-boost-your-energy-naturally

Field, T. (2016). Yoga research review. *Complementary Therapies in Clinical Practice, 24*, 145–161. https://doi.org/10.1016/j.ctcp.2016.06.005

Franzen, P.L. & Buysse, D.J. (2008). Sleep disturbances and depression: Risk relationships for subsequent depression and therapeutic implications. *Dialogues in Clinical Neuroscience, 10*(4), 473–481. Retrieved from https://www.ncbi.nlm.nih.gov/pmc/articles/PMC3108260/

Galbiati, A., Giora, E., Verga, L., Zucconi, M., & Ferini-Strambi, L. (2017). Worry and rumination traits are associated with polysomnographic indices of disrupted sleep in insomnia disorder. *Sleep Medicine, 40*(1), e105. https://doi.org/10.1016/j.sleep.2017.11.304

Komaroff, A.L. (Ed.) (2016). *Boosting your energy: How to jump-start your natural energy and fight fatigue*. Boston, MA: Harvard Health Publishing.

Musiek, E.S., et al. (2018). Circadian rest-activity pattern changes in aging and preclinical Alzheimer disease. *JAMA Neurology, 75*(5), 582–590. https://doi:10.1001/jamaneurol.2017.4719

Paddock, C. (2017, September 7). Just 25 minutes of yoga, meditation "boosts brain function, energy." *Medical News Today*. Retrieved from https://www.medicalnewstoday.com/articles/319333.php

University of British Columbia. (2017, July 24). Using money to buy time linked to increased happiness. *ScienceDaily.* Retrieved from https://www.sciencedaily.com/releases/2017/07/170724161258.htm

Whillans, A.V., Dunn, E.W., Smeets, P., Bekkers, P.R., & Norton, M.I. (2017). Buying time promotes happiness. *Proceedings of the National Academy of Sciences*, published ahead of print. https://doi.org/10.1073/pnas.1706541114

In Unit 7, you learned about making appropriate word choices. As you learn new vocabulary, consider the audience you are writing for, the register you should use, and the genre you are working within to decide when to use a word.

B. VOCABULARY Here are some words and phrases from Reading 1. Complete each sentence with a word or phrase from the box. You may need to change the form of the word or phrase to make the sentence grammatically correct.

alleviate *(v.)*	depletion *(n.)*	immune system *(n.)*
calorie *(n.)*	derive from *(v. phr.)*	meditation *(n.)*
chronic *(adj.)*	fatigue *(n.)*	resilience *(n.)*
conducive *(adj.)*	hydrated *(adj.)*	sluggish *(adj.)*

1. Eating too much food, particularly junk food, can make you feel _____ and have trouble concentrating.

2. Eating healthy food, getting plenty of exercise, and sleeping enough hours are all _____ to feeling energetic and happy.

3. A good diet and plenty of rest can help _____ feelings of being tired all the time.

4. Energy _____ candy and chocolate is released quickly, and people often feel tired again soon.

5. Some people use _____ to boost their energy levels and maintain a feeling of calm and low stress.

6. Drinking enough water every day will keep you _____ and prevent excessive sleepiness.

7. Severe _____ can be caused by too much exercise or a poor diet, resulting in the desire to sleep all the time.

8. Stress can reduce the effectiveness of your _____ and make you feel tired.

9. My friend is tired all the time because he has a _____ disease that affects his energy levels.

10. People who develop _____ to anxiety and recover quickly from stress may also have better energy levels.

11. Working for long periods of time without a break can lead to energy _____ and poor performance.

12. According to the government of Canada, an active 30-year-old man needs about 3,000 _____ in order to have enough energy for his daily tasks.

iQ PRACTICE Go online for more practice with the vocabulary.
Practice > Unit 8 > Activity 3

C. IDENTIFY Circle the answer that best completes each statement.

1. The main source of people's energy is _____.
   a. the exercise they do
   b. the chores they finish
   c. the sleep they get
   d. the food they eat

2. Exercise stimulates your body and mind by _____.
   a. relaxing your muscles and their energy-producing units
   b. boosting blood circulation and the amount of available oxygen
   c. releasing high levels of stress hormones
   d. increasing your stress and anxiety

3. Burnout and feeling tired all the time can be the result of _____.
   a. having too many chores or work projects
   b. paying other people to do your little jobs around the house
   c. buying your way out of unpleasant experiences
   d. redistributing your main responsibilities

4. A healthy routine for getting a good night's sleep includes _____.
   a. using a smartphone, laptop, or tablet to help you fall asleep
   b. planning for at least six hours of sleep per night
   c. going to bed and getting up around the same time every day
   d. interfering with your natural body clock

D. IDENTIFY Correct these false statements with information from Reading 1. Write the number of the paragraph where the correct information is.

1. We need to eat as many calories as possible if we don't want to feel tired all of the time. (Paragraph: ____)

   _____

2. When we feel tired, we should eat foods with a high glycemic index so that the sugar content is broken down quickly and ready to be used by our bodies. (Paragraph: ____)

   _____

3. People who drink a lot of coffee are very sensitive to caffeine, and a small amount helps improve concentration and alertness. (Paragraph: ____)

   _____

4. If people want to feel energized by physical activity, they need to run very far or work out until they are tired. (Paragraph: ____)

   _____

5. Reading for 25 minutes is better than doing yoga for 25 minutes if you want to improve your mood, energy level, and ability to think clearly. (Paragraph: ____)

_____

6. People who do their own chores have a greater sense of well-being compared to people who pay for services to do the chores they don't like. (Paragraph: ____)

_____

7. Everyone needs the same amount of sleep each night if they want to feel refreshed. (Paragraph: ____)

_____

8. Using a bright screen just before bed helps your natural body clock and creates a state of relaxation. (Paragraph: ____)

_____

E. **EXPLAIN** Answer these questions to complete a set of notes based on information found in the reading.

Pay attention to diet

1. What happens if we don't eat enough calories?
2. What happens if we eat too many calories?
3. Why is hydration important?
4. How does drinking coffee affect people?

Do some light exercise

1. What does exercise produce in your muscles?
2. What does exercise improve your body's ability to do?
3. How do moderate amounts of stress hormones affect you?

Put time aside for yoga and meditation

1. How do yoga and meditation boost energy levels?
2. What can yoga or meditation do if you feel tired because of stress?
3. How can yoga help people with high-intensity jobs?

Learn to delegate tasks

1. What happens to people if they can't deal with their responsibilities?
2. What did Elizabeth Dunn say about improving a sense of well-being?

Don't underestimate sleep

1. Why is it important for people to get enough sleep?
2. What are some possible results from disrupted sleep?
3. What can healthful habits help you do?

CRITICAL THINKING STRATEGY

Applying new learning to problems

When you learn new information from a reading, you can apply that information to other scenarios to develop solutions to various problems. The goal of reading a text isn't simply to understand what an author has written. You can apply what you learn from a text to other situations. For example, you might take general, abstract ideas you read about and apply them to a specific, concrete problem. You might also take an example from a reading, compare that example to a similar issue, and develop a practical solution to fix that issue. The ability of taking something you learned in a reading and applying it to another situation shows that you have a deep understanding of the original text. With practice, you can become skilled at using your knowledge to solve problems in different situations.

In Activity F, you will use what you learned in Reading 1 to respond to a variety of scenarios. Using the information from the reading in this way will help you have a better understanding of the text and how it applies to solving problems.

iQ PRACTICE Go online to watch the Critical Thinking Video and check your comprehension. *Practice > Unit 8 > Activity 4*

F. **DISCUSS** Read the following scenarios. Then go online to find information that can help solve the problems in each situation. Using the information you find online and in Reading 1, think of a response to each scenario. For each response, provide a short quote to support it and indicate the source of your information. Discuss your responses and sources with a partner.

1. Sofia's mother makes her a large lunch to take to college every day. She enjoys eating all of it, but she feels sluggish in the afternoon and has trouble staying awake in class.

   What should Sofia do to help her concentrate in the afternoons?

   Supporting quote: _____

   Source of information: _____

2. Antwan loves candy, and his favorite mid-morning snack is a chocolate bar. At first, he feels great after his snack, but he soon feels tired again. He is worried it is affecting his job.

   What should Antwan do to feel more alert in the mornings?

   Supporting quote: _____

   Source of information: _____

3. Michael is a police officer, and his job is very stressful and intense. Lately, he has been feeling anxious and depressed. These feelings are also making him tired most of the time.

   What could Michael do to improve his mood and energy levels?

   Supporting quote: _____

   Source of information: _____

4. Pei Chen is an international student, and she keeps in touch with her family and friends via social media. Usually, she checks her messages on her phone right before she falls asleep. However, lately, she hasn't been sleeping very well.

   What could Pei Chen do to improve her sleep?

   Supporting quote: _____

   Source of information: _____

iQ PRACTICE Go online for additional reading and comprehension.
Practice > Unit 8 > Activity 5

? WRITE WHAT YOU THINK

A. DISCUSS Discuss the questions in a group. Think about the Unit Question, "What affects people's energy levels?"

1. Are eating well, doing exercise, trying yoga, practicing meditation, delegating tasks, and getting enough sleep realistic ways to boost energy levels for people in today's world? Why or why not?

2. Do you have enough energy to do the things you want to do? What are you doing, or could you be doing, to boost your energy levels?

3. Why do so many people feel stress in their daily lives? How does stress impact people's energy levels? Can stress ever have a positive impact on people's energy levels?

B. COMPOSE Choose one of the questions from Activity A and write a response. Look back at your Quick Write on page 226 as you think about what you learned.

Question: _____

My response: _____

_____

_____

_____

A chart is a useful tool for organizing your notes and annotations from a reading. Creating such a chart makes studying easier. Charts can also make it easier to paraphrase and summarize a text for a report or essay. There are various charts you can use depending on the type of text and the type of writing you plan to do.

Main ideas and details chart

This type of chart helps you identify and understand the relationship between main ideas and details. Record the main ideas in the reading on one side of the chart and the most important details on the other.

Main ideas	Details
What people drink affects energy levels.	Fatigue is a symptom of dehydration. Drinking water can help relieve tiredness. Caffeine in coffee improves concentration.

Cause and effect chart

This type of chart helps you identify and understand the causes (the events in a story or the steps in a process) and the effects (the results of those events or steps).

Cause	Effect
Moderate release of stress hormones	Feel more energized and alert

Connections to the text chart

This type of chart helps you remember and understand the text in a more meaningful way because you are connecting the text with something you already know.

You can make connections between the reading and:

- things or events in your own life (**text to self**)

- other information you have read (**text to text**)

- issues, events, general knowledge in the world (**text to world**)

Ideas in Reading 1	Connections
Adults should sleep for around seven to nine hours per night in order to feel refreshed.	**Text to self:** During final exam time, it is hard for me to get more than six hours of sleep per night, and I often feel tired during the day.
	Text to text: I read an article that said a lack of sleep can cause high blood pressure and heart disease. People can also gain weight and be at risk for diabetes.
	Text to world: With people's busy lifestyles today, not many people probably get the recommended seven to nine hours of sleep per night.

A. IDENTIFY Write the number of each corrected statement from Activity D (pages 231–232) next to the main idea that it supports.

Main ideas	Details
a. Food and drink impact energy levels.	1
b. Physical activity affects energy levels.	
c. Help with tasks and responsibilities influences energy levels.	
d. Adequate sleep has a relationship with energy levels.	

B. IDENTIFY Complete this chart for Reading 1 with the missing cause or effect.

Cause	Effect
1. eat too many calories	system overload and sluggish feeling
2. dehydration	
3. caffeine in coffee, tea, and cocoa	
4.	temporary increase in physical strength
5.	increased circulation and oxygen-carrying capacity
6. techniques such as mindful breathing	
7. 25 minutes of yoga or meditation	
8.	burnout and constant fatigue
9. seven to nine hours of sleep	
10.	state of alertness and inability to sleep

C. EXTEND Complete the chart by identifying text-to-self, text-to-text, and text-to-world connections you can make to the information in Reading 1.

Ideas in Reading 1	Connections
Food and drink impact energy levels.	Text to self:
	Text to text:
	Text to world:
Physical activity affects energy levels.	Text to self:
	Text to text:
	Text to world:
Help with tasks and responsibilities influences energy levels.	Text to self:
	Text to text:
	Text to world:
Adequate sleep has a relationship with energy levels.	Text to self:
	Text to text:
	Text to world:

iQ PRACTICE Go online for more practice organizing notes and annotations in a chart. *Practice > Unit 8 > Activity 6*

READING 2

The Scientific Reasons You Feel More Tired During Winter (And How to Combat It)

OBJECTIVE ▶

You are going to read an article from the website *Stack* about why people feel more tired during the winter. Use the article to gather information and ideas for your Unit Assignment.

PREVIEW THE READING

A. PREVIEW What do you think the article will say about how winter affects people's energy levels? Check (✓) your answer.

☐ People feel tired during winter because of the cold weather.

☐ People feel tired during winter because it is harder to travel around in snow.

☐ People feel tired during winter because of a lack of sunlight.

B. QUICK WRITE Why do you think people feel more tired during winter? Write for 5–10 minutes in response. Use ideas and evidence that you already know about to support your argument. Remember to use this section for your Unit Assignment.

C. VOCABULARY Check (✓) the words or phrases you know. Then work with a partner to locate each word or phrase in the reading. Use clues to help define the words or phrases you don't know. Check your definitions in the dictionary.

deficiency *(n.)* ⅋+	**nutrient** *(n.)*
dreary *(adj.)*	**optimal** *(adj.)* OPAL
fortified *(adj.)*	**rampant** *(adj.)*
hibernate *(v.)*	**sedentary** *(adj.)*
inflammation *(n.)*	**supplement** *(n.)* ⅋+
it is possible to *(phr.)* OPAL	**there are a number of** *(phr.)* OPAL

⅋+ Oxford 5000™ words   OPAL Oxford Phrasal Academic Lexicon

iQ PRACTICE Go online to listen and practice your pronunciation.
Practice > Unit 8 > Activity 7

WORK WITH THE READING

 A. INVESTIGATE Read the article and gather information on what affects people's energy levels.

THE SCIENTIFIC REASONS YOU FEEL MORE TIRED DURING WINTER (AND HOW TO COMBAT IT)

People living in northern latitudes are exposed to less daylight in winter

1   When the winter months hit, many of us feel the need to **hibernate**. Suddenly, getting out of bed in the morning is a Herculean task. Mid-day fatigue rises to another level. Going to the gym—a task that was easy during the summer and fall—now feels nearly impossible. Is this just your imagination? Probably not. Odds are it is winter-related fatigue. There are scientific reasons people feel more tired during winter than they do during other seasons. The good news is you can take steps to fight the fatigue and stay energetic, even during the darkest days of winter.

Less Sun Makes Us More Sleepy

2   Stepping outside on a sunny day is one of life's simple pleasures. It's also something we don't get the chance to do very often during winter. For one, the days get shorter during winter. This is especially true for those living in northern cities. For example, take a city like Cleveland, Ohio. On June 21 (the summer solstice), the sun was in the sky for 15 hours, 10 minutes, and 21 seconds. On December 21 (the winter solstice), the sun was in the sky for 9 hours, 10 minutes, and 11 seconds. That's over six hours of less daylight.

3   While everyone enjoys a nice day, sunlight is closely tied to human biology. Melatonin is a hormone produced by the pineal gland inside the brain. Melatonin regulates sleep and wakefulness. When we're in the dark, our bodies produce more melatonin. Winter is a dark time, so our bodies produce more melatonin in response. This leads to excessive feelings of fatigue and tiredness. According to the Mayo Clinic, "the change in season can disrupt the balance of the body's level of melatonin, which plays a role in sleep patterns and mood" (Mayo Clinic Staff, 2018).

4   Sunlight is also our major source of vitamin D. Human skin creates significant amounts of vitamin D when it's exposed to sunlight. Those who live in northern latitudes tend to have lower vitamin D levels, especially during the winter months. When the weather is cold and the days are short, there are fewer opportunities to get outside. Vitamin D **deficiency** is **rampant** in our society, and not just in colder climates. A recent study found that more than one-third of the student-athlete population at the University of Southern California had low levels of vitamin D (Bachman, 2016).

5   Vitamin D has a huge impact on how we feel. It plays a role in bone health, cell growth, blood pressure, immune function, and reduction of **inflammation**. It also plays an important role in performance and recovery. "Vitamin D is so

important for performance. We used to think it only impacted bone health, but more and more studies have shown that it acts like a hormone and actually has a role in muscle function. It's very important for athletes," says Dr. Maren Fragala, Director of Athlete Health and Human Performance for Quest Diagnostics.

6   Vitamin D has been found to impact performance in a variety of ways. A recent study conducted by Precision Nutrition found that when athletes entered a workout with "**optimal** serum vitamin D concentrations," they went on to recover faster and more efficiently (Koslo, n.d.). "More pre-exercise vitamin D meant less post-exercise muscle weakness and better recovery through the entire recovery process. Less pre-exercise vitamin D meant more weakness and worse recovery," the study's authors wrote.

7   A different study, published in the journal *PLoS One*, found that vitamin D levels were strongly correlated with the performance of professional soccer players (Koundourakis et al., 2014). "Findings suggest that vitamin D levels are associated with the ergonometric evaluation of muscle strength [. . .] sprinting capacity and VO2 max in professional soccer players," the authors wrote. Low levels of vitamin D increase fatigue and make recovery take longer. No wonder getting to the gym on a regular basis feels so difficult during winter!

Fighting Winter Fatigue

8   **There are a number of** simple steps you can take to boost your energy during the cold, **dreary** months. Getting enough vitamin D is a great start. How much vitamin D do you actually need? The Institute of Medicine recommends 600 International Units (IU) per day for most adults, but many sports dietitians recommend higher amounts for athletes. A recent article from *The Wall Street Journal* states that "some sports dietitians encourage athletes to get 1,000 to 2,000 IU [of vitamin D] daily" (Bachman, 2016).

9   Sunlight is obviously the best option, but getting enough vitamin D from sunlight is especially tough during winter. According to the National Institute of Health (2016), skin exposed to sunlight through a window does not produce vitamin D. That means you have to actually go outside to collect vitamin D from sunlight. This might sound tough during winter, given that the days are short and the weather is nasty. However, your skin does receive vitamin D even on cloudy days—just not as much as it would on a day with blue skies. If you are able to go for a walk or jog outside a few times a week, that should help.

10   **It is also possible to** get vitamin D from your diet, but relatively few foods contain a significant amount. Examples of foods high in vitamin D include egg yolks, fatty fish, and **fortified** products like cereals and milk.

11   Since adequate amounts of vitamin D can be hard to come by, many take it in the form of a **supplement**. If you go that route, select a vitamin D3 supplement, since that form most closely approximates the vitamin D naturally produced by the body.

12   Besides vitamin D, regular exercise is a surefire way to boost energy levels. This might sound counterintuitive, but research backs it up. A study from the University of Georgia found that **sedentary** adults who engaged in as little as 20 minutes of low-to-moderate aerobic exercise three days a week for six weeks experienced a significant uptick in their overall energy levels (Parker-Pope, 2008). I get that you might not want to drive to the gym in a blizzard and knock out a 60-minute workout. But doing something always beats doing nothing. Winter is a perfect time to use convenient at-home workouts such as yoga.

13   Diet is another important factor. It often feels easier to eat fruits and vegetables during the summer months, but winter is when your body really craves its **nutrients**. Keep your plates colorful and include a variety of produce to help keep your energy levels high.

14 Light therapy lamps (or boxes) are another option. "A light therapy box mimics outdoor light. Researchers believe this type of light causes a chemical change in the brain that lifts your mood and eases other symptoms of seasonal affective disorder," writes the Mayo Clinic (Mayo Clinic Staff, 2016). For people curious about trying light therapy, Amazon offers a wide variety of such products for under $100. If you're interested in learning more, the Mayo Clinic has an informative page on the topic.

Light therapy lamps mimic outdoor light

References

Bachman, R. (2016, January 25). Elite athletes try a new training tactic: More vitamin D. *The Wall Street Journal*. Retrieved from https://www.wsj.com/articles/elite-athletes-try-a-new-training-tactic-more-vitamin-d-1453745154

Koslo, J. (n.d.). Research review: Can vitamin D make you a better athlete? *Precision Nutrition*. Retrieved from https://www.precisionnutrition.com/research-review-vit-d-recovery

Koundourakis, N.E., Androulakis, N.E., Malliaraki, N., & Margioris, A.N. (2014). Vitamin D and exercise performance in professional soccer players. *PLoS One, 9*(7): e101659. https://dx.doi.org/10.1371/journal.pone.0101659

Mayo Clinic Staff. (2016). Seasonal affective disorder treatment: Choosing a light therapy box. *Mayo Clinic*. Retrieved from https://www.mayoclinic.org/diseases-conditions/seasonal-affective-disorder/in-depth/seasonal-affective-disorder-treatment/art-20048298

Mayo Clinic Staff. (2018). Seasonal affective disorder (SAD). *Mayo Clinic*. Retrieved from https://www.mayoclinic.org/diseases-conditions/seasonal-affective-disorder/symptoms-causes/syc-20364651

National Institute of Health. (2016). Vitamin D: Fact sheet for consumers. Retrieved from https://ods.od.nih.gov/factsheets/VitaminD-Consumer/

Parker-Pope, T. (2008, February 29). The cure for exhaustion? More exercise. *The New York Times*. Retrieved from https://well.blogs.nytimes.com/2008/02/29/the-cure-for-exhaustion-more-exercise/?hp

B. VOCABULARY Here are some words and phrases from Reading 2. Complete each sentence with a word or phrase from the box. You may need to change the form of the word or phrase to make the sentence grammatically correct.

deficiency *(n.)*	inflammation *(n.)*	rampant *(adj.)*
dreary *(adj.)*	it is possible to *(phr.)*	sedentary *(adj.)*
fortified *(adj.)*	nutrient *(n.)*	supplement *(n.)*
hibernate *(v.)*	optimal *(adj.)*	there are a number of *(phr.)*

1. _____ things you can do to increase your energy levels during the winter, such as go outside in the sun, eat more fruits and vegetables, and start some light aerobic activity.

2. When people don't get enough sunlight, they can suffer from vitamin D _____, which can make them feel tired after exercise.

3. If you have a _____ lifestyle, you can gain more energy by getting some light exercise three days a week.

4. To get more vitamin D, people can drink _____ beverages, such as cow's milk or soy milk.

5. Vitamin D plays an important role in reducing _____, which can be the result of heavy exercise and injured muscles.

6. Bears _____ during the winter because it is cold and there isn't much food for them to eat.

7. Your body needs lots of _____ during the winter, so it is important to eat plenty of fruits and vegetables.

8. _____ increase your levels of vitamin D by going for a walk outside, even on a cloudy day.

9. During the winter, feelings of fatigue are _____ because of the dark weather and shorter days.

10. People often feel less energetic on a _____ day with a dark sky and rain.

11. If you don't have enough vitamin D in your diet, you can take a daily _____ in the form of a pill.

12. If people have the _____ amounts of vitamin D, it is easier for them to recover from exercise.

iQ PRACTICE Go online for more practice with the vocabulary.
Practice > Unit 8 > Activity 8

C. CATEGORIZE Read the statements related to the main ideas in Reading 2. Write *T* (true) or *F* (false). Then correct any false statements.

_____ 1. People have more energy when their bodies produce more melatonin during the winter.

_____ 2. People who live in northern latitudes typically have higher levels of vitamin D during the winter months.

_____ 3. Having higher levels of vitamin D before exercising helps people have less muscle weakness and better recovery from their workouts.

_____ 4. Your skin can't produce vitamin D if you are outside on a cloudy day during the winter.

_____ 5. People can get vitamin D from foods such as egg yolks, fatty fish, fortified cereals, and fortified milk.

_____ 6. Light therapy lamps are similar to outdoor light, and they can cheer people up during the winter.

D. IDENTIFY Write the number of the paragraph in Reading 2 where each detail can be found.

Main Idea	Details	Paragraph
Lack of sunlight causes fatigue	a. Lower amounts of vitamin D can result in muscle weakness and difficulty recovering from exercise.	
	b. The pineal gland produces more melatonin during the winter.	
	c. In northern cities, the days are shorter during the winter.	
	d. People in northern areas usually have lower levels of vitamin D.	
	e. Professional soccer players with higher levels of vitamin D have better performance.	
	f. Vitamin D can act as a hormone and help muscles function.	

E. IDENTIFY Use this chart to record notes on the final part of Reading 2, "Fighting Winter Fatigue." Write only the most important details.

Main Ideas	Details
1. Getting vitamin D is harder in the winter (Paragraph 9)	- - -
2. Other sources of vitamin D (Paragraphs 10 & 11)	- -
3. Other ways to boost energy levels in the winter (Paragraphs 12, 13 & 14)	- - -

F. IDENTIFY Scan Reading 2 for statistical information. Answer the questions.

1. In Cleveland, how many hours of daylight are there on the summer solstice?

2. In Cleveland, how many hours of daylight are there on the winter solstice?

3. How much vitamin D should most adults have per day?

4. How much vitamin D should athletes have per day?

5. According to a study from the University of Georgia, how much exercise should sedentary adults do to increase their overall energy levels?

6. How much do most light therapy lamps or boxes cost?

G. **EXPLAIN** Based on the information in Reading 2, what answers can you infer to the following questions?

1. Why is it harder for people to go to the gym during the winter?

_____

2. Compared to Cleveland, how much daylight is there in Edmonton, a city 600 kilometers north of the U.S. border, on the summer and winter solstices?

_____

3. Why do athletes need more vitamin D than the average person?

_____

4. Why can't people get vitamin D from sunlight through a window?

_____

5. Why do companies fortify products such as cereals and milk with vitamin D?

_____

6. Why does eating a wide variety of produce help keep your energy levels high?

_____

WORK WITH THE VIDEO

A. **PREVIEW** What are carbohydrates?

VIDEO VOCABULARY

starch (n.) a white carbohydrate food substance found in potatoes, flour, rice, etc.; food containing this

molecule (n.) the smallest unit, consisting of a group of atoms, into which a substance can be divided without a change in its chemical nature

ingest (v.) to take food, drink, etc. into your body, usually by swallowing

absorb (v.) to take in a liquid, gas, or other substance from the surface or space around

iQ RESOURCES Go online to watch the video about carbohydrates.
Resources > Video > Unit 8 > Unit Video

B. IDENTIFY Watch the video two or three times. Match each word in the box with the description that best defines it. Then answer the questions that follow based on the information in the video.

carbohydrates	cellulose	fructose	glucose	starch	sucrose

1. _____: the simplest sugar; a single molecule with 6 carbon, 6 oxygen, and 12 hydrogen atoms

2. _____: it gives honey its sweet flavor; it has the same atoms as glucose, but arranged in a different way

3. _____: table sugar; glucose and fructose paired together

4. _____: longer chains of thousands of molecules of glucose joined together

5. _____: rigid straight chains of glucose that provide structure in plants

6. _____: long chains that can twist to fit a lot of glucose in a small space; a good energy store

7. What happens to long starch molecules after they are eaten?

8. According to the video, which kind of carbohydrate should form most of the carbohydrate in our diet? Why?

C. EXTEND Are carbohydrates a good source of energy? Do different carbohydrates affect energy levels differently? Use the information in the video, as well as your own knowledge and ideas, to support your response.

WRITE WHAT YOU THINK

SYNTHESIZE Think about Reading 1, Reading 2, and the video as you discuss these questions. Then choose one question and write a response.

1. The two readings and the video mention a number of things that affect people's energy levels, such as diet, exercise, exposure to sunlight, and carbohydrates. Out of everything mentioned in the readings and the video, what do you think affects people's energy levels the most? Why?

2. Is there something that wasn't mentioned in the two readings or the video that has a strong effect on people's energy levels? What is it? Is it more important than what was mentioned in the readings and the video? Why or why not?

3. What would you recommend to someone who wanted to improve their energy levels?

Some adjectives and verbs are often followed by certain prepositions. These common word combinations are called **collocations**. Being familiar with these patterns can increase your accuracy as you write and speed up your reading comprehension. These charts show some common collocations found in Readings 1 and 2.

Adjective + preposition

Adjective	Preposition	Example
depleted	of	People who feel **depleted of** energy can try drinking a cup of coffee to wake themselves up.
conducive	to	Doing too much work is not **conducive to** feeling happy and energized.
ready	for	If you eat a good diet and get plenty of sleep, you'll be **ready for** your day's activities when you wake up.
curious	about	Mark was **curious about** light therapy as a cure for his seasonal affective disorder.

Verb + preposition

Verb	Preposition	Example
derive	from	The energy we **derive from** food is measured in calories.
depend	on	The ideal amount of sleep for people **depends on** someone's age as well as other factors.
worry	about	Some people **worry about** the food they eat and its effect on their energy levels.
correlate	with	High levels of vitamin D **correlated with** better performance for professional soccer players.

Cause or effect

The collocations *result from* and *be caused by* are used to introduce a cause. *Lead to* and *result in* are used to introduce an effect. They are all common in academic writing.

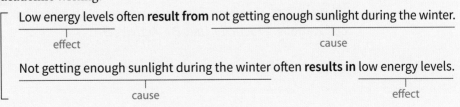

ACADEMIC LANGUAGE

The corpus shows that *derived from* and *depend on* are often used in academic writing to show causal and other relationships. *These supplements are derived from fish oil.*

_____ **OPAL**
Oxford Phrasal Academic Lexicon

A. APPLY Complete each sentence with the appropriate preposition. If you need help, look at the Vocabulary Skill Box or scan Readings 1 and 2. Then check (✓) the sentences with collocations used to express cause or effect.

☐ 1. Eating whole grains and vegetables can help you feel alert and ready _____ more active tasks.

☐ 2. Fatigue can be caused _____ a chronic condition that is difficult to cure.

☐ 3. Jonathan engages _____ 30 minutes of yoga every day, and it helps him feel good.

☐ 4. If I quit drinking coffee, I'm worried _____ feeling sleepy at work.

☐ 5. Too much melatonin in the body leads _____ a general feeling of tiredness.

☐ 6. Watching videos on your smartphone interferes _____ your ability to sleep well.

B. COMPOSE Combine the phrases (cause, effect, and collocation) into one sentence. Change the verbs and nouns as necessary to create a grammatical sentence.

1. not get enough quality sleep / feel tired all the time / result from
   Feeling tired all the time results from not getting enough quality sleep.

2. a sense of fatigue / not drink enough water throughout the day / can result from

3. poor time management / burnout and feeling tired all the time / may lead to

4. light therapy lamps or boxes / positive changes in brain chemistry / can be caused by

5. a lack of daylight during winter / changes in the body's melatonin levels / may be caused by

6. drink a cup of coffee / feel more awake and alert / can result in

C. COMPOSE Find five new adjective + preposition or verb + preposition collocations in Readings 1 and 2. Then write a sentence in your own words for each of the five new collocations.

iQ PRACTICE Go online for more practice with adjective/verb + preposition collocations. *Practice › Unit 8 › Activity 9*

WRITING

OBJECTIVE ▶ At the end of this unit, you will write a cause and effect essay about what affects people's energy levels. Your essay will include information from the readings, the unit video, and your own ideas.

WRITING SKILL Writing a cause and effect essay

People often write to understand the reasons behind something or the results of something: causes and effects. The piece of writing can either focus on the causes of a situation or event or it can focus on the results of a situation or event.

The **causal analysis essay** looks at multiple causes leading to one major result. It usually begins by describing a particular situation and then analyzing the major causes.

Thesis statement: Poor sleep, high stress, and a bad diet can lead to a lack of energy.

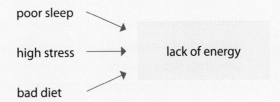

The **effect analysis essay** examines how one major situation has a number of different results. It usually begins by describing a particular situation and then analyzing the major effects.

Thesis statement: Too much caffeine can result in difficulty sleeping, headaches, and nervousness.

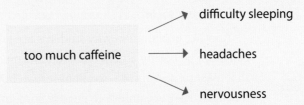

There are two common problems to watch for in a causal analysis or effect analysis essay.

1. The relationships between cause and effect must exist and be logical. Avoid mistaken causal relationships—jumping to conclusions without first checking the logic of your argument.
   - ✗ Drinking large amounts of tea and coffee leads to happiness.
   - ✗ Eating high glycemic foods, such as candy, immediately results in illness.

2. The causal relationships must be supportable with details such as facts, examples, statistics, quotations, and anecdotes.

A. WRITING MODEL Read the model essay written in response to an English composition class assignment. Then answer the questions with a partner.

English Composition 101 Midterm Essay Assignment

Why do some students have very low energy and difficulty concentrating? Write an essay analyzing why some students have trouble staying awake during class.

Class Time Is Often Sleepy Time

by Stuart Tanaka

There is a serious problem that is growing on university campuses. In ever greater numbers, undergraduate students are finding it difficult to stay focused in class. It is routine to see students closing their eyes during lectures or staring out the window. While some students hide behind their books, others move around in their chairs, trying to keep alert. Why are students struggling to make the most of their class time? The reasons for this struggle to stay awake lie in student jobs and university classes.

One culprit for this lack of focus in class is the increasing number of students who are holding down part-time or even full-time jobs while they are in school. As the cost of living continues to rise and tuition fees increase, students are finding it necessary to have a job in order to make ends meet. However, often the only jobs available to students are low-paying ones that require long hours in order to make the money necessary to go to school. The long hours cut into study time, forcing students to study later and later into the night. It is not rare for a student to arrive home from a part-time job at 9 p.m. and then be faced with another four or five hours of homework. It is hard to imagine being bright and energetic for an early morning class after that.

Another explanation why students are not focusing in class is that classes can often be boring affairs that students must endure. One reason may be that most professors are excellent researchers, but not necessarily the best teachers. They are unable to engage students in learning and instead lecture from prepared notes in a traditional manner. Students today are what have been called *digital natives*, used to multitasking on the Internet, listening to music on their smartphones, and watching videos on their tablets. To suddenly ask them to listen to lectures read aloud in a monotone voice leads to wandering minds.

Schedules packed with work and study, along with classes that do not engage students' attention, lead to difficulties focusing in class. Something must change if students are to get the most out of their programs of study. Students need to make a commitment to work fewer hours, and universities need to make a commitment to improve classroom lectures.

1. What type of essay is this?

   ☐ causal analysis essay   ☐ effect analysis essay

2. What is the thesis statement for this essay? Underline it.

3. What is the first topic sentence? Underline it twice.

4. Note the first major cause and its effect in the margin.

5. What is the second topic sentence? Underline it twice.

6. Note the second major cause and its effect in the margin.

7. What is the concluding statement? Underline it.

B. **IDENTIFY** Complete this cause and effect chart for each main body paragraph of the essay in Activity A.

Working part-time or full-time jobs is making students tired and unable to focus	
Cause	Effect
1. rising cost of living	
2.	students need a job
3. students usually have low-paying jobs	
4.	students have to study late at night
5. students study late at night	
6.	
7.	
8.	
9.	
10.	

C. **EXTEND** Imagine you have been assigned to write an essay based on one of the readings in this unit. Choose Reading 1 or Reading 2 and create a cause and effect chart in response to one of these essay questions.

1. What are some reasons people feel tired during winter?

2. What can people do to boost their energy levels?

3. What are the effects of a poor diet?

4. Why are some people tired all the time?

D. WRITING MODEL Read the model cause and effect essay. Then fill in the diagram that follows with the major effect in the rectangle, the main causes in the ovals, and the associated important details on the lines. Some of the information has been completed for you.

Tips for Graduate Students to Keep up Their Energy

In recent years, the multiple demands put onto graduate students seem to be getting heavier and heavier. These demands, such as the pressure to pass exams, the requirement to write a thesis or dissertation, and the need to have a part-time job, can drain students of their energy. Some students may even feel trapped in an exhaustion from which there is no escape. However, there are measures that students can take to beat that feeling of being tired all the time. Namely, getting lots of exercise, sleeping well, enjoying healthy drinks, and staying positive all help maintain the high levels of energy that students need on a daily basis.

Exercise is known to boost energy levels. While students may find it hard to carve out the time to exercise, 30 minutes of exercise three times a week is enough to keep fatigue at bay. A great time to get mobile is early in the morning. Students can try a light jog or a brisk walk before breakfast. This exercise will get their blood flowing and carry oxygen to the brain, helping them feel bright and alert for the rest of the day. Another tip is to not be sedentary all day. While studying for long periods of time, students should get up and walk around. For example, after every hour of studying, students should stand up and go for a five-minute walk before hitting the books again. Finally, stretching before bed is another way for students to keep themselves in top form. It can help tired muscles get the oxygen they need to support an active lifestyle.

Along with exercising, getting enough good quality sleep is very important for students who are feeling tired all the time. The key to getting good quality sleep is having a comfortable mattress. A lumpy, second-hand futon or a ten-year-old mattress from home might be the culprit preventing a good night's sleep. It is important for students to speak with a sleep expert and find the right mattress for their sleeping style. In addition, students should avoid using electronics before going to bed. It might be fun watching YouTube videos before bed, but the glowing blue light from the screen has been known to have a negative effect on sleep quality. Lastly, a regular sleeping schedule is vital for maintaining normal energy levels. Most people need at least eight hours of sleep a night. Thus, pulling an all-nighter one night and then sleeping for 12 hours straight the next night is not a good idea. The best plan is to go to bed every night at 10:30 and wake up at 6:30 the next morning, fresh and ready to start the day.

Good hydration is another factor that can help maintain energy levels. The first and best choice is plenty of water. To avoid feeling sluggish and dehydrated, students should aim to drink at least eight glasses of water a day. Another good drink for a quick pick-me-up is green tea. Green tea is rich in antioxidants, and it has less caffeine than coffee. Being sugar free, it is also a much better choice than soda or energy drinks, and students can avoid the sugar crash that comes with consuming those types of sweetened beverages. It is also a good investment for students to have a good quality juicer. Having enough vitamins and minerals is key to staying energetic, but many students are not able to eat the recommended seven to eight servings of fruits and vegetables. However, with a juicer, students can drink their vitamins and minerals and find the energy they need for studying.

Finally, having a positive mental attitude is the most important factor contributing to staying energetic. There are many challenges to being a student, but it can help if problems are seen as opportunities for learning. By seeing setbacks as learning experiences, students are less likely to feel depressed and drained. For example, when students fail tests, they can analyze those tests so that they can do better next time. Another tip to help keep students' energy up is to remember to smile. It may seem silly at first, but it is hard to feel tired if you are smiling. Finally, it is important to see the good in people. Professors may seem like they want you to do too much work, but there may be reasons behind what they are doing. For example, those early morning quizzes might be to ensure that students make it to class on time, with the result of helping them learn more in the end. Holding people in a positive light will help students stay in a good mood, resulting in these students feeling less drained and exhausted.

All in all, graduate students can keep up their energy levels with plenty of exercise, good quality sleep, healthy drinks, and positive attitudes. It might be hard at first, but putting these four pieces of advice into practice is sure to boost energy levels. Once the benefits of having high energy levels start to be enjoyed, living a healthy lifestyle will be natural.

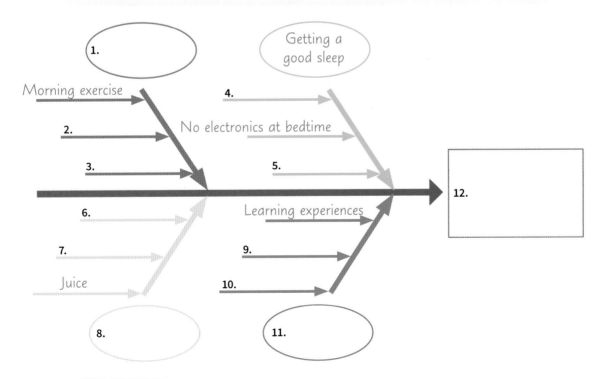

iQ PRACTICE Go online for more practice with writing a cause and effect essay. *Practice › Unit 8 › Activity 10*

Cause and effect connectors show the exact relationship between your ideas and give your writing coherence.

The **coordinating conjunction** *so* follows the cause and is connected to the effect in a sentence. It does not usually start a sentence in formal academic writing.

Some people do not get enough exercise, **so** they suffer from low energy levels.

The **subordinators** *because*, *due to the fact that*, and *since* connect to the cause in a sentence. They are used in dependent (adverbial) clauses. Notice the use of the comma when the dependent clause comes first.

Some people have low energy **because** they do not get enough exercise.

I have low energy levels **due to the fact that** I don't eat enough complex carbohydrates.

Since you feel so tired, you should stay home and rest.

The **transitions** *as a consequence*, *as a result*, *because of this*, *consequently*, *for this/that reason*, and *therefore* all follow the cause and are connected to the effect.

Some people do not get enough exercise. **Consequently**, they suffer from low energy levels.

Some people do not drink enough water; **for this reason**, they feel tired during the day.

iQ RESOURCES Go online to watch the Grammar Skill Video.
Resources > Video > Unit 8 > Grammar Skill Video

TIP FOR SUCCESS

In order to sound fluent, use connectors only when you need to demonstrate a clear relationship between ideas.

A. IDENTIFY Draw an arrow from each cause to its effect.

Cause and effect		
1. She feels tired every day.	←	She's not getting enough sleep.
2. I feel energetic while I work.		I drink coffee in the morning.
3. Some people eat too many processed and refined foods with a high glycemic index.		Some people suffer from low energy levels and fatigue.
4. There isn't much daylight during winter.		People's bodies produce less melatonin and vitamin D.
5. Habitual coffee drinkers build up tolerance to caffeine.		Caffeine may not help people who drink a lot of coffee to concentrate.
6. He feels burned out and tired all the time.		He is overwhelmed by his responsibilities because he has no one to help him.
7. Marta has a strong immune system.		Marta practices yoga and meditation regularly.
8. Joe always sees problems as opportunities for learning.		He rarely feels depressed or frustrated.

B. COMPOSE Rewrite the sentences in Activity A using these connectors. Change nouns to pronouns as needed to make your sentences sound natural.

1. for this reason
2. because
3. therefore
4. due to the fact that

5. because of this
6. as a consequence
7. since
8. so

iQ PRACTICE Go online for more practice with cause and effect connectors. *Practice > Unit 8 > Activity 11*

iQ PRACTICE Go online for the Grammar Expansion: Transitions showing contrast. *Practice > Unit 8 > Activity 12*

UNIT ASSIGNMENT Write a cause and effect essay

OBJECTIVE ▶

In this assignment, you will write a cause and effect essay that examines factors that can positively or negatively affect people's energy levels. As you prepare your essay, think about the Unit Question, "What affects people's energy levels?" Use information from Reading 1, Reading 2, the unit video, and your work in this unit to support your paragraph. Refer to the Self-Assessment checklist on page 254.

---

iQ PRACTICE Go online to the Writing Tutor to read a model cause and effect essay. *Practice > Unit 8 > Activity 13*

PLAN AND WRITE

A. BRAINSTORM Make a list of all the different things that affect people's energy levels that you read about in this unit. Then complete the activities.

1. Sort your list into things that have a positive impact on people's energy levels and things that have a negative impact.

2. Circle three or four factors in each list that have the greatest impact, and compare your choices with a partner. Then decide on which factors have the best effect on people's energy levels and which factors have the worst.

B. PLAN Follow this step to plan your cause and effect essay.

Decide if you want to focus on things that positively or negatively impact people's energy levels. You can use the three or four positive or negative factors you brainstormed earlier in your cause and effect essay.

iQ RESOURCES Go online to download and complete the outline for your cause and effect essay. *Resources > Writing Tools > Unit 8 > Outline*

C. WRITE Use your planning notes to write your cause and effect essay.

1. Write a cause and effect essay on what affects people's energy levels.

2. Look at the Self-Assessment checklist below to guide your writing.

iQ PRACTICE Go online to the Writing Tutor to write your assignment.
Practice > Unit 8 > Activity 14

REVISE AND EDIT

iQ RESOURCES Go online to download the peer review worksheet.
Resources > Writing Tools > Unit 8 > Peer Review Worksheet

A. PEER REVIEW Read your partner's essay. Then use the peer review worksheet. Discuss the review with your partner.

B. REWRITE Based on your partner's review, revise and rewrite your cause and effect essay.

C. EDIT Complete the Self-Assessment checklist as you prepare to write the final draft of your cause and effect essay. Be prepared to hand in your work or discuss it in class.

SELF-ASSESSMENT	Yes	No
Does the essay build a convincing argument using facts, reasons, and examples?	☐	☐
Does the essay use cause and effect connectors effectively?	☐	☐
Are collocations with prepositions used correctly?	☐	☐
Does the essay include vocabulary from the unit?	☐	☐
Did you check the essay for punctuation, spelling, and grammar?	☐	☐

D. REFLECT Discuss these questions with a partner or group.

1. What is something new you learned in this unit?

2. Look back at the Unit Question—What affects people's energy levels? Is your answer different now than when you started the unit? If yes, how is it different? Why?

iQ PRACTICE Go to the online discussion board to discuss the questions.
Practice > Unit 8 > Activity 15

TRACK YOUR SUCCESS

iQ PRACTICE Go online to check the words and phrases you have learned in this unit. *Practice > Unit 8 > Activity 16*

Check (✓) the skills you learned. If you need more work on a skill, refer to the page(s) in parentheses.

CRITICAL THINKING ☐ I can apply new learning to problems. (p. 233)

READING ☐ I can organize notes and annotations in a chart. (p. 235)

VOCABULARY ☐ I can use adjective/verb + preposition collocations. (p. 245)

WRITING ☐ I can write a cause and effect essay. (p. 247)

GRAMMAR ☐ I can use cause and effect connectors. (p. 252)

OBJECTIVE ▶ ☐ I can gather information and ideas to develop a cause and effect essay analyzing two or three factors that affect people's energy levels.

{+ The **Oxford 5000™** is an expanded core word list for advanced learners of English. The words have been chosen based on their frequency in the Oxford English Corpus and relevance to learners of English. As well as the Oxford 3000™ core word list, the Oxford 5000 includes an additional 2,000 words that are aligned to the CEFR, guiding advanced learners at B2–C1 level on the most useful high-level words to learn to expand their vocabulary.

OPAL The **Oxford Phrasal Academic Lexicon** is an essential guide to the most important words and phrases to know for academic English. The word lists are based on the Oxford Corpus of Academic English and the British Academic Spoken **English corpus.**

The **Common European Framework of Reference for Language (CEFR)** provides a basic description of what language learners have to do to use language effectively. The system contains 6 reference levels: A1, A2, B1, B2, C1, C2.

UNIT 1

acquisition *(n.)* {+ OPAL C1
ambiguity *(n.)* C2
bilingual *(adj., n.)* C1
cognitive *(adj.)* {+ C1
contemporary *(adj.)* {+ OPAL B2
cue *(n.)* {+ B2
depending on *(v. phr.)* A2
enhanced *(adj.)* {+ OPAL B2
equip *(v.)* {+ B2
exploration *(n.)* {+ OPAL B2
fallacy *(n.)* C2
immersion *(n.)* C2
involve *(v.)* {+ OPAL A2
is based on *(adj. phr.)* OPAL A2
lingua franca *(n.)* C2
measure *(v.)* {+ OPAL B1
motivation *(n.)* {+ OPAL B2
plummet *(v.)* C2
refer to *(v. phr.)* OPAL A2
specialist *(adj.)* {+ OPAL B2
spread the myth *(v. phr.)* B2
stereotype *(n.)* {+ C1
the likelihood of *(n. phr.)* OPAL C1
tolerance *(n.)* {+ C1

UNIT 2

accumulate *(v.)* {+ OPAL C1

algorithm *(n.)* C1
at stake *(prep. phr.)* C1
automate *(v.)* C1
benefits *(pl. n.)* {+ OPAL A2
demand *(n.)* {+ OPAL B2
discrimination *(n.)* {+ OPAL C1
entry-level *(adj.)* C2
expertise *(n.)* {+ OPAL B2
freelancer *(n.)* C2
gig *(n.)* {+ B2
hypothetical *(adj.)* OPAL C1
job security *(n. phr.)* B1
labor *(n.)* {+ B2
on the margins *(prep. phr.)* C2
scraps *(pl. n.)* C2
substitute *(v.)* {+ OPAL C1
supply *(n.)* {+ OPAL B1
take a cut *(v. phr.)* C2
take advantage of *(v. phr.)* B2
the degree of *(n. phr.)* OPAL B2
the other end of the spectrum *(n. phr.)* OPAL C2
transaction *(n.)* {+ C1
wage *(n.)* {+ B2

UNIT 3

alteration *(n.)* OPAL
bias *(n.)* {+ OPAL B2
campaign *(n.)* {+ B1
concoct *(v.)* C2

credible *(adj.)* {+ C1
distort *(v.)* {+ C1
document *(v.)* OPAL B2
error-prone *(adj.)* C2
ethical *(adj.)* {+ OPAL B2
inherent *(adj.)* {+ OPAL C1
leave in the dark *(v. phr.)* C2
legitimate *(adj.)* {+ C1
manipulate *(v.)* {+ C1
misleading *(adj.)* {+ C1
prominent *(adj.)* {+ C1
provoke *(v.)* {+ C1
scale *(n.)* {+ OPAL B2
scrutinize *(v.)* C2
skyrocket *(v.)* C2
take … with a grain of salt *(v. phr.)* C2
tempting *(adj.)* {+ C1
transformation *(n.)* {+ OPAL C1
unprecedented *(adj.)* {+ C1
visualize *(v.)* C1

UNIT 4

confront *(v.)* {+ C1
conserve *(v.)* {+ OPAL C1
consolidate *(v.)* {+ C1
crucial *(adj.)* {+ OPAL B2
daunting *(adj.)* C2
devastating *(adj.)* {+ C1
devote *(v.)* {+ B2

dominate *(v.)* 🔑+ OPAL B2
erosion *(n.)* C1
extinct *(adj.)* B2
genetic *(adj.)* 🔑+ B2
inevitable *(adj.)* 🔑+ B2
inhabit *(v.)* C1
intensively *(adv.)* C1
mediator *(n.)* C2
mission *(n.)* 🔑+ B2
mundane *(adj.)* C2
navigate *(v.)* B2
orbit *(n.)* B2
plan B *(n.)* C1
quarantine *(v.)* C2
reassemble *(v.)* C2
urgency *(n.)* C1
vulnerability *(n.)* 🔑+ C1

UNIT 5

accommodate *(v.)* 🔑+ B2
anticipate *(v.)* 🔑+ B2
appealing *(adj.)* 🔑+ C1
concede *(v.)* 🔑+ C1
controversy *(n.)* 🔑+ B2
counterintuitive *(adj.)* C2
criteria *(pl. n.)* 🔑+ OPAL B2
division *(n.)* 🔑+ OPAL B2
encounter *(v.)* 🔑+ OPAL B2
fatal *(adj.)* 🔑+ C1
form bonds *(v. phr.)* B2
hybrid *(adj.)* C1
in decline *(prep. phr.)* B2
intentionally *(adv.)* C1
isolated *(adj.)* 🔑+ B2
mingle *(v.)* C2
negotiate *(v.)* 🔑+ B2
neutral *(adj.)* 🔑+ OPAL B2
nomadic *(adj.)* C2
pop up *(v. phr.)* C1
proponent *(n.)* C2
regulated *(adj.)* 🔑+ B2

reinforce *(v.)* 🔑+ OPAL B2
specialized *(adj.)* 🔑+ OPAL B2

UNIT 6

abundant *(adj.)* C1
adjust *(v.)* 🔑+ OPAL B2
anticipate *(v.)* 🔑+ B2
appliance *(n.)* B2
aptitude *(n.)* C2
consequence *(n.)* 🔑+ OPAL B1
conservation *(n.)* 🔑+ OPAL B2
constraint *(n.)* 🔑+ OPAL C1
contaminated *(adj.)* C1
convene *(v.)* C2
craftsmanship *(n.)* C2
device *(n.)* 🔑+ OPAL A2
disposal *(n.)* 🔑+ C1
dubious *(adj.)* C1
elimination *(n.)* C1
founder *(n.)* 🔑+ B2
incinerate *(v.)* C2
obsolete *(adj.)* C1
participant *(n.)* 🔑+ OPAL B2
permeate *(v.)* C2
sustainable *(adj.)* 🔑+ B2
the concept of *(n. phr.)* OPAL B2
thrive *(v.)* 🔑+ C1
tinker *(v.)* C2

UNIT 7

allegedly *(adv.)* 🔑+ C1
breakthrough *(n.)* 🔑+ C1
conceal *(v.)* 🔑+ C1
disrupt *(v.)* 🔑+ C1
encompass *(v.)* 🔑+ C1
facilitate *(v.)* 🔑+ OPAL C1
fundamental *(adj.)* 🔑+ OPAL B2
impact *(n.)* 🔑+ OPAL B1
in particular *(prep. phr.)* OPAL B1
innovation *(n.)* 🔑+ B2

lens *(n.)* 🔑+ B2
magnification *(n.)* C2
ornamental *(adj.)* C2
presence *(n.)* 🔑+ OPAL B2
prior to *(adj. phr.)* OPAL B2
provision *(n.)* 🔑+ C1
retain *(v.)* 🔑+ B2
sector *(n.)* 🔑+ OPAL B2
sequence *(n.)* 🔑+ B2
stimulus *(n.)* 🔑+ C1
substance *(n.)* 🔑+ OPAL B1
textile *(n.)* C2
texture *(n.)* 🔑+ C1
transition *(n.)* 🔑+ OPAL B2

UNIT 8

alleviate *(v.)* C1
calorie *(n.)* B1
chronic *(adj.)* 🔑+ C1
conducive *(adj.)* C2
deficiency *(n.)* 🔑+ C1
depletion *(n.)* C2
derive from *(v. phr.)* B2
dreary *(adj.)* C2
fatigue *(n.)* C1
fortified *(adj.)* C2
hibernate *(v.)* C2
hydrated *(adj.)* C2
immune system *(n.)* B2
inflammation *(n.)* C2
it is possible to *(phr.)* OPAL A1
meditation *(n.)* 🔑+ C1
nutrient *(n.)* B2
optimal *(adj.)* OPAL C1
rampant *(adj.)* C2
resilience *(n.)* C2
sedentary *(adj.)* C2
sluggish *(adj.)* C2
supplement *(n.)* 🔑+ C1
there are a number of *(phr.)* OPAL A1

AUTHORS AND CONSULTANTS

AUTHORS

Nigel A. Caplan is an associate professor at the University of Delaware English Language Institute. He holds a Ph.D. in Education from the University of Delaware with a focus on literacy and an M.S.Ed. in TESOL from the University of Pennsylvania. He has taught English learners in several U.S. universities as well as in the UK, France, and Germany. His research and professional interests include genre-based writing pedagogy, functional grammar, and ESL teacher preparation. He is also co-author of two books in the *Inside Writing* series.

Scott Roy Douglas is an associate professor in the University of British Columbia's Okanagan School of Education. He holds a Ph.D. in Education from the University of Calgary with a specialization in teaching English as a second language. Over the years, he has had the privilege of working with additional language learners throughout the world, from the Middle East to Asia. His research interests include English for academic purposes teaching and learning, short-term study abroad, additional language assessment, and teacher development.

SERIES CONSULTANTS

Lawrence J. Zwier holds an M.A. in TESL from the University of Minnesota. He is currently the Associate Director for Curriculum Development at the English Language Center at Michigan State University in East Lansing. He has taught ESL/EFL in the United States, Saudi Arabia, Malaysia, Japan, and Singapore.

Marguerite Ann Snow holds a Ph.D. in Applied Linguistics from UCLA. She teaches in the TESOL M.A. program in the Charter College of Education at California State University, Los Angeles. She was a Fulbright scholar in Hong Kong and Cyprus. In 2006, she received the President's Distinguished Professor award at CSULA. She has trained ESL teachers in the United States and EFL teachers in more than 25 countries. She is the author/editor of numerous publications in the areas of content-based instruction, English for academic purposes, and standards for English teaching and learning. She is a co-editor of *Teaching English as a Second or Foreign Language* (4th ed.).

CRITICAL THINKING CONSULTANT James Dunn is a Junior Associate Professor at Tokai University and the Coordinator of the JALT Critical Thinking Special Interest Group. His research interests include critical thinking skills' impact on student brain function during English learning as measured by EEG. His educational goals are to help students understand that they are capable of more than they might think and to expand their cultural competence with critical thinking and higher-order thinking skills.

ASSESSMENT CONSULTANT Elaine Boyd has worked in assessment for over 30 years for international testing organizations. She has designed and delivered courses in assessment literacy and is also the author of several EL exam coursebooks for leading publishers. She is an Associate Tutor (M.A. TESOL/Linguistics) at University College, London. Her research interests are classroom assessment, issues in managing feedback, and intercultural competences.

VOCABULARY CONSULTANT Cheryl Boyd Zimmerman is Professor Emeritus at California State University, Fullerton. She specialized in second-language vocabulary acquisition, an area in which she is widely published. She taught graduate courses on second-language acquisition, culture, vocabulary, and the fundamentals of TESOL, and has been a frequent invited speaker on topics related to vocabulary teaching and learning. She is the author of *Word Knowledge: A Vocabulary Teacher's Handbook* and Series Director of *Inside Reading, Inside Writing*, and *Inside Listening and Speaking*, published by Oxford University Press.

ONLINE INTEGRATION Chantal Hemmi holds an Ed.D. TEFL and is a Japan-based teacher trainer and curriculum designer. Since leaving her position as Academic Director of the British Council in Tokyo, she has been teaching at the Center for Language Education and Research at Sophia University in an EAP/CLIL program offered for undergraduates. She delivers lectures and teacher trainings throughout Japan, Indonesia, and Malaysia.

COMMUNICATIVE GRAMMAR CONSULTANT Nancy Schoenfeld holds an M.A. in TESOL from Biola University in La Mirada, California, and has been an English language instructor since 2000. She has taught ESL in California and Hawaii and EFL in Thailand and Kuwait. She has also trained teachers in the United States and Indonesia. Her interests include teaching vocabulary, extensive reading, and student motivation. She is currently an English Language Instructor at Kuwait University.